A   D   A

W9-CLK-671

NORTH

Turtle Mt. ▱ Ind. Res.

DAKOTA

Ft. Berthold
Ind. Res.

Devils Lake
Ind. Res.

Standing Rock
Indian Res.

Sisseton

Cheyenne River
Ind. Res.

Former Lake
Traverse
Ind. Res.

SOUTH DAKOTA

Lower Brule
Ind.
Res.

Crow Creek
Ind. Res.

Pine Ridge
Ind. Res.

Rosebud
Ind. Res.

NEBRASKA

Plate

River

Red Lake
Ind. Res.

White Earth
Ind. Res.

MINNESOTA

La Pointe
Ind. Res.

Lanse & Vieux
Desert Ind. Res.

Lac Du Flambeau
Ind. Res.

Lac Court Oreille
Ind. Res.

Menominee
Ind. Res.

WISCONSIN

L. SUPERIOR

L. MICHIGAN

MICHIGAN

River

IOWA

ILLINOIS

INDIANA

KANSAS

MISSOURI

KEN.

DO

scalero
d. Res.

Osage
Ind. Res.

Quapaw

Plains

OKLAHOMA

Five

Civilized

Tribes

Tribes

ARKANSAS

TENN.

Mississippi

MISS.

ALA.

CO

TEXAS

LOUISIANA

LEGEND

■ Indian Reservations

▨ Former Indian Reservations

Hagstrom Map Company, Inc. N.Y.

The Story of the Red Man

LONGMANS, GREEN AND CO.
55 FIFTH AVENUE, NEW YORK
221 EAST 20TH STREET, CHICAGO
TREMONT TEMPLE, BOSTON
128 UNIVERSITY AVENUE, TORONTO

LONGMANS, GREEN AND CO. LTD.
39 PATERNOSTER ROW, E C 4, LONDON
53 NICOL ROAD, BOMBAY
6 OLD COURT HOUSE STREET, CALCUTTA
167 MOUNT ROAD, MADRAS

THE RED MAN ON THE PRAIRIES

The Story of

THE RED MAN

By
FLORA WARREN SEYMOUR
A.B., LL.B., LL.M.
MEMBER OF THE BOARD OF INDIAN COMMISSIONERS

LONGMANS, GREEN AND CO.
LONDON · NEW YORK · TORONTO
1929

For
G. S. S.

CONTENTS

LIST OF ILLUSTRATIONS

PLATES

ix

MAPS

The Story of the Red Man

The Story of
THE RED MAN

CHAPTER I

History Dawns for the Indian

A BROWN–SKINNED native of a tropical southern island was idling on the beach one October morning when he caught sight of something that roused him to instant alertness. It seemed like the great white wings of an immense bird, coming toward him from the wide ocean side of his little isle, across waters into which his canoe did not venture.

Other natives gathered about him to see the white wings skimming across the surface of the waves. As they came nearer the watchers saw a great canoe above which the pinions soared and dipped. The canoe approached the shore; the wings fell motionless; from the strange craft there came still stranger creatures — men with pale faces and gay robes and shining glitter of steel all about them.

A great tree-like stick was placed in the sand upon the beach. A silken banner fluttered in the air. The newcomers fell upon their knees.

"Surely these are spirits," whispered the awed natives to one another.

"*Los Indios!*" exclaimed Columbus in triumph. "We have found the eastern Indians by travelling westward across the ocean."

Thereafter for many years the newly discovered world and its inhabitants were the central features of European development. America's gold and treasure made Spain for a space the richest and most powerful of nations. Zeal for conquest in the name of King or Church brought many Europeans to the new land. Dissensions political or religious sent many others forth seeking a new home across the waters. European history from this time on can be told only in the light of the promise and opportunity America had to offer.

But what of the early American ? What was his part in all this great melodrama of conquest and exploration and settlement ? Unfortunately he had no written language, no historian to leave to future ages his version of the tale.

In the records we catch a glimpse of him here and there, fighting or fraternizing, making trade or treaty or brandishing the tomahawk. We can only guess how he would have told the story. What would he have said of the Spaniard who came for gold and jewels and found in the southwestern desert the little fields of corn that were far more valuable ? How did he feel about the Frenchman who adopted his canoes and trails and immemorial places of portage, roaming far across the northern forest in the search for fur ? What portent did he see in the English colonists who learned of him the worth of the maize and potatoes, the beans and pumpkin and tobacco new to European palates, and who devoted broad stretches of land to their cultivation, pushing on and on into the wild country and subduing it to tillage ?

We shall find little related of the effect of all this upon the native American. The Indian was in the Stone Age when Europe burst in upon him. When De Soto was marching across the lowlands of the South, when Raleigh was skirting the Virginian coasts, the native had barely learned a little metal working, chiefly for purposes of ornament; his weapons and utensils were of wood and stone, grass and clay. Life with such simple aids as he had devised was hard and precarious even in the more fertile sections of the country. In the more desolate regions it was hardship intensified beyond anything a twentieth-century imagination can grasp.

Even worse than his lack of tools was the utter absence of domestic animals. His faithful dog indeed bore him company, as Alexander Pope related. If the creature was not in actual physical attendance it might be because he had served more intimate needs in the form of a stew or a roast. On occasions he even helped to drag a *travois*, but was neither strong enough nor steady enough to fill a great place as a beast of burden. Horses for travel and transportation, cattle for ready and dependable food supply, sheep for this and for clothing, would have filled a sad lack in pre-Columbian days.

The Indian of the fifteenth century, if he ventured away from the water-ways, did so on his own moccasins. If his household goods attended him, they must be no more in weight than his wives and children could carry. If he stalked the game in the forest, he might, with good fortune, prove that his weapons of stone hatchet and arrow were more powerful than those nature had bestowed upon the bear or the catamount. If he won in such a contest, he could next try his skill upon the warriors of the nearest tribe.

Pre-Columbian life was thus very full of adventure. It was still more full of wonder. Everything that the Indian did not understand was magic — usually dark magic, to be feared and propitiated. Spirits lurked in ambush everywhere. They were usually malevolent and frequently tricky in the extreme. Life was a game in which the cards were marked, and triumph lay in over-reaching one's opponent.

Of course it was the greatest magic yet seen when wings of white cloth brought the big canoes over the salt waters; when centaurs appeared and were seen to divide themselves into two animals, one four-footed and the other in human shape; when these white-faced men-creatures wielded long sticks that burst into smoke and explosion, killing bird or beast far beyond reach. Surely these were gods, more powerful than any spirits yet en-countered in sky or stream or storm. Unfortunately this was an advance notice which later performances did not always justify.

The utter strangeness of what was about to happen neither white man nor red could realize at the time. By a single stroke of destiny the Indian was snatched out of the Stone Age and into an era that has always defied analysis, so compounded is it of new and old, of ways native and ways adopted, of greater strength and deep-ening dependence.

II

MEANWHILE the nations of Europe contended for do-minion over the new continent. A papal bull and a line of demarcation straight downward through the Atlantic divided the newly discovered worlds between Spain and Portugal, the westward half falling to Spain. But from the other nations there was heard dissent. " If Father Adam has made a will disinheriting any of his children, let the paper be brought forth," the French monarch demanded. Exploration, in his judgment, was needed to give a valid title to the land. Elizabeth of England went further. Occupation and settlement, she said, must be added to exploration before the ownership was indefeasible. In due time all these set about establishing themselves in the new country.

First came the Castilian hosts. When Cortez and his band had won their way to the citadel of Mexico, and Pizarro's fiery array had humbled Peru, stories began to spread in Spain of the wonders to the north of the Gulf of Mexico. Cabeza de Vaca told of El Dorado — the Golden One — whose bath in the river sent the stream on its way laden with the glittering metal. Ponce de Leon, Narvaez, De Soto, on the Floridan peninsula and across to the Mississippi; Fray Marcos and Coronado toiling through the southwestern deserts in search of the Seven Cities of Cibola — the Spanish trail is marked across our land in blood and bravery.

In the North the French call a roll of daring — Cartier thinking the mouth of the St. Lawrence the long-sought Northwest Passage; Champlain pushing on beyond and laying the foundations for Quebec and Montreal; Joliet, Marquette, La Salle, portaging from the Great Lakes over to the mighty interior river. So come the men of France to cross the trail of the Spaniard on the lower reaches of the Mississippi.

And eventually, after hard struggle, the English gain a foothold on the rocky Atlantic coast. A chill land Cabot finds, above the great gulf of the St. Lawrence. It is to the south that colonies will in time be established; on the rugged New England shores where the settlers will vie with the French for ascendancy over the natives; in the central land of the Iroquois, where the finger lakes lead over westward to the Great Five; along the Susquehanna, the Potomac, the James; and down to meet the lower Spanish trail. Sir Walter Raleigh and the lost colony, which left but the word Croatan carved upon a tree to explain its departure; Captain John Smith with his romantic tales of the Indian "princess" Pocahontas; Massasoit greeting the Pilgrims on the shore of his wintry bay — the romance of England in new America clusters about the wondering natives.

For the newcomers, however, it was another and fresher field for the rivalries and jealousies of the land they had left behind; a wider battle-ground on which to wage the old unending wars.

The possibility that the original inhabitants of the land were its owners was not taken into consideration. Possession was very far from being nine points of the law. The simple savage, all agreed, should be happy to welcome the invader and accept from him the blessings of an organized government and an established religion.

This rule was not evolved expressly for America. It was as widely accepted as any idea mankind had ever entertained. The triumph of the nation over the tribe, of the better organized over the unfederated, was simply the inevitable march of the odd process we call civilization. Like the French King, we have no access to the forgotten courthouse where Father Adam's will was filed for probate. But we may be sure that the document, if discovered, would authorize his descendants to establish their form of family rule over any less powerful group they might encounter. Certainly they have been acting on that principle ever since.

Essentially this is only the rule that " he should take who has the power and he should keep who can." But in practice there is a little more of the tinge of justice behind the universal conviction that the Romans had a right to Gaul, or the Spaniards to Florida, or the Belgians to the Congo. The nation that would replenish the earth must eventually find more earth to be replenished. The missionary who would carry the good tidings must go forth into all the world to do so. The patriot who loves his land labors willingly to extend her sway to " lesser breeds without the law." And above all, the spirit of adventure will have its way. Once the dread of the monsters of the deep was overcome, and the way shown by one intrepid voyager, no force known to mankind could have held back the eager followers.

III

So WITH their varied motives, good and bad, selfish and selfless, they came to the new land. Spain sent her *conquistadores* to pursue the flickering flame of treasure across leagues of jungle and thicket. She sent, only slightly later, the devoted *padres,* whose long robes trailed in dust or stream, caught on jagged rock or clutching briar, while they pressed ahead to plant the Cross among the unheeding heathen of the new land. The two streams, of cruel conquest in the name of booty, and of firm but peaceful rule in the name of religion, mingled and ran side by side.

Across eastern America the trail was brilliant but doomed. Hernandez de Soto, swaggering through the forests to perish on the shores of the mighty river, typifies the whole. In his journeyings he met many sections of the varying groups of Indians we have later learned to call the Five Civilized Tribes — Choctaw, Chickasaw, Creek, and the lesser members of the Muskhogean groups — but he left them only a fleeting memory of restlessness and cruelty. His followers straggled back past the villages of those unusual people, the Natchez, who were later to meet annihilation at the hands of the enraged French settlers of the lower Mississippi. But of these exceptional folk — who, if old chroniclers are to be believed, were unique among the Indians of our country by reason of a well-developed caste system — De Soto's men had no tale to tell. Their story of an Indian *cacica,* or princess, who of her vast wealth bestowed upon the soldiers great ropes of pearls, must have been a large morsel for even that credulous age to swallow.

So Spain established a nominal title, at least, to the flowery peninsula and to much land lying to the north and west; so she established the town of Saint Augustine, which today looks down with the pride of antiquity upon the mushroom growths fostered by "realtors" among the palms and pines. But on the whole she left, through three centuries of nominal occupation, startlingly little impression on either country or natives.

In the Southwest the hold was firmer. New Spain, centred in the City of Mexico, reached out a hand to the north. Fray Marcos had seen from a height the ancient Zuñi village which had answered with death the exactions of his forerunner, the Barbary slave Esteban. He did not approach to risk a repetition of the tragedy, but turned and hurried back to New Spain "with more fright than food." Today one may look upon the ruins of that old village as a score of years of patient excavation have brought it again to the light of day; and may fancy Fray Marcos pulling his robe closer about him and clutching the cross to his bosom, as he hears from the shuddering messenger the tale of destruction. It was a painful introduction to the land of the terraced houses, where the more settled tribes built their tiny stone rooms in places easy of defence against the wilder roving bands.

This was in 1539; and the next year brought the ill-starred Coronado expedition and its brief conquest of some of these pueblo strongholds. But it was not until the very close of the century that Juan de Oñate took formal possession of the country along the upper Rio Grande in the name of the sovereign of Spain and of the Holy Faith which was to give its name, a few years later, to the little capital of New Mexico. Santa Fé disputes with Saint Augustine the claim to being the oldest city within the limits of the United States. The claim flourishes by averring that an Indian village existed upon the site before the Castilian made it his. It is an odd thought that two Spanish towns vie for dignity in a nation that has done more than any other to drive Spain from the western world.

It was in this Rio Grande country that the Spanish land policy began to formulate itself. These Indians, agricultural in life, were more amenable to the discipline which *padres* and soldiers sought to enforce. Hence their name of Village or Pueblo Indians, by which we know them today. Royal edicts recognized their right to as much of the land as they really occupied. Around each of the villages to which they were to be confined by a diplomatic mixture of kindness and compulsion, they were to be in possession of a certain measured acreage. All beyond was " waste land," to be used as the sovereign saw fit. The nomadic tribes — Navaho and Apache and Comanche and Ute — were *Indios salvajos* and as such had no rights to land. The Christianization of the Village Indians made them wards of the crown, to be protected in land ownership.

In 1680 the Indians found this protection of nearly a century a little too enveloping. The subsurface grumblings broke out into open and fierce rebellion. Their leader, Popé, who from the northernmost pueblo of Taos directed the outbreak, was for a brief space the triumphant emperor. The Castilian was driven down the Rio Grande and for a dozen years the natives rejoiced in their freedom. The priests were speedily dispatched; the records of the little colony were burned to the last leaf, in the plaza at Santa Fé; and those who had undergone Christian baptism cleansed themselves by a ceremonial rinse in yucca suds.

Twelve years later, Diego de Vargas led the hosts of Spain back to a fresh conquest, and before long the short-lived rebellion was over. Only the Province of Tusayan, the far-off Arizona where dwelt the Hopi folk, remained unsubdued. To this day they eschew the Spaniard and all his works.

Spanish development in Alta California was much later. When we speak of the " old missions " there, it is by a sort of poetic license, for they were practically the last manifestation of Spanish activity in our part of the world. The devoted Franciscan Junípero Serra began the mission at San Diego in 1769, and the building of the Camino Réal northward to San Francisco Bay went on while the English colonies on the Atlantic coast were winning their freedom from the mother country. The highway was still in the building when Mexico followed the example of the northern colonists and declared her independence of Spain. Her jealousy of all things Spanish led, before long, to the secularization of the missions. They soon fell into neglect and were deserted by the natives who had been gathered into these important industrial and agricultural communities. They were " old " missions indeed, in a very short time after the change of rule.

IV

MEANWHILE in the North, all unwittingly, the French were polishing a sparkling jewel for the British crown. The Spaniards sought gold, conquest, and the conversion of the natives into peaceful and industrious contributors to the coffers of both Church and State. The French found a different sort of native and a different terrain. They brought to the enterprise a different spirit and purpose. Trade and diplomacy actuated the explorers and missionaries of New France. The "black robes," instead of gathering the Indians into centers, roamed with the nomad bands, sharing their bitter hardships or enduring from them fearful tortures, even to martyrdom. Father Jogues, wandering with the Hurons, captured by the Iroquois and made to run the savage gauntlet, his comrades killed, his own frame racked with brutal mutilations, is to the end the devotee of his holy cause. Ransomed by the Dutch at Albany and slipped on board a ship returning to his home land, he received the adulation of court and people, only to return to the new world and the agonizing death awaiting him there. Many a similar tale of wilderness journeyings may be culled from the *relations* which the fathers wrote to the heads of the order, back in France.

So with the explorers and colonists, and above all with those who sought trade with the tribes of the forest and the lakes. From the Abnaki on the coast to the Algonquin tribes above and beyond the Great Lakes, the Frenchman was known and often welcomed as a brother. For one Caughnawaga, where a group of " praying Indians " were drawn into a community, there were countless adoptions of roving and adventure-loving French into the savage bands.

About the time the Spaniard was fleeing down the Rio Grande to escape the volcano of Pueblo Indian wrath, Robert Cavelier de la Salle was taking possession of the vast and fertile valley of the Mississippi in the name of the French King. La Salle's dust was mingling with the dust of the Texas plain when, a few years later, the Castilian recorded on the white surface of El Morro rock his expedition for the reconquest of New Mexico. But the Frenchman's last journey left its impress, and in a few years came the establishment of the new French province, Louisiana.

Not at New Orleans alone, guarding the mouth of the great river, but all along its course are the ineffaceable symbols of that vast French penetration into the heart of a continent. Radisson crossing the Minnesota woodlands, the Verendry brothers reaching out across the land of the Chippewa to the Mandan villages on the upper Missouri, Du Luth with his fur trade, the little French villages growing up among the tribes of the Illini confederation, French friendship below with the Muskhogean tribes — all contributed to the power of New France. Friendliness was the keynote of French settlement and French diplomacy. It was a wide though far from stable empire.

V

FRENCH to the north and west; Spaniard to the south; and last to the rugged eastern coast came the straggling little English colonies that were to grow into a nation. From the outset they had a loftier intent toward the natives than either of the others. In fact we may say that their western road was paved with good intentions, like another famous and well-travelled thoroughfare. But, in the outcome, their arrival was more of a menace to the natives than the glittering weapons of the *conquistadores* or the waving banners of the *fleur de lis*. For they came not to seek spoils or souls, nor even primarily to establish relations of barter, but with the definite intention of making homes for themselves in the wilderness.

In general, they recognized the Indian ownership of the land and made treaty — so far as treaty can be made in such circumstances — in order to obtain possession of what they needed for their settlements. But settling down on the land and owning it to the exclusion of anyone else was a new idea to the Indian mind; an idea that did not readily find lodgment. It is to this day quite foreign to the Indian's feeling and instinct, despite the example and precept of the centuries.

The colonists, being used to royalty, found Indian " kings " from whom they made purchases of territory. " King Philip" in New England, old " King Hendrick " among the Mohawk, the " Emperor Powhatan " in the title-loving Virginia country, were envisaged by the newcomers as maintaining in their rude villages a royal state and power. Even the poor little homesick Pocahontas, in England with her English husband, became the " Indian Princess " or the " Lady Rebecca."

The history of each colony reads about the same — toleration at first, yielding more and more to suspicion, antagonism, insult, and at last, open warfare. In the New England and central colonies, the war was with the Indians as French allies as well as in their own right. In the South, French and Spanish assured Indian enmity if it would not have arisen otherwise. But even without these European rivalries, conflict was inevitable.

Two different types of life were contending; and the savage type was bound to give way.

In New England the Pequot conflict on the lower Connecticut and the wars of King Philip ended with the colonist in possession and the Indian factor practically eliminated. The natives who had been won to Christianity by the devoted Eliot and Gookin suffered with their unconverted brethren. The few who remained could readily be left to the French and to the terror-dealing Mohawk.

In New York the one stroke of colonial diplomacy may be attributed to that remarkable character, Sir William Johnson, who won his way into the confidence of those same dreaded Mohawk tribesmen, and, bringing under the influence of his seat at Fort Johnson the different tribes allied with them, made the League of the Iroquois serve as a buffer between the English and the French with their Huron allies. The followers of Penn, in a way, gained their early immunity from Indian outbreak through the same agency. In fact, it was fear of their masters, the Iroquois, quite as much as the celebrated Penn treaty, that kept the Delaware quiet so long as they remained east of the Alleghanies. When they had gone westward and no longer had to call themselves " women " at the command of their savage conquerors, they bore quite a different character.

Below the Potomac another confederacy faded from view. Here again the wide depredations of those terrifying Iroquois had their result. The dissensions of Powhatan and his people with the English colonists were only partly responsible for the disappearance of the natives. Still farther south the English settlers made contact with groups that touched also the Spanish and the French, and were modified by them in varying degree. Five large bands were to draw back across the mountains, while the smaller groups became broken and lost, partly in war and partly by amalgamation with the slaves of the region. One group, the Tuscarora, went north to join the Great League, and change the Five Nations — as the English called them — into the Six Nations gathering about the council fire at Onondaga.

So, with always the exception of the powerful League of the Iroquois, Indian life east of the Alleghanies tended either to retreat westward before the advance of English settlement, or to disappear from view entirely.

VI

So MUCH, in briefest survey, of two centuries and a half of European venturing. To the Indian, the advance of the stranger had meant far more than the sharing of his hunting grounds or his retreat from the settler. It had brought a transformation, immediate and far-reaching. Gladly the red man welcomed the easier travel, the deadlier weapons, the more convenient goods and utensils which the newcomer made known to him. Deeper and more significant were the changes which these wrought in the very fabric of Indian existence.

The horse was at once an inestimable blessing and the presage of destruction. It held the possibility of distance that could never otherwise have been traversed; accumulations of goods that without this aid could never have been amassed or transported from one place to another. So far, it was justly regarded as the symbol of wealth, the most prized of possessions.

But ease in travel meant more and livelier warfare. It widened the circle of enemies. It diminished the length and breadth of the continent even more surely, and much more fatally, than the Iron Horse did centuries later.

Horse and gun together changed the location of many a tribe in these days. We get glimpses, here and there, of tense drama; — the Chippewa driving the Sioux beyond the headwaters of the Mississippi; agriculture deserted for the chase and the warpath; the *Indios salvajos* becoming ever and ever a more fearful menace to the trembling village folk of the desert. And, under the influence of such greatly increased powers of destruction, the range of the buffalo shrinks, shrinks to its concentration on the rolling central plains.

So these great gifts of the white man brought their greater dangers.

Even less easy to comprehend, at the time, was the inevitable loss of independence. This had nothing to do with the soil and its possession, with Indian kings or white rulers. It was a matter of economic and social organization. The white man could adapt the gifts of the Indian to his own life and economy. Appreciating the value of corn or beans or potatoes, he was soon able to raise these native crops upon a scale of which the Indian himself had never dreamed. Noting the fine adaptation of the Indian canoe to the ways it must follow, he could learn the art from the inventor, and pursue it with superior weapons and speed so as to outstrip the original in usefulness.

With the Indian, the case was far different. He could not reproduce these wonders which the newcomer brought. He must get them by favor or force, by barter or expropriation. If the Indian with the gun were more powerful than the Indian with bow and arrow, then the stranger who could supply the gun was most powerful of them all. If the English half-axe were of keener temper than the stone hatchet, then by one means or another the native warrior must keep his weapons bright. Beads and gay calico, flour and fire-water — the white man seemed to have these in boundless supply. In return for them, to promise peace or lands, to bring store of furs from the forests, seemed little enough.

The goods which the white man alone could furnish made life for the red man much more prosperous and secure in his struggle with the adverse forces of nature. But they checked his own early efforts toward manufacture, substituting wares which he could not learn to duplicate. When a generation or two had gone by, he was all but utterly dependent upon his trade with the newcomer. He had put forever behind him the resources of his old days of want and peril. In exchange for surer weapons and tools he had unconsciously bartered his birthright of freedom.

Ever so easy is that descending pathway. . .

VII

LITTLE noticed, and always underestimated, the inevitable mixture of races began with the first explorers and went steadily onward. With many of the tribes it was a point of etiquette to offer temporary wives to all guests whom they wished to honor. The chief would bring his surplus squaws or a selection of his marriageable daughters, from which the leaders of the party might choose.

Now European etiquette has always enjoined compliance with the wishes of one's hosts. A visit a year or two later would afford ample evidence of acquiescence in the native custom. Indeed it is only the very few visitors who ventured to refuse the proffer who have left us written record of the matter. But lighter skin, blue eyes, and hair with a tendency to curl are a record even less to be controverted.

Very early in Spanish rule do we find problems arising out of this persistent blood mixture. We find rules made for *meztizos,* of mixed Spanish and Indian blood; for *mulattoes,* mixed Spanish and negro; for *zambos,* mixed Indian and negro; for *coyotes,* an even more complicated mixture of all three. Before long there was a new race growing up in the Southwest.

Today for sentimental reasons we like to forget the Indian origin of the American citizen whom we call " Mexican," and the undoubted Mexican mixture in the southwestern Indian whom we speak of as " full-blood." But the facts of history are not with us in this.

The same process went on in the North, and spread to far wider lands because of the roving nature of those French who so loved the savage life that they became " more Indian than the Indian himself." The tribes of the St. Lawrence practically merged into the French Canadian as the years went on. The denizens of the forests about the Great Lakes were only slightly behind in the amount of French blood they shared. Ottawa, Menominee, Chippewa, Potawatomi, Cree, welcomed the French *voyageur, coureur du bois,* and trader as equal sharer in their lives. Among the Miami, the Illinois tribes, and the Sauk they had firm and friendly footing. Even the Sioux, retreating before the better armed Chippewa, received a French strain from very early years. There are sections of our country today where the terms French and Indian are almost interchangeable, and very justly so.

While the English were generally less ready for such racial mixture, the hostility was legal rather than actual. The Iroquois, mingling with English, Dutch, French,

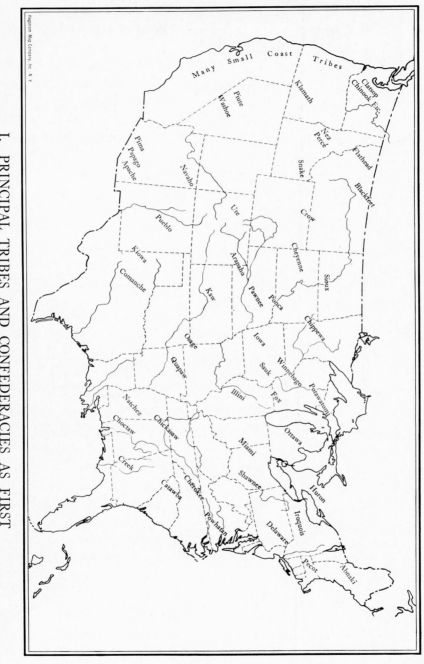

I. PRINCIPAL TRIBES AND CONFEDERACIES AS FIRST
ENCOUNTERED BY THE WHITE MAN

Many Small Coast Tribes

Clatsop
Chinook Etc.

Piute
Washoe

Klamath

Nez
Percé

Flathead

Pima
Papago
Apache

Navaho

Snake

Blackfeet

Pueblo

Ute

Crow

Kiowa

Arapaho

Cheyenne

Sioux

Comanche

Kaw

Pawnee

Ponca

Osage

Chippewa

Quapaw

Iowa

Sauk

Winnebago

Natchez

Illini

Fox

Potawatomi

Choctaw

Chickasaw

Miami

Ottawa

Creek

Cherokee

Shawnee

Huron

Catawba

Powhatan

Iroquois

Delaware

Pecot

Abnaki

and the miscellaneous groups that settled the Mohawk Valley, speedily became a people that would almost defy racial analysis.

Not to be overlooked, either, was the mingling that went on with the slaves of the colonists. Many of the lost tribes of the seaboard were merged into the colored population. The Indians of North Carolina today claim that the legends of Uncle Remus belong to them and not to the African.

So by intermarriage, by adoption, and by capture, the mixture went on apace. In two centuries and a half, with those tribes having white contact, being an Indian was much more a matter of the way of living than of racial distinction.

VIII

OUR HISTORIES tell us of the duel of centuries between France and England. Transferred to the theatre of the New World, it raged with occasional lucid intervals from the time when Champlain and his Huron in 1609 first made the Iroquois acquainted with firearms, until the treaty of Paris in 1763 marked the final withdrawal of the French from America.

To the Indian this European contest fitted in with an older and more lasting warfare of his own. The League of the Iroquois was formed before ever English or Dutch sails came up the Hudson. Independent of affairs or nations across the sea, it waged its deadly, and usually triumphant, fight against the surrounding tribes. To the Iroquois it was merely incidental that the French allied themselves with the Indians to the north, while they themselves maintained diplomatic relations with King George's men. White colonists were only one factor in a widespread game which they played with an art no courtier need despise. "They constantly received the bounty of both parties without much regarding the professions of either," says Charlevoix.

The seventeenth century was a story of recurring raid and foray. Denonville's punishment of the Seneca and the building of the ill-starred fort at Niagara was followed by an Iroquois northward raid that left Canada desolate. Frontenac, who thought to divide and conquer the British, found all he could do in saving his harried colonists from the nearer danger. So the scales hung, tipping first to one side then to the other.

The Treaty of Utrecht in 1713 brought something nearly like peace between the contending European powers and their native allies. For a generation formal warfare was all but laid aside. Then the War of the Austrian Succession was the signal for fresh hostility in the New World as well as the old. This conflict subsided only to make way for another. In the middle years of the century it became apparent that another struggle was at hand. It was to be the death struggle this time.

Promising the colonists their allegiance — as also did the Delaware — at the Albany Congress of 1754, the Iroquois repented and wavered when Oswego fell and it seemed that the fortunes of France were to be in the ascendant. One by one the tribes of the League turned to the French and to their allies of the forests and the lakes; until only the Mohawk, easternmost among the New York Indians, held to their friendship with Sir William Johnson, their brother, superintendent, and powerful friend. One by one the tribes turned back again to England, as the star of France sank and disappeared.

The "Farre Indians" and the tribes of the country above the St. Lawrence had lost their European allies. So much the better would be the situation for the Iroquois diplomat. For all his great achievement and his mighty talk, the white man was merely the pawn in the red man's game.

IX

SUCH, too, were the vaulting thoughts of one of the "Farre Indians." No sooner had the curtain fallen upon the drama of the vanquished Gaul than it rose again, and an actor in warpaint and feathers bestrode the stage magnificently. Pontiac had no sense of serving as epilogue to the play that had just ended; no prescience that he would in time be viewed as prologue to the new drama of America. As chief of the Ottawa and trusted counsellor to their allies the Potawatomi and the Chippewa, as one who had been courted and consulted by French generals, and feared by English, he felt it his destiny to drive the invader from the land and restore his Indian people to their old freedom.

His painted warriors went tirelessly through the forests and along the streams. From the shores of Superior to the banks of the Ohio, from the finger lakes east of Niagara to the wilderness of the Wisconsin woods the belts of wampum carried his message. It was eagerly received. Ready hands took up the hatchet. There was unity, there was courage, there was a definite and intelligent plan.

The future of the Mississippi Valley — yes, of America herself — lay for a moment in the hand of the Ottawa chief Pontiac.

CHAPTER II
The Prologue: Pontiac

I

SEVENTEEN SIXTY–THREE. The ships of King Louis have faded from sight across the broad Atlantic. England and Spain have divided between them the whole of North America, with the Mississippi River to serve as a boundary. England adds Quebec as fourteenth on her roster of American colonies. East and West Florida swell the number to sixteen.

For the original thirteen, she decrees that their settlements shall never be pushed farther west than the headwaters of the streams emptying into the Atlantic. This will keep a strong barrier between her possessions and that land named Louisiana for the French king and now claimed by the Spanish. Between the Alleghanies and the Mississippi the land, untouched by the whites, is to remain forever "Indian country."

There are fewer than two million of these head-strong, restless folk who are speedily becoming more American than British. Surely there is room for them and to spare, between the pine forests along the St. Croix and the Georgia savannahs. They have now but four settlements that can be called cities, even by a most liberal use of the word. And these four are at immense distances — Boston, New York, Philadelphia, Charleston. They are sundered not only by the great stretches of land in which travel is toilsome in the extreme, but quite as effectually by their differing histories, occupa-

22

tions, aims, and ways of living. All draw their very life
from England and from English trade. The mother
country sees no reason why these people should ever
want to penetrate beyond the great mountain barrier.

It is a pretty scheme, but the colonists have already
stood upon Pisgah and viewed the promised land.

Doubt not they will enter in. . .

II

THE copper-skinned American has even less of unity
than English polity ascribes to his colonial brother. One
of our great hallucinations reveals itself in our talk of
" the American Indian " as a single people. They are
less so than the French, Spanish, and Italian, whose
common Roman ancestry gives them certain resem-
blances in physique and language.

Certain racial characteristics are shared by all the
Indian tribes: the dark straight hair and the brown
skin, though the tint of the latter varies from a near-
yellow to a near-black. Other traits vary greatly from
tribe to tribe. Those who know the Indian would not
mistake the Ute for the Navaho, or a Nez Percé for a
Crow.

Culturally, they were alike in that none had reached
the stage of political and economic interdependence
which creates a state and a settled national life. But
below that level there were an infinite variety of grada-
tions, from the powerful federation of the Iroquois to
the lone wanderers making their pitiful struggle against
starvation in the wastes of the Great Basin country.

Linguistically, they were of half a hundred different
language stocks, and of two or three hundred different
tongues, within the borders of the United States as we

now know it.   It is this division which scientists usually follow, tracing tribal relationships through their likenesses of speech.   Wide variations of both physique and culture are found within the same language group.   Differences of location make the likeness of tongues at times almost incredible, pointing to wide separations and long migrations centuries before the European reached these shores.   Indeed, any plan of classification will raise almost as many questions as it settles.   We must be careful not to let the term Algonquian, or Siouan, or Muskhogean, grow to mean other than a language relation.

At this time, when the American colonies were beginning to learn in the school of war that they could achieve something that looked toward unity, their Indian relations were chiefly with three large groups — central, south, and west.   In New England and Virginia, as we have seen, the native factor had been all but ruled out of the game.

South of Virginia were the peoples who came later to be known as the Five Civilized Tribes.   The fifth of these was still in the making, for the Seminole were, as their name indicates, "runaways" from the Creek Nation, who hid themselves in the Florida swamps and made common cause with other fugitives, refusing the civilization to which their brethren offered a greater degree of hospitality.   The other four — Cherokee, Creek, Choctaw, and Chickasaw — were on the way to becoming agricultural people when the first explorers found them, in a rich country where vegetation was plentiful and game easy to procure.   They had known the Spanish to the south and the French to the west, as well as the English crowding in between them and the coast.   Scotch and German traders had early come and settled among them. The result was that even at this early day they were far from being totally Indian. Already their leaders were of half blood or less.

Of the five all but the Cherokee were linguistically of the Muskhogean group. These Cherokee were southern cousins of the Iroquois, but never a part of that famous League. Another Iroquoian band, the Tuscarora, had terminated their warfare with the Carolina settlers by going north, a generation before, and allying themselves with the League as a sixth in that powerful group.

For the present we may leave these southern peoples to keep on their way of advancement in the road of the white man. Later on they will make a President for us, and will harass a Supreme Court intolerably. In the meantime, our concern is with the middle lands.

III

Above the Potomac and the Ohio, the Indians with whom the early colonists came into contact were as a rule either Iroquoian or Algonquian. The unrelenting warfare which the League of the Iroquois had been waging for many a generation had spread their domain wider and wider. Unwittingly they had done much to clear the way for the Atlantic colonists. The cry " A Mohawk ! " was the sure way to strike deadly terror to the heart of every Indian of the villages of New England; it carried no less horror to the Powhatan group below the Potomac. So great was the prowess of these dusky warriors, so widespread their dominion over Indians far and near, that they had readily persuaded the French priests that they had conquered and put to death two million fighting men. Two thousand might have been a better estimate; for the New World was ever but sparsely populated by its original inhabitants. The loss of two thousand braves would have meant the virtual annihilation of not one, but several tribes.

During the long French-English contest the Iroquois held a strategic position between the two opposing forces. Their interest lay with the English, with whom they traded in the skin of the beaver and other pelts. Their own forests had been denuded of much of their wild life, but as intermediary between the white man and the tribes of the wilder western regions the Iroquois could reap power and profit. The French needed no such middlemen; they sent out to great distances their *coureurs de bois*. The English were content to accept trade as it came to them at the border.

The long story of the raids and counter-raids that went on between the valleys of the Mohawk and the Susquehanna, and the shores of the St. Lawrence, shows the Indian as the play of all these opposing forces shaped his natural instincts and activities. The wavering allegiance of the Iroquois when the French seemed on the eve of victory, their return to the English when the fortunes of war were about to change, their consciousness of power, their pride in battle and dignity in council, have done more, perhaps, than any other factor to create the popular estimate of the Indian. From the same story we can read both good traits and ill, can draw a picture of a treacherous savage or of a noble and wronged child of nature.

The latter part of the colonial story centres about Sir William Johnson, who, from his great estate upon the Mohawk River, surrounded by settlers, exerted an influence that reached far to red man as well as white. To the Mohawk themselves, his immediate neighbors, he was bound by the closest of ties; for many years his

MASKED HUNTING

After an Engraving by De Bry

SCALPING AND MUTILATING

After De Bry

home at " Fort Johnson " was presided over by an Indian chatelaine. The first of these was Caroline, daughter of the Mohawk " King " Hendrick. On Caroline's
death Sir William chose her spirited sixteen-year-old
niece Molly Brant, to act as " the Indian Lady Johnson." Thus Sir William made secure his alliance with
the Mohawk, the easternmost of the Six Nations.

" During my stay," wrote an Englishwoman who came
to paint the portrait of the doughty colonist, " he had
Indian chiefs to dine with him several times. Their
attire was the same as white people's and for the most
part they conversed in English. This disappointed me,
because I wished to sit at table with genuine Indians in
blankets and leggings and talking nothing but gibberish
through an interpreter."

Beyond the Mohawk Valley the " Long House," as
the Iroquois called their country, stretched out toward
Niagara. Next came the Oneida, with their adopted
cousins from the south, the Tuscarora. West of them
the Onondaga cherished the sacred council fire that had
burned for many a generation as a symbol of their un-
dying League. Among the farther finger lakes dwelt
the Cayuga; while westward still, and hardest to hold
in allegiance, the stormy Seneca guarded the outer gateway of the League domain.

Beyond the Great Lakes were the " Farre Indians,"
who, like those to the east and south, had many a time
felt the avenging hand of the warring Iroquois.

These were chiefly of Algonquian stock, but the relationship does not imply a federation. Tradition made
the Delaware the oldest of them all, to be addressed as
" grandfathers." These friends of Penn had now retreated to the Ohio Valley. They had made the Albany
Congress of the colonists an occasion for shaking off the

yoke of the Iroquois and for renouncing forever the
hated decree that they must call themselves "women"
and forego fighting. Many times in the future they
were to prove that in their days of subjection they had
by no means lost the art of warfare.

Beyond the Delaware lived the Shawano or Shawnee,
whose name of "Southerners" indicates something of
their involved early history of alternate friendship and
conflict with the Carolina tribes. They had recently
wiped out the Catawba and had come north to rest on
their laurels. But they were not to let their reputation
as fighters grow dim. They too, later on, were to have
the honor of making a President. Those remarkable
twin brothers, Tecumseh and the Prophet, would soon
see the light of day in a wigwam down the Ohio.

It was from the north that the Miami had come to
their haunts along the reaches of the Wabash River.
Beyond them, spreading out to the Mississippi, were the
already diminishing tribes we speak of collectively as
the Illinois.

North of these folk of the river valleys were the many
tribes that centred about the Great Lakes. These of
course had long known the French and had gained
power from the acquaintance. Since the days of Champlain, the Wyandot or Huron, at the head of Lake Erie,
had made common cause with the French against English and Iroquois. West of them, the Potawatomi,
Ottawa, and Chippewa, large groups, related, always
loosely allied, spread throughout the Michigan region
and no one knew how far back into the Red River country and the lake land of the upper Mississippi. Menominee, Winnebago, Kickapoo, Sauk and Fox, roamed the
forests between Lake Michigan and the many waters
of Minnesota.

Anything like exact knowledge of the numbers of these tribes was unobtainable. A French trader who had roamed up and down the land with his wares, remaining in Detroit and taking the oath of allegiance to England, had made a list of all the tribes known to his people. He estimated their warriors as about fifty-six thousand in number. This came close to being an enumeration of all the tribes east of the Mississippi. It contained many names unknown to the English and not easily identifiable then or now.

According to Parkman, in this upper region which lay within the sphere of Pontiac's influence, the number did not at this time exceed ten thousand fighting men. But this is admittedly only an estimate; " the wandering tribes of the north defy all efforts at enumeration."

IV

THE capitulation signed after the fall of Quebec provided for the surrender of all the frontier forts which the French had maintained throughout the western territory. A chain of these ran along the Great Lakes from Niagara around to Green Bay on the western shore of Lake Michigan. Fort Schlosser lay just above the great Falls; Presqu'Isle stood where the town of Erie is now located. Sandusky guarded the western end of Lake Erie. Most important of them all was Detroit, founded by Cadillac in the first year of the century. Northernmost was Michillimackinac, destined in its watery wastes to be more than once the scene of drama and romance. Past it one sailed to reach the last outpost on Green Bay.

From Presqu'Isle the route went south, always seeking the water-courses. Fort Bœuf and Fort Venango led the way down to the site of Fort Duquesne. But that French stronghold had been surrendered and destroyed several years before, and Fort Pitt built upon its site by the conquering British. It was a strategic point upon the river as was Detroit upon the lakes. These two were the focal points of attack.

As French forts they had been to the Indians places of friendly intercourse, where gifts of arms and ammunition, or manufactured goods and implements, might easily be procured. They did not need to be strongly garrisoned because they were not really in enemy country. Only rarely did some distant tribe become hostile to the French; and then there were usually plenty of friendly bands to keep the recalcitrant ones in order.

All this was changed when the cross of St. George was raised over the forest strongholds. The English had not learned the lesson that it is easier to catch flies with honey than with vinegar. When the Indians came for gunpowder they received but grudging welcome.

Reflection should have told these blundering soldiers that, when a handful of men are surrounded by a sea of hostile warriors, it is wiser to keep peace by cajolery than to rely upon arms. They were to learn the lesson in bitterness before very long.

Such treatment as this was no more than the Indians had already anticipated. Indeed the retreating French had prophesied it; and the friendliness of the Canadian villages emphasized the difference between the old allies and the new invaders. Even without such a leader as Pontiac, border warfare would have been inevitable. With a mind like his to plan and an eloquence like his to persuade, what might have been but annoyance became deadly menace.

Pontiac was about fifty years old at this time and an

hereditary chief of the Ottawa. He was said to have a Chippewa mother, a fact which may have given him a wider sweep of influence. But it was not through heredity or custom that he led many diverse tribes of Indians into a long combat, sustained with a courage and a pertinacity rare in Indian annals. It was by right of his personality that he was leader.

Confederation is not natural to the Indian; nor is obedience even to one's own chief enforceable. Individualistic in the extreme, the red man joins his fellows or not, as he wishes; pursues his own desires, and leaves the scene of battle at his own discretion. Not for him are battle formation and lines of march, formal charges and attacks. He fights on the very simple and practical plan of doing as much harm as possible and getting as little injury as possible in return. To the European, war was a game to be prosecuted according to certain set rules. To the aboriginal American it was a matter of getting the better of one's opponent in the speediest and least dangerous way.

It is all the more remarkable, then, that there have at intervals arisen among these tribes, men who could unite all these diverse and untamed elements and fuse them to a single purpose, not by authority, but by the weight of character and ability. Though his plan was to fail and his life was to end ignominiously, yet, in Pontiac, there is something of the genius of a Napoleon.

He had been a consistent friend of the French, and tradition says that he led the Ottawa and Chippewa warriors at Fort Duquesne at the time of Braddock's defeat. Our first authentic view of him, however, is when Major Robert Rodgers' Rangers journeyed across the wilds to carry to the outlying posts the tale of the capitulation of Quebec. Pontiac parleyed with them and heard with evident discomfiture the news of the defeat of his French allies.

"I shall stand in your way till morning," he told the Rangers; and for a time the Rangers were uneasy in expectation of a midnight attack. But Pontiac decided to bide his time, and smoked the calumet before he submitted to the passage of the newcomers on their way to Detroit.

Very soon it was plain that the English would not treat as an ally this red master of the woods. Lost was the deference his French brothers had given him. Their forecast of the English attitude was all too true. British rule would mean no good for the red man.

So Pontiac sent his runners far and wide, bearing belts of wampum with their message of portent. Soon all the western tribes above the Ohio were ready for the warpath. Some of the lower Mississippi were not too far for alliance. Of the Iroquois to the east, the Seneca listened eagerly. Only the most strenuous efforts of Sir William Johnson kept the other members of the League from joining with the dusky emperor of the lake region.

The spring of 1763 was set for the beginning of warfare. Rumors of impending ill came to Major Gladwyn, in command of the little garrison at Detroit. At first he refused to credit them.

Tradition has it that an Indian girl called Catherine, who had won his favor, revealed to him the plan which Pontiac and his braves had decided upon. Coming to the fort with a pair of moccasins which she had beaded for him, Catherine told the commandant to expect a visit from the warriors in apparently friendly guise. Admitted to the fort to smoke the calumet with their English friends, they would await a given signal to bring out their concealed weapons for use upon the unsuspecting soldiers. At every wigwam they were busy sawing and filing off the barrels of their guns, that they might be concealed beneath their blankets until the moment of attack. This definite story could not fail to put Gladwyn upon his guard.

It proved to be true. On the seventh of May Pontiac and his warriors presented themselves before the gate of the little fort. They gained admittance as usual. But it was not the usual group of indolent loungers that met Pontiac's alert gaze. To a man the soldiers were armed and ready for action. Off in the barracks sounded the roll of a drum.

"Why," inquired Pontiac, "do I see so many of my father's young men standing in the street with their guns ? "

Gladwyn, through his interpreter, replied that it was for discipline and drill. A conversation ensued in which both sides sparred for advantage. The warriors about Pontiac waited for the throwing of the belt of wampum that would be the signal for an attack upon the whites. At the end of a spirited speech, it seemed to all that the moment had come.

But Gladwyn had his own signal ready, and an ominous clash of arms without the building dissuaded the cautious chief from open warfare. There was nothing for it but to go ; and go they did.

"On Monday next," was the parting promise, " we shall return with our squaws and our children, that we may all smoke the pipe of peace together and dance in token of our friendship." There was heartfelt relief as the line of sullen warriors filed out of the fort.

On Monday they came again, to find the gates locked and barred. The inhabitants of the little French-Canadian town which surrounded the fort returned from morning Mass to find their village common filled with a throng of Indians, shouting and demanding admission to the soldier town. Major Gladwyn appeared, and said that while Pontiac himself might enter, he must leave his great crowd of followers behind.

Pontiac knew that his mask of friendship was no longer a disguise. He threw it off as he turned to his savage band. War was declared in that moment. They ran off, as Gladwyn wrote, " yelping like so many devils." They improved the moment by scalping the few English who were to be found dwelling in the Canadian village — an old woman and her children; a retired army sergeant who dwelt on an island in the river.

Pontiac himself, tense with wrath, returned to his canoe and to his village of Ottawa on the eastern bank of the river. The order to remove the encampment was speedily given and as speedily obeyed. That night, on the western shore, in view of the little fort, the campfires shone on the wild fierce contortions of the war dance.

Dawn brought a horde of savage warriors upon the fort — Ottawa, Potawatomi, Chippewa, Wyandot. They did not charge openly, but sheltered by the vegetation or by the nearby buildings of the town they poured a rain of bullets upon its walls.

For six hours their deadly fire was kept up. Then there was a slackening, and under pretense of parley Captain Campbell, the second in command, was persuaded to come out from the fort. He was long a friend of the Indians and anticipated no danger. Instead of meeting them in council he found himself made a prisoner.

" My father," said Pontiac, "will sleep tonight in the lodges of his red children." Captain Campbell was to enter upon his last sleep among these red children, too, before the summer was over.

Major Gladwyn's belief that this was but a temporary outbreak, a burst of ill feeling that would soon pass away, was dissipated. From all directions the savage warriors thronged in to give their aid. Day after day was ushered in with the sound of the war cry and the whirr of bullets.

The siege had begun.

v

THE FORESTS and valleys must have been full of Pontiac's messengers. He is said to have kept two secretaries, one to read his messages and one to write the answers. He cleverly kept one from learning what the other was about, and thus his vast designs were known only to himself.

While the fusillade continued at Detroit, and one of their two small schooners had slipped away to carry the news of the siege and seek reinforcement at Niagara, every one of the little outposts in the wilderness was suffering a similar attack. Everywhere, except at the two major posts of Detroit and Fort Pitt, the Indian allies were successful.

Up at Michillimackinac a ruse similar to that tried at Detroit wrought the ruin of the garrison. On King George's birthday the gates were open and the unsuspecting soldiers were lounging about as the Chippewa gathered in the customary manner, to play a game of la crosse just outside the walls. The sport heightened in speed and interest until a ball, apparently by chance, soared over the wall and into the fort itself.

Whooping as if with the excitement of the game, the whole assemblage rushed within the walls. The squaws, already gathered inside, were ready with the guns which they had smuggled in under their blankets. The shrieking of play turned to the deadly war-whoop.

"In an instant," reported the captain, "they killed Lieutenant Jamet, and fifteen rank and file, and a trader named Tracy." Captain Etherington himself, with a dozen others who had been amusing themselves outside the fort, was taken prisoner. In the little village every English trader was hunted down and killed, save one, Alexander Henry, whose thrilling narrative of that bloody day outdoes the writers of fiction.

This was early in June. Sandusky had already been burned. Presqu'Isle fell, and such of its men as were not slaughtered were brought in to Pontiac at Detroit, prisoners. Le Bœuf and Venango made brief resistance. Throughout the whole region English traders were plundered and killed wherever they might be found.

At Green Bay the better temper of the Indians and better judgment of the commander made it possible for the little garrison to retreat in safety. Passing Michillimackinac on their journey eastward they were able, through the offices of a friendly French priest, to take with them Captain Etherington and the few survivors from the fort there. When, in mid-August, they reached Montreal, there were no British soldiers left in the vicinity of the Great Lakes save the few in the beleaguered garrison at Detroit.

There is scarcely a chapter in Indian history which tells of so persistent an onslaught as Pontiac and his warriors kept up all this summer. The Wyandot and Potawatomi grew tired of the siege and asked for peace. Prisoners were exchanged and these warring groups withdrew. But the Ottawa and the Chippewa did not slacken.

A detachment sent from Niagara by water earlier in the summer had met capture and annihilation. At the end of July there was a more successful attempt at the long desired reinforcement; Captain Dalyell, coming in under cover of night, brought two hundred and eighty men and a much needed supply of provisions and ammunition.

With more courage than wisdom, Dalyell urged that the time had come to strike a decisive blow against Pontiac. Major Gladwyn was reluctant to give his consent; by this time he began to comprehend something of the nature of Indian warfare. But Dalyell persisted.

"He then said he thought I had it in my power," Gladwyn wrote, "to give Pontiac a Stroke; and that if I did not Attempt it now, he would Run off, and I should never have another Opportunity; this induced me to give in to the Scheme, contrary to my Judgment."

So Captain Dalyell marched out to his death and to the utter defeat of Bloody Bridge where a horde of painted savages lay in ambush awaiting the British troops. The few survivors next day found their way back to the gates.

Still the garrison held out; still the bullets of the red warriors beat upon its walls.

The long summer wore on. . .

VI

THE FORCES of the red men were later in reaching Fort Pitt. All during May runners were coming in bearing the news of the attack on Detroit; of the surrender of the smaller forts and of the annihilation of one little garrison after another; of the wiping out of all the English traders in the Indian villages between the Ohio and the

Mississippi. Captain Simon Ecuyer, the Swiss officer in charge at Fort Pitt, wrote to Colonel Bouquet at Philadelphia that he was convinced it was no simple outburst of a single tribe. He realized that it was a general uprising. The settlers on the frontier were to understand this thoroughly before the summer was old.

June was nearly over before Fort Pitt with its little band of soldiers and its groups of refugee settlers — women and children as well as men — was actually besieged. One day a delegation of Delaware appeared and drove off the stock outside the fortress. They showered the intervening space with bullets, but from a distance too great for serious injury.

Next morning they came up to the walls in friendly fashion to warn the whites they must withdraw before " the bad Indians " should arrive in force. The " Six Nations," they said, " would soon be there to plunder and destroy."

Ecuyer, equally diplomatic, assured them calmly that he expected at any moment six thousand English soldiers who were marching to his aid. It was his innings. The Indians withdrew for a few days discomfited by their failure to frighten the enemy into a retreat.

Meanwhile the few wretched survivors of Le Bœuf struggled in with their tale of horror. At Venango none were left to tell the story. The Seneca had made a clean sweep. Ecuyer prepared for a siege.

The next month was filled with a series of minor attacks and depredations. The main forces of the Indians, however, were still so engaged upon the smaller forts and at Detroit that sufficient numbers could not be brought for a decisive onslaught. They could and did completely cut off communication with the settlements to the east. No messenger that was sent out from Fort Pitt reached his destination.

After another fruitless parley, siege was begun in earnest. All day long, from all sides, a continuous fire was poured upon the feeble little fort. How long it would last no one could tell. When, a week later, the Indians apparently vanished, the garrison could not at first guess the reason for this interval of peace.

Bouquet's army was on the way, and the red warriors had gone to intercept it.

All summer long the border settlements in Pennsylvania, Maryland, and even Virginia had known the terror of the torch and the scalping knife. The influence of Sir William Johnson kept eastern New York tranquil, but in the west the Seneca and Cayuga raiders made a path of devastation. Beyond the Susquehanna there was constant peril; farms were ravaged, settlements burned, and those inhabitants of the frontier who escaped death or capture took refuge at Carlisle or in the two little forts, Bedford and Ligonier, which lay on the route to Fort Pitt.

Bouquet with his scant five hundred soldiers made his slow way past the two little forts, leaving his sick with them — an equivocal reinforcement but all that could be spared. The Indians who had blockaded Ligonier for weeks vanished as the army approached; but a day's journey farther on, white man and red met in the battle of Bushy Run.

The first day threatened for the English troops such a fate as Dalzell had met at Bloody Bridge. But Colonel Bouquet, on this tortuous march, had learned something of the Indian method of warfare. This was no foe that would advance in line and receive his fire. The soldiers, grouped in a square for the protection of their sick and wounded, were attacked on all sides by enemies who were but glimpsed here and there as naked bodies leaped agilely from behind the shelter of tree or rock. The casualties of that day of fighting were more than sixty. Night brought only a temporary lull and the war-whoops began again before the first glimmer of dawn could be seen.

Obviously only some stratagem could bring the Indians into a position to be attacked. Colonel Bouquet drew in his lines; and under cover of the forest two companies, appearing to give way, in reality crept around to the other side of the attacking Indians who, believing that they had gained the victory, were pressing joyously in upon the shrinking square.

A volley from the rear, and the bayonets of the Scottish Highlanders, turned the course of the fight. The united companies were now able to drive off their assailants. The Indians fled in all directions. Sixty red warriors were left dead upon the field; but the English loss had been twice that number.

So fighting, Colonel Bouquet and his men reached Fort Pitt on the tenth of August; and that beleaguered garrison was relieved.

But the border warfare that had devastated the settlements went on with little check. There was no force of soldiers to stop it, for it spread over the whole western frontier. In Pennsylvania the situation was unhappy in the extreme, for the pacific Quaker authorities of the colony were far removed from danger and temperamentally inclined to fondness for the Indian.

In the conflicts which divided the white inhabitants of the colony we see the two extremes of opinion which have always complicated the dealings of the white man with the red. On the one hand are the remote and comfortable, visualizing the Indian as the wronged and noble owner of the lands — always the distant lands — who should be treated with all the indulgence given an orphaned child. On the other side are the pioneers in immediate contact with all the hideous details of Indian warfare, whose vision of abstract justice is blinded by the bloody scalps of women and children. These embittered realists are as sure there is no good Indian but a dead Indian, as the untouched theorist is positive that the red man can do no evil the white man is not bound to extenuate and condone.

Truth, to be sure, lies somewhere between these two extremes; but the seekers for truth are never in the majority.

So the scalping-parties roved, and the settlers raged; and the hideous tortures of the valley raids stood beside the unprovoked attack on quite friendly and peaceable converts at Conestoga, whose only offence was their red skins.

A truce was made at Detroit by October, though sporadic attacks still made vigilance imperative. Fort Pitt was now safe. Aside from these two spots devastation was everywhere, and the loss in fighting men, in forts, and in territory, warned the British that they must put forth every effort if they were to hold the land the French had ceded.

The honors of the year 1763 were with Pontiac.

VII

THE NEXT year brought a turn to affairs. It was obvious that the English troops must take the offensive if they were to bring about any measure of peace or security for the borders. Three separate lines of endeavor each had its share in bringing to Pontiac and the warring tribes some realization of the futility of their conflict.

Sir William Johnson sent out his wampum messages and met at Niagara such of the Indians as were now willing to make peace. It was a huge gathering of many tribes from vast distances. Johnson had the wisdom to refuse a general council and to treat with each tribe separately. Many times the calumet went round; and more than all, the concluding gifts of ammunition and supplies confirmed the Indians in the judgment that they would do well to transfer their allegiance from the French to the English King.

Colonel John Bradstreet took a force along the Great Lakes for the pacification of such tribes as he might meet. He was the usual courageous blunderer. He satisfied himself with a nominal peace and a formal statement of allegiance. He was content with the bare assertion that those with whom he treated spoke for all the Indians of the West. Apparently it did not occur to him to ask that the many captives in Indian villages be returned to their people. Complacently he sent messengers southward to assure Bouquet that he had completed the work of peacemaking.

Bouquet's honor as a soldier was touched by this high-handed assumption of authority where no authority had been delegated. More than this, his native common sense told him that the Indians were not pacified until they gave substantial evidence of that state by rendering up their prisoners. He must complete the work himself.

Bouquet's expedition in the fall of 1764 penetrated the very heart of the country of the Delaware and Shawnee, along the Ohio, and convinced these warlike tribes that further resistance would be folly. They begged for a council. They assured Bouquet, with all their native eloquence, that the warfare had been entirely the fault of the tribes to the west and of the tempestuous spirits of their younger men. This is the time-honored council talk of the Indian. We shall hear it for a century longer among tribes then unkown to the white man.

Bouquet was not to be cajoled by fair words. He sternly told the Indians he would give them twelve days in which to bring in their captives. There were hundreds; some had been prisoners for years. There were children who had almost forgotten any life but that of the wigwam and who failed to recognize the parents who looked so piteously through the ragged ranks to find their own.

Convinced at last that the Indians had carried out his instructions in good faith, Bouquet gave them the hand of friendship. To conclude a peace treaty, however, he bade them go to Sir William Johnson. This they were now quite ready to do.

Thus one by one the tribes that Pontiac had rallied about him acknowledged their defeat. Only in the farther west, along the Mississippi, was there hope for continued resistance. Pontiac had now, to his dismay, received assurance from French sources that the King of France would not return with his war canoes to retake his western empire. This he was reluctant to believe.

Again down the valleys went his messengers with their belts of wampum. But the Illinois tribes and those of the lower Mississippi were not of the dauntless breed that had beset the tribes the year before. Nor would the traders along that great river any longer furnish him ammunition and weapons.

Even to New Orleans went his ambassadors, where they learned beyond a doubt the bitter truth that the French war canoes would no longer spread their white sails in American waters. They came back to their leader, dejected and sullen.

So at last came Pontiac to smoke the pipe of peace with Sir William Johnson and to exchange the belts of wampum that symbolized his submission.

" Father, when our great father of France was in this country, I held him fast by the hand. Now that he is gone I take you, my English father, by the hand, in the name of all the nations, and promise to keep this covenant as long as I shall live."

Pontiac died a year or two later at the hands of an Illinois tribesman; and so great was the revenge taken by his fellows for this injury that whole tribes along the Mississippi and the Illinois were wiped out by the eager warriors from the north who had thrilled to the savage eloquence and exulted in the vaunting pride of their leader.

Pontiac left his real impress, not in Indian victory or defeat, but in the drawing together of the American colonists in the face of a common enemy. The tragedy of his high ambition and his downfall was fitting prelude to the Revolution which was to remake America.

CHAPTER III
The Revolution on the Border

I

PONTIAC had proved to be as instructive a school-
master as young America had known. The rod
was the accepted symbol of instruction in those days.
Britain had learned that warfare may be something different from the formal procedure taught by the drill
sergeants. She had discovered that Indian fighting was
not to be despised because no massed armies lined themselves up to receive attack.

The colonists, especially those on the frontier, had
had a practical illustration of the adage that in unity
there is strength. They had come to realize that English
troops were a far-off defence when the war-whoop was
sounding across their lonely clearings.

The Indians had learned the lesson that the British
were stronger than the French. This was a useful lesson
so far as it kept them at peace with Great Britain; but
it proved unfortunate when the colonists fell out with
the mother country. It has ever been the red man's luck
to stake his all on the losing side.

The years sped on toward the Revolution. Sir William Johnson's peace held in the North. True, the
Shawnee on the Ohio and the Cherokee in their mountain
fastnesses kept up a warfare that was almost continuous, for forty years from the beginning of " the old
French War" in 1855. But for the present it was an
intermittent and unorganized affair, rising to no heights

45

that made necessary a call on England for troops. The red man forgot his enmity with the soldiers across the sea, while his resentment grew daily against the pressing settlers who came ever to the westward.

Sir William Johnson had designed to settle this question of boundary for the Iroquois in the Fort Stanwix Treaty of 1768. A line drawn north and south through New York and northwesterly across the upper part of Pennsylvania was to set a limit for the white man. For their cessions east of that line the Indians received fifty thousand dollars.

This agreement averted open warfare for the moment. But encroachments and complaints did not cease. Sir William held another council in 1774 when the dark clouds of dissension were gathering, not only between white and Indian, but between England and her colonies as well.

The outlook must have been a sad one for this doughty colonial. Not one, but many loyalties held him. England had honored him with titles and position. America had brought him broad acres and an almost royal sweep of power over hill and valley. All along the beautiful Mohawk were settlements that had grown up through his activity, people who looked to him as leader and patron. And to the red man he was friend and brother, admitted into the councils of the Iroquois as no white man had been before him.

For the six hundred Indians who gathered at Johnson Hall in the midsummer of 1774 it was a meeting to deliberate upon the threatened outbreak in the Ohio Valley, to be known later as Lord Dunmore's War. But to Johnson's wider vision this was but a small part of the trouble that was impending. Anxious must have been his days as he pondered upon the choice that was drawing nearer and nearer. The time must come when he would throw the weight of his influence on the side of the old land or the new. Either way lay loss and sorrow and the destruction of his beloved valley.

But to him the choice did not come. After a hard day of talk and persuasion, of sustained mental and emotional effort in the intensity of the July sunshine, he fell suddenly ill. Two hours later the Iroquois were bewailing the downfall of that great tree "with many roots sunk deep in the soil of our affection."

There were some who said that, foreseeing the inevitable conflict, Sir William hastened his own end. Of this there is no direct proof. He had been a man of courage and decision. His prestige among both white men and red would have done much to determine the course of war in the borderlands. Now his decision need not be made; and his influence could not be passed on to the heirs of his property and his position. Sir John Johnson, his tardily legitimated son by a Dutch bound-girl, inherited the estate but refused the headship of Indian affairs; the latter was assumed for the time by Colonel Guy Johnson, Sir William's nephew and son-in-law. Neither could approximate the power of the older man.

Already the air was hot with anger and the dust of rebellion was thick in the gusty winds.

II

BETWEEN Pontiac, the Indian leader of the previous decade, and the red man whose figure was now to tower above the confused mêlée of border warfare, there is a difference so wide that comparison is almost ludicrous. Pontiac was the untamed savage genius of the forest; Joseph Brant was the courtier and the diplomat. Pontiac fought among a naked, yelling mob in warpaint and feathers. Brant led his Indians as a division of the British Army and held the commission of a colonel in His Majesty's troops. Pontiac died in a drunken orgy; Brant spent his declining years translating the New Testament into the Mohawk language.

It is hard to think of Joseph Brant — Thayendanegea — as a pure Indian. The Iroquois tribes had by this time suffered dilution from innumerable sources, red and white. Their custom of adopting such captives as they did not kill had given their Indian strain a heavy mixture even before the advent of the white man. And with the coming of French and Dutch and English, of traders and settlers of every nationality, of run-away bondsmen and of white prisoners captured in the frequent forays, the European mixture had been continuous and ever expanding. Still, of specific white ancestry for Brant we have little record. His father was said to be a full-blood Mohawk. His mother may have been a half-blood. He was born on the Ohio, but the life of which we have record begins with his boyhood in the Mohawk Valley, where his sister Molly, a year or two his senior, was the " Indian custom " wife of Sir William Johnson.

The white men who attained influence and power among the Indians in the early days accomplished a double object in taking unto themselves dusky spouses. They not only obeyed the scriptural injunction that it is not good for man to be alone, but they selected their helpmeets with a keen eye to tribal influence. Sir William's first Indian wife was the niece of the powerful old Mohawk chieftain Hendrick, and on her death Molly Brant, another of the same dominant family, became the mistress of his household, and was known afar as " the

Indian Lady Johnson." Though she did not hold a legal right to this title she apparently enjoyed all the position and influence that legal sanction might have given her. In the shelter of Johnson Hall and under the influence of his vigorous *de facto* brother-in-law, Joseph Brant grew to manhood.

We hear of him as a lad, but a fighter, at the Crown Point battle in 1755, when old Hendrick aided William Johnson on his way to a knighthood. School — Dr. Wheelock's school for red and white at Lebanon, Connecticut, the forerunner of Dartmouth College — must have come after that. There seems little time in Brant's active life for formal education, but that he received it there is no doubt. Soon we hear of him as secretary to a missionary, and later as aid in Sir William's movements against Pontiac.

There is an interval of quiet, in which, after the time-honored fashion, he marries and settles down. He is a peaceful member of the Episcopal congregation at Canajoharie. Dr. Wheelock writes of him in 1767:

"He now lives in a decent manner, and endeavors to teach his poor brethren the things of God, in which his own heart seems much engaged. His house is an asylum for the missionaries in that wilderness."

For a time Brant parted company with the English Church. His wife dying, he sought to marry her half-sister. Even in the wilderness this infraction of the canon law could not be countenanced. Brant sought a dissenting minister to perform the ceremony. Later on this digression seems to have been condoned for he was a good churchman in the evening of his life.

All this bears odd comparison with Pontiac's tepee and plurality of squaws. Indeed it compares much to Brant's advantage with Sir William's notable lack of punctilio in his marital relations. Brant not only learned the ways of the white man but he learned to follow them more faithfully in some respects than the white man himself.

So when he goes to Europe with Colonel Guy Johnson, Sir William's successor as superintendent of Indian affairs, Joseph Brant is by no means abashed in the presence of English courtiers and statesmen. At times he doffs his correct European clothing and wears a costume suggestive of the North American forest; but he does it in the manner of one who treads a stage. So garbed, he sits to Romney for his portrait, clasping in his right hand a highly polished tomahawk on which his name has been admirably engraved. Boswell — none other than Johnson's Boswell — becomes his friend and admirer, and writes of him in *The London Magazine*. Our Joseph is a social success.

Diplomatically he is equally triumphant. Surveying the power and size of London, he decides that his fortunes will be cast with the English King. Rumor has it that he refuses to kiss that King's hand, alleging his own royal descent as entitling him to the standing of an equal. He must have smiled to himself as he said it, mentally comparing his forest pathway along the Mohawk Valley with the crowded streets of King George's capital.

He promises Lord George Germain that the Six Nations will continue firm in their allegiance to the King their Father. And it may be added that the promise is far better kept than those which were proffered in return by that trumpery poltroon whom fate and family had put in control of colonial matters in these days of destiny.

So returns Colonel Joseph Brant to the land of his

JOSEPH BRANT

By Courtesy of the Smithsonian Institute

nativity. He is a fine figure of a British officer — tall and spare, dignified and suave. His near-Indian garb is elegantly beaded and of the costliest material. He throws back his blanket of "superfine blue" that we may not fail to see his silver mounted cutlass and his shining silver epaulets.

He will have occasion to use the cutlass. It is the month of July, and a certain famous Declaration has just been promulgated.

III

The use of Indian troops in warfare has always been a subject of controversy. The conscienceless enemy incites the savages to rapine and slaughter; and this is most reprehensible. But if our own brave and friendly Indian allies revert to their historic methods of warfare and bring in a harvest of bloody scalps we must condone them for their good intent. In a word, it makes all the difference in the world whose ox is gored.

Both England and the colonies looked very dubiously upon the use of savage warriors, but in the end used them. England was the greater sinner in this regard, because she had the friendliness of a greater number of tribes. The visit of Brant and other leaders to England, on the eve of war, was part of a definite plan of *rapprochement*.

Yet this is the sort of thing Pitt perpetrated in Parliamentary halls:

"But, my lords, who is the man, that, in addition to the disgrace and mischiefs of the war, has dared to authorize and associate to our arms the tomahawk and scalping knife of the savage ? to call into civilized alliance the wild and inhuman inhabitants of the woods ?

to delegate to the merciless Indian the defence of disputed rights, and to wage the horrors of his barbarous war against our brethren ?   My lords, these enormities cry aloud for redress and punishment."   To justify this censure he was obliged to gloss over the fact that the British had already made alliance with the savage in the " old war " against the French.

"Good Heavens ! " said one of the peers of England when he heard of this denial.   " Did Pitt really deny it ? Why I have here lying by me letters of his that sing pæans on the advantages we gained by employing Indians in the Canadian war."   In truth, the die had been cast in this matter, long before.

England was not in the happiest of positions.   There was a large and vociferous party at home unfriendly to the war.   Europe was full of hostile eyes watching for the slightest advantage.   The residents of Canada, which she must make the base for a good deal of her American warfare, were anything but British.   Their ten years of nominal allegiance to the British flag concerned them little.   The turbulence of the colonies to the south concerned them even less.   Altogether it is not surprising that mid-European mercenary troops and mid-American natives carried the cross of St. George through most of the years of conflict.

The colonists, who knew from actual experience what Indian warfare meant and how difficult it was to control, were less ready to commit themselves to such a course. But it was not long before it seemed inevitable and General Washington was writing to the President of the Congress:

" In my opinion it will be impossible to keep them in a state of neutrality; they must, and no doubt soon will, take an active part either for or against us.   I submit to

Congress whether it would not be better immediately to engage them on our side."

The Massachusetts legislators had before this approached the little remnant of the Stockbridge, a Mohican group that had taken the side of the British against the French and had nearly been annihilated. In New York, General Schuyler was still reluctant, hoping for neutrality. That harried colony whose borders included Royalist New York City and the council fires of the Iroquois, was not to enjoy so easy a solution of its difficulties.

This was the break-up, as it proved, of that far-famed League of the Iroquois which had held sway over almost a quarter of the continent before its shores had been invaded by the white man. For the Oneida, influenced by the counsel of two patriotic missionaries, Kirkland and Deane, sent word to the Americans that they would not interfere in this war between brothers.

"Brothers," they wrote to the Governor of Connecticut, "possess your minds in peace respecting us Indians. We cannot intermeddle in this dispute between two brothers. The quarrel seems to be unnatural. You are two brothers of one blood. We are unwilling to join on either side in such a contest, for we bear an equal affection of both Old and New England."

A part of the Tuscarora followed their example. Before the war was old, neutrality had proved the usual will-o'-the-wisp, and the Oneida were soon definitely aiding the "Bostons," as the American troops were called.

The Mohawk, however, and all the western members of the League — Onondaga, Cayuga, Seneca — followed the lead of Brant and the Johnson family. Tryon County, as the vast region of the New York hinterland

was called, became an armed camp.   Actual warfare
began with the battle of Oriskany.

Burgoyne, travelling from Montreal down Lake
Champlain and the Hudson Valley, had Indian troops
under his command; but they proved a poor reliance
after he had taken Ticonderoga and was struggling
through the dense woods south of that fort.   At Albany,
according to the plan, he was to meet Howe advancing
north from New York City, and St. Leger, who, with a
force including many Indians led by Brant, had started
out from Oswego to cross central New York.

The meeting did not come about.   Howe never
started north, but went instead in another direction.
St. Leger started indeed, but got no farther than Fort
Stanwix.

With him were the seven hundred braves whom Brant
commanded.   Mary Jemison, a white woman who had
lived among the Seneca from childhood, told of the flam-
boyant predictions which had induced them to enter the
combat.

" They were sent for to see the British whip the rebels.
They were told that they were not wanted to fight but
merely to sit down, smoke their pipes, and look on.   The
Seneca went to a man; but, contrary to their expectation, instead of smoking and looking on, they were
obliged to fight for their lives."

Their expectations of a gala day were dimmed when
they encountered dogged old General Nicholas Herkimer
and the militia of Tryon County at Oriskany.   It was
one of the bloodiest days of the war.   Herkimer, his horse
shot from under him, his leg shattered, mortally
wounded, had himself propped up against a tree and sat
there directing the battle.   His knowledge of military
technique was not great; but his dogged resolution held

together his untrained and untried settlers through hours of frightful slaughter.

When ammunition gave out there was hand-to-hand fighting with bayonet and tomahawk. Hundreds fell on both sides before a sortie from the fort and a downpour of rain ended the day. The British Greens and Rangers retreated speedily but in military order. The Indians, shouting their call to retreat, dispersed in all directions. The Seneca returned to their homes in deepest mourning, expressing their humiliation by " the most doleful yells, shrieks, and howlings, and by inimitable gesticulations."

For the war generally, Oriskany had its importance in defeating the plan to reinforce Burgoyne and so making necessary his capitulation to the Americans. For the Iroquois and for the border settlements of New York it meant the beginning of years of raid and foray and devastation.

" The Indian," said De Witt Clinton, " hung like the scythe of death on the rear of our settlements."

IV

FOR YEARS the name of Joseph Brant was a symbol of merciless cruelty and relentless warfare. But as the soberer judgment of time prevailed, it began to appear that he shared this bad eminence with others not of his race. Brant was execrated as the arch-fiend of the massacre of the settlers along the Wyoming Valley in upper Pennsylvania. In reality Colonel John Butler was the leader in that particular atrocity. He gave his Seneca full sway for their zeal to avenge the defeat of Oriskany.

Brant had enough to answer for in the Cherry Valley affair; for Wyoming we must yield the glory to " Queen

Esther," of the celebrated French-Indian family of Montours. By her spirited rendition of the war-song while with a club she dashed out the brains of sixteen captives held for her by the warriors, she fairly earned her distinction as "the fiend of Wyoming."

One by one the little settlements were wiped out — Coblestown, Springfield, Andrustown, German Flatts. The year of 1778 closed with the devastation of Cherry Valley. Colonel Walter Butler, son of the ravager of Wyoming, was in command; but Brant was with him, aiding in the raid of those who had so recently been his neighbors. Brant felt he could not have the heart to share in some of the deeds of that day.

" I have those with me," he said, " who are more savage than the savages themselves." They proved it abundantly at Cherry Valley.

These encounters cannot be called battles, for refugee families running for shelter are not armies. The word massacre is used quite too freely in discussing Indian warfare, but here it seems a fair representation of the case. Such armies as the colonies had were very busy elsewhere in this time of turmoil.

Occasionally the border folk were able to rally a few men and guns and give battle, as at Minisink, in the following summer. Brant's force of Indians and of Royalists disguised as Indians had burned the settlement and destroyed several small stockades and were retreating up the Delaware when they met a body of militia.

" However," wrote Brant to Colonel Bolton, " the rebels soon retreated, and I pursued them until they stopped upon a rocky hill, round which we were employed, and very busy, near four hours. We have taken forty-odd scalps and one prisoner. I suppose the enemy

II. PONTIAC'S POINTS OF ATTACK

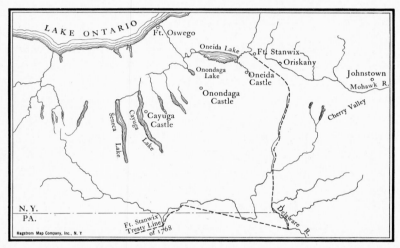

III. CENTRAL NEW YORK IN REVOLUTIONARY DAYS

IV. SCENE OF TECUMSEH'S BATTLES

have lost near half of their men and most of their officers. They all belonged to the militia, and were about 150 in number."

It was not until Clinton marched down the Susquehanna, and Sullivan came to meet him at Tioga Point, that there was any promise of an alleviation of the continual raiding.

Brant and his Mohawk, Butler and his Seneca, were unable now to stem the tide. Defeating them at Newton, the American army swept its way through the whole country of the Indians, destroying villages and cornfields, burning granaries, leaving the whole garden land of the Iroquois in desolation. The region, at Washington's injunction, was to be "not merely overrun, but destroyed." General Washington thus describes the rout:

"The Indians, men, women, and children, are flying before him (Sullivan) to Niagara, distant more than one hundred miles, in the utmost consternation, distress and confusion, with the Butlers, Brant and others, at their head."

This was the destruction of the Long House of the Iroquois. There was no longer food or shelter for them in the beautiful valleys they had so long possessed. For the present they quartered themselves upon the British Army at Niagara where huts were built for their shelter.

In spite of this exile raiding went on about as vigorously as before. The surrender of Cornwallis did not end it. For a year and a half longer British and Indians together ravaged the valleys of New York until Tryon County was desolation itself. Twelve thousand farms had reverted to brush and bramble. Red and white cultivation alike were wiped out.

The war ended in defeat for the British. For their

Iroquois allies it was more than defeat. Forgotten were those facile promises of 1775 when the red man was assured of boundless lands and booty and rivers of rum. The British soldiers had a home across the sea to which they might withdraw. The red men saw their homes in desolation and the white conqueror very unwilling to permit re-entrance. At Washington's request a kinder policy was advocated; but even so only a handful came back to their old haunts. The others took refuge in Canada.

Joseph Brant it was who had the courage, the persistence, the diplomacy to win at last from the forgetful English some fulfillment of their promises. Today the Canadian Six Nations centre about Brantford, the town that bears his name and shelters his place of burial. His was an unusual life and an unusual character. He brought to a striking close the long story of the League of the Iroquois.

The groups that returned to their New York valleys made treaty with the Americans in 1784 and again in 1794. A half-dozen tiny reservations were thus secured to them and are possessed today by their descendants. To this day they maintain their claim of independence and point to a treaty which will before long be ready to claim a sesquicentennial of unbroken observance.

But the council fire at Onondaga went out in the fires of the Revolution, and the sachems no longer gather about it in council.

v

BELOW the Long House region events of even greater moment were filling the years. The country between the Ohio and the Tennessee Rivers was the " dark and bloody ground " which was the home of no tribe, but the hunting ground of all. The Iroquois, as the strongest, laid claim to it; and the British government held itself to have succeeded to that claim after the treaty of Fort Stanwix in 1768.

An Indian claim, however, is only as good with other Indians as the force of arms behind it; and anyone succeeding to the equity of the Iroquois would have to defend the title against all the other tribes who roamed and fought over the hillsides and down the rich valleys. Heedless both of Indian opposition and of the English proclamation line the restless Virginia pioneers began to push their way westward.

Besides the disregarded Proclamation which was designed to keep the colonists east of the mountains, Great Britain had given further offence in the Act which placed much of the Illinois country under the sway of the Province of Quebec. From England this probably looked all right on the map; but to the American pioneers it was an insulting rebuff. That this land west of their own borders should be handed over to the control of the French and Indians with whom they had fought so long and so bitterly, was not to be endured. The echoes of a century and a half of savage warfare could not be expected to die out in a decade.

So over the mountains they went — Sevier and Robertson to create the short-lived State of Franklin along the water-courses of Tennessee; Daniel Boone and his buckskin-shirted array to those rude cabins and forts that were the beginning of the Commonwealth of Kentucky. One of the early fruits of this pioneering was Lord Dunmore's War.

Logan was the Indian who won most renown as the scourge of these outlying cabins. His affecting speech resounded from every Friday afternoon platform during the McGuffy period of our national education. It recounted his early love of the whites; the brutal murder of all his relatives by Colonel Cresap; the many scalps Logan had taken in revenge; and announced an intention to die fighting and alone —

" Who is there to mourn for Logan ?   Not one ! "

The facts were that Colonel Cresap was guiltless of the outrage; that Logan's wife and family were not among the victims; and that his squaw probably mourned him with the customary loud lamentations when he finally succumbed after a life of long and continuous fighting with the Demon Rum. But the white man is prone to agree with the Iroquois in ranking oratory very high in the list of virtues. Logan's supposed speech has wrung tears from many an auditor who did not inquire whether it was truth or poetry.

Cornstalk, the Shawnee chief, was apparently much more of a warrior and much more of a hero than Logan. At the battle of Point Pleasant, on the Kanawha River, he commanded a thousand Indians against about the same number of whites under General Andrew Lewis. In the fall — it was the year 1774 — he made treaty with Lord Dunmore and promised to keep peace with the whites. He did so for a time — longer, be it said, than they kept peace with one another.

The colonists felt sure that the Royal Governor Dunmore had deliberately failed to meet with the other section of the army at Point Pleasant, and that in making treaty with the Indians he was bespeaking their aid against the settlers rather than for them. Events moved on to the governor's flight and the border warfare merged into the Revolution as one stream flows into another.

Three years later Cornstalk appeared at Point Pleasant to tell the settlers that his people would no longer

be held back from war. He was seized as a hostage.
When his aides murdered the family of a settler, he was
killed in turn. About the honor of this proceeding we
would best say little. For its wisdom we have even less
defence. Of course the Shawnee thereafter kept the warpath beaten hard with their hurrying moccasins. They
did not stop fighting until a dozen years after Britain
had given up the struggle.

The British head of this western warfare was Hamilton, the commander at Detroit. The story goes that he
offered bounty for scalps and none for prisoners, with
the pleasing result that the Indians would march their
captives north, making them carry the loot, to a point
not far from the fort. Then they would murder their
prisoners and come in with the fresh and bleeding trophies which would ensure royal payment. This may be
true. Those who ally themselves with savages must
adopt the savage methods of warfare, and Hamilton's
correspondence exhibits him receiving scalps and " sing-
ing the war-song " with the Indians he sent out to battle.
Brant, who by his education and associations had lost
all the native gusto for murder as such, found to his sorrow that he could not keep back his Mohawk and Seneca
to his own standard of fighting.

In Hamilton's defence it should be reported that the
British told equally ghastly tales about the Americans,
and that Washington was supposed to thirst for gore as
avidly as any Mingo of them all. Propaganda was a
term that had not been applied to war in those days;
but as a fact it had existed since man invented language.

Whether or not they preferred scalps to prisoners, the
forts in the Northwest certainly gave aid and comfort
to the Indians and furnished them with arms and ammunition to prosecute the warfare on the border. In the

remote villages of Cahokia and Kaskaskia and Vincennes the French settlers cared little about the failure
or success of British armies, but they were never averse
to a profitable trade with the Indians. That was their
reason for existence.

The story of how young George Rogers Clark walked
in on the fort and town of Kaskaskia and calmly announced a change of allegiance is an early classic. With
his small force all but marooned in the wilderness of
unfriendliness, he played the American game of bluff
so coolly and so intelligently that he won the French
inhabitants to his side and made an impression upon the
surrounding Indians that brought them flocking in to
seek peace.

" I determined," he wrote, " to send no message to
the Indians for some time, but wished interviews to happen between us through the means of the French gentle-
men, and appear careless myself. . . I had been always
convinced that our general conduct with the Indians was
wrong; that inviting them to treaties was construed by
them in a different manner from what we expected, and
imputed by them to fear, and that giving them great
presents confessed it. I resolved to guard against
this. . . As the Indians in this quarter had not yet been
spoiled by us, I was resolved that they should not be."

" A Daniel come to judgment," indeed ! It fell out
as he planned. The Indians took counsel of the French
traders and presented themselves in great numbers at
Cahokia. One band tried to capture Clark by treachery,
but he had their leaders seized. Then, in the midst of
the great throng of warriors, uncertain and grumbling
over the arrest of some of their number, Clark ordered
his little party to assemble that evening for a dance.
This exhibition of indifference completed his conquest

of the red man's imagination. They came gladly next morning for a grand council, entreating that they might be received as friends. They laid the blame upon the English for sending " evil birds " flying through the land, and begged that the white wampum belt of peace might take the place of the bloody emblem of war.

The next day — for great lapse of time is an essential part of Indian council ceremony — Clark told in the symbolic language fitted to the occasion of the reasons for the war between the Big Knives and the English. He flung down before the chiefs a bloody belt and a white one and bade them make their own choice.

" Don't take up the one belt with your hands, while your hearts drink up the other," he counselled sternly. Next day they were glad to take up the white belt of peace and to entreat his mercy for the chiefs who had plotted against them.

Five weeks of such treaty-making brought friendly relations with tribes over a vast range of territory. As far to the northwest as Pittsburgh the change in the temper of the Indians was apparent. British power had received a setback. English and Sioux united in the following year, and the fighting continued. But the tall young redhead captain of the Long Knives had left his impress upon the tribes of the Illinois region.

Along the Ohio the story of raid and slaughter went on and on, even after the surrender of Cornwallis. On the Muskingum the Moravian Indians were murdered by enraged settlers who felt that pacifists had no right to exist while the world was at war. Neither Indian nor white man could understand or trust these people who believed in the literal acceptance of the command to love one another.

VI

BELOW the dark and bloody ground we come to the Cherokee hills. The Cherokee had listened to the song of the British siren and were more than ready for fight. In fact they had been fighting all along; the nominal change of standards meant little.

These southern cousins of New York's Six Nations were already taking on much of the ways and of the blood of the white man. Their towns and villages had assumed something of the air of permanency; they were increasingly interested in agriculture as well as the chase. When they swooped down from the west and raided the villages of the border dwellers of the Carolinas, they knew that a return raid from hastily assembled militia would soon devastate their own corn fields and gardens. Repeat this indefinitely and you have the story of a generation among the Cherokee. General Wayne of the Americans, by his humane treatment of the prisoners he took in 1782 when the Cherokee attacked him to their own loss, did much to detach their interest from the waning British fortunes; and Sevier helped to widen the breach by increasing the number of " friendlies."

Of the neighboring Creek, some joined with the Cherokee in these continued outbreaks; others preserved a friendliness to the colonists of South Carolina and Georgia, even when the colonists themselves changed their allegiance; and some cast in their lot with Spain when that country thrust herself into the situation by declaring war upon England in 1779.

It was not that Spain loved the colonists more but England less. She saw a chance to regain her ancient province of Florida, which she had carelessly bartered

away in 1763. She did not send any armies to the New
World but she sent word to New Orleans and the land
beyond the Mississippi that her people were at liberty to
jump in and grab off whatever was loose. She got what
she wanted, and for another forty years the boundary
between Florida and the United States was a bone of
contention.

Dominant over the Creek in this period was the picturesque and versatile Alexander McGillivray who
dwelt in great state upon the Coosa River in Alabama.
He managed to be at one and the same time " emperor "
of the Creek and the allied Seminole and Chickamauga,
Superintendent-General for Spain over the Creek and
Seminole, Colonel in the British Army, agent of the
United States with the rank of Brigadier-General, and
an extremely prosperous trader with a French partner.
By the exercise of diplomacy he not only had all the
emoluments of these different ranks but even wore the
different uniforms as best suited occasion and company.
He was said to travel always with two servants, and
even more than Pontiac he must have been in need of
skilled advice to keep his right hand from knowing what
his left hand was doing.

His blood was as various as his loyalties. His grand-
father was a French captain, who had married a daughter of the ruling Creek family. Her Spanish blood had
no doubt aided in making her celebrated for her beauty.
Their daughter married a Scotch youth of wealthy family
who lived long among the Creek and waxed prosperous.
Their son Alexander, born about 1839, was thus of four
nationalities; he possessed, according to one writer, " the
polished urbanity of the Frenchman, the duplicity of
the Spaniard, the cool sagacity of the Scotchman, and the
subtlety and inveterate hate of the Indian." General

Robertson, who knew him well, said that the Spaniards
were all devils and McGillivray the most Satanic of the
lot — " half Spaniard, half Frenchman, half Scotchman,
and altogether Creek scoundrel." But his cleverness it
would be hard to deny. When we add that he was about
as truly an emperor as an Indian tribe is likely to have,
by virtue of his sagacity and the devotion which his
Creek people gave him, we need not wonder that the
course of the tribe through these years is devious and
not easy to understand.

McGillivray visited the newly made first President of
the United States in New York in 1790 and took the
oath of allegiance to the nation. He was liberal enough
in interpreting the terms of his treaty, however, to keep
up official relations with Spain for the remaining three
years of his life. His people and their connection with
Spain were to be a continuing source of perplexity to
America when Weatherford, his nephew, succeeded to
headship in the tribe and to almost as unusual a career
in war and diplomacy.

VII

WARFARE and treaty-making alternated along the border
during the decade following the formal close of the Revolution. By 1795 most of the tribes had made actual
capitulation, and a brief space ensued in which all took
breath for the century to come.

The greater part of the Iroquois, their League shattered and their Long House destroyed, had betaken
themselves to Canada. Those who stayed in their old
haunts had learned too well the lesson of the war to ask
further instruction. They remained at peace; a peace
still unbroken.

The Mississippi Valley seemed little changed, but those first rough cabins of the settlers in Tennessee and Kentucky were omens of a vast and irresistible sweep of population that in time would engulf the entire continent. Disunion, intertribal warfare, the enervating effect of French trade and of fire-water, the ravages of the Iroquois, had long since worked a powerful change upon many of the tribes in this great midland. They had lost their native vigor long before Daniel Boone struggled through the hills. But the steady tread of the thousands who followed that hardy trail-blazer would do much to hasten and complete the process of disintegration and ruin.

British power still lay on the forts to the north. We may be sure they did nothing to mollify Indian resentment against the American. Another Indian leader, held by many to tower immeasurably over all others the race has produced, was later to appear in this region as the embodiment of Indian aspiration. Tecumseh's father was killed at Point Pleasant. His brother fell by his side in fighting against Wayne in 1794. Already he was a young man of promise as warrior and leader.

Southward the menace of Spanish intrigue joined with the advance of settlement to keep the tribes uneasy. The Choctaw had already begun that western march which was eventually to bring the Five Tribes of the South together beyond the Mississippi. Some were to go peaceably; some were to go by force. Many were to fall by the wayside.

When the Constitution was made, the states having possessions of lands beyond the Alleghanies relinquished them to the Federal Government. The southern colonies did so with the proviso that their land east of the mountains should be cleared of Indians and the country

reserved for the white men.   Beyond the range the Indian was still to be supreme.   In the diplomacy that
made the treaty of peace between England and America,
this land was still visioned as a buffer between the
United States and Spain's trans-Mississippi empire.

But the vision in America, as the old century passed
away, was of a land of rich soil and great water-ways.
The pioneers saw a country filled with farms and towns
where the gun of the hunter would soon give way to the
plough.

The Indians began to catch a glimpse of that vision
too; but with much more misgiving.   Old Daniel Boone
had already found Kentucky too crowded and had betaken himself and his rifle beyond the big river.

CHAPTER IV
The People of the West

I

AND NOW the curtain rises on a scene very different from anything that has gone before. East of the Alleghanies the Indians have been acquainted with English settlers for nearly two centuries. In the northern forest country they have given the French their furs in trade and their daughters in marriage for a half century longer. Down on the Rio Grande they have acknowledged the sway of the Spaniard for quite as long a time.

But in this vast unknown land that lies between the Mississippi River and the Rocky Mountains, while there is a tradition that white men live in the East, it is little more than a tradition. In the South the Pawnee occasionally make a raid and bring back horses captured from the people of New Mexico. In the North French traders make their way about now and then, and the nearer tribes know of their existence. Farther back there are great tribes and groups of tribes that have not seen the face of a white man.

What could the treaty of 1763 mean to the restless Cheyenne, the tempestuous Blackfoot, the marauding Crow? The untamed son of the prairies would have stared in wonder at the notion that he had changed from a subject of France to a subject of Spain. Being subjected even to a chieftain of his own tribe was very far from entering into his plan of living. No apprehension

69

of change visited the plains when the inhabitants of New
Orleans and of the little French village of St. Louis began to hear the rumor that Spain had re-ceded Louisiana
to France. No misgiving came to the western hunter of
the buffalo when the ministers of Jefferson, seeking to
assure the Mississippi Valley pioneers of an outlet by
the purchase of the city at the river mouth, found themselves forced to include in the bargain the unexplored
lands north and west.

A foolish and wasteful bargain, Americans thought.
And the Indians thought about it not at all.

More on their minds were the intertribal wars and
migrations that make up their unwritten history,
stretching back into the dim vistas of the mystical.
From the north, from the sources of the Mississippi
where the numerous and fierce Chippewa were all powerful, came an impetus that kept the various Siouan
tribes moving southwestward. When the advent of the
French armed the Chippewa the movement was accelerated. In the early tradition of the Sioux and tribes
of their sort is a recollection of a day when some dependence was placed upon agriculture as a means of livelihood; but this was forsaken before the light of history
dawns upon the region.

Beyond the Siouan groups which, in addition to the
seven-branched Sioux or Dakota, included Ponca,
Osage, Assiniboine, Oto, Missouria, and the more sedentary Mandan, were the far westward cousins of the Algonquian family. Three in number they were, and all
warlike rovers along the eastern fringes of the mountains — Blackfoot, Cheyenne, and Arapaho. From the
south, coming up across the plains with a generally
northeasterly trend, were the Caddoan group — Caddo,
Aricara, Pawnee. Farther west, in the mountains and

the desert beyond, were Shoshoneans — Ute, Comanche, Crow, and Shoshoni or Snake.

But this is getting beyond the border of the Louisiana country, so far as an unknown land can have a border. Westward is the wilderness that is later to be known as the Oregon country, leading in the northwest to the Pacific Coast, where Captain Gray has only recently discovered the mouth of the Columbia River — the legendary River of the West. Farther down that coast, Father Junípero Serra and his followers have strung a line of mission establishments along the *Camino Réal*.

So the white man is at the fringes of the country, all around; but within, the Indians dispute the land only with the bear, the buffalo, and with one another. And very different folk they are from the Indians of the Mohawk or the Ohio or the Tallahassee.

The fact that they have known the white man not at all is only part of the difference. This is a stranger land, less watered, less timbered, less hospitable to man and vegetation. The Missouri makes a water-way for the northern part of this domain. The Platte, wavering and unstable, for the great part of the time does little more than indicate a path. All the land is a broad, treeless plain covered with the verdure that feeds innumerable roving herds of buffalo.

For the Indian of the plains the buffalo was the source of things material and spiritual. His legends clustered about the great shaggy beasts, their thundering masses, their continued migrations. His ceremonials were based upon the yearly hunt which occupied all of the tribe for most of the summer. His tepee was made of buffalo hide, his implements of buffalo horn, his food was buffalo meat, "jerked" by the squaws for winter rations.

The buffalo even created a common language for the

tribes of the plains, who met upon the hunt, when for their own good it was expedient to refrain temporarily from warfare. It was a language of signs and gestures; with its aid Sioux could talk to Comanche, Crow to Osage.

In this interchange of the hunt they gained some community of religious interest as well. These plains folk were the people of the sun dance, testing the young warrior by torture and pain. The dance had a long and involved ritual which served many tribal purposes, religious, political, and social.

Long before they had actually seen the white man, however, the Indians of the plains had felt his influence. The horse brought by the Spaniard had made immediately easier the pursuit of the buffalo and the movement of an Indian community from place to place. East of the Mississippi the term " an Indian village " means a definite location, a place where Indian homes, however sketchy in architecture, are at least attached to the ground with a reasonable expectation of remaining there. Among these buffalo Indians a " village " is a collection of tepees, now sheltering its dark-skinned families, and in an hour or two packed up by the squaws and trundling off to its next night's location. The village means the group or community, plus such shelter as they may carry around with them. Horses have helped to make these villages thoroughly ambulatory.

Now, at the dawn of the nineteenth century, even guns are beginning to make their way into the northern part of the plains, through the medium of French or British traders coming from the north. It was these flaming deadly sticks of the white man that made it possible for the Chippewa to drive their ancient enemies the Sioux away from the Lakes region. When more

THE BEAR DANCE
After Catlin's Portfolio

THE BUFFALO HUNT
After C. Bodmer

tribes have received these weapons, the natives will begin to find that the hordes of buffalo are not beyond exhaustion after all. These marvellous gifts of the white man carry their penalties as well as their benefits.

La Verendrye, striking across the woods from the Superior country in the first quarter of the eighteenth century, passed the Turtle Mountains in the northern part of that land that now bears the name of Dakota and reached the villages of the Mandan on the upper Missouri. Now, at the beginning of another century, there were coming up that stream three little vessels bearing a strange message and a strange flag.

II

A RUNNER had come out to the Osage from St. Louis. He brought a writing to tell them that they had a new "Father" and that henceforth Washington was to be the seat of authority for their land. The Osage had no welcome for the stranger or his tidings. For years they had known the French and enjoyed their trade. They had even at times crossed the Mississippi to fight other tribes on behalf of their French friends. They had accepted the Spanish indifferently, in effect unaware of change. The Osage response to the news was a simple one. They put the letter into the flames and dismissed it from their minds.

News travels quickly in Indian country. "Moccasin telegraph" has little to ask from the white man's keys or wires. When the two open periogues and the larger keel boat that carried the Lewis and Clark party swung out into the Missouri, rumor was already spreading across the prairies like a flame. When they had left behind them the little French village of St. Louis, the

smaller French village of St. Charles, and the almost in-
finitesimal French village of La Charette, in one of whose
" seven small houses " Daniel Boone was sometimes to be
found, the tribes farther up along the Missouri knew that
the white men, with gifts and flags and much strange
talk, were on their way up the stream.

Above the mouth of the Platte the Oto and Missouria
chiefs gathered in council. Constant warfare had so
depleted their numbers that these two tribes had joined
in permanent alliance in order to muster force enough
to resist other red warriors.

Six chiefs headed the motley band and each received
from the American party a medal designed for this trip,
bearing upon one side a picture of the President. A
flag was presented with appropriate injunctions issued
through an interpreter, bidding the Indians preserve the
peace not only with the white children of his white
father, but with the red folk about him as well. The
Oto promised, the more readily perhaps because of their
own weakness and their recent appeal to the nearby
Pawnee for protection. Smaller medals for the minor
chiefs, presents for all the tribesmen assembled, afforded
them much satisfaction; while the firing of the air-gun
convinced them that the white man had strong medicine.

Of this place where the Oto assembled they made report, through the interpreter, that it was " central to the
chief resorts of the Indians; one day's journey to the
Oto; one and a half to the great Pawnee; two days from
the Maha (Omaha) ; two and a quarter from the Pawnee
Loup villages; convenient to the hunting grounds of the
Sioux; and twenty-five days' journey to Santa Fé."
Commemorative of the occasion, they gave the place the
name of Council Bluffs.

The friendliness of Oto and Missouria, of Pawnee and

Omaha, meant no warmth of graciousness in the Sioux, farther up the river. Since their old enemies to the north were allied with the French, the Sioux had espoused the cause of the British from the moment of their emergence from the wilderness to a place in the sun of history. A striking incident of the retreat of the British from Green Bay Fort, in the days of Pontiac, had been the appearance of a Sioux warrior who pledged the support of his nation to England because she was an enemy to France.

The same principle, in the Sioux mind, applied to the present situation. These intruders had made friends with the Pawnee, their inveterate enemies to the south. They would bear careful watching.

"I went formerly to the English, and they gave me a medal and some clothes," said Weucha, the great chief of the Yankton Sioux; "when I went to the Spanish they gave me a medal but nothing to keep it from my skin; but now you give me a medal and clothes. But still we are poor; and I wish, brothers, you would give us something for our squaws." A series of appeals from the lesser chiefs repeated the plaint.

"All these harangues," the diarist reported, "concluded by describing the distress of the nation; they begged us to have pity on them; to send them traders; that they wanted powder and ball; and seemed anxious that we should supply them with some of their great father's milk, the name by which they distinguished ardent spirits."

What the Yankton Sioux begged, the Teton Sioux all but demanded. There were sharp words and a drawn sword, and a vivid moment when it seemed that the outcome would be anything but peaceful. The white men withdrew to a little island which they called Badhumored Island in memory of the encounter.

The next day the Sioux band, led by repentance or curiosity, urged a renewal of negotiations. Thereafter there were dances and feasts. The ceremonial dish of dog's meat was passed around and the pipe smoked. Still some of the warriors, after all the proper speeches had been made and promises offered, were unwilling to see the boats pursue their journey up the Missouri. They sat firmly upon the ropes which held them to the shores, until their chief, his pride stirred by an appeal of the captains to his authority, forcibly displaced the red men and let the vessels depart.

The Ricara (Aricara), ready to give promise for promise and corn for calico, still made the mental reservation that when the white man was gone they would probably have to listen to their friends and business associates the Sioux, from whom they received British goods in return for the products of the gardens of their squaws. Like the Mandan who lived above them on the Missouri, the Ricara were tending toward the sedentary and agricultural life and roamed less than the peoples below.

They would keep their eyes open too. It was late autumn now in a region where snow and ice come early. It looked as if their enemies the Mandan would have an unusual chance to observe these strange visitors. They could not push up the icy river much longer.

III

THE YOUNG Indian woman sat just outside the circle of the campfire, very quietly. The men who were talking, close up by the flame, probably thought she was asleep, with her tiny baby in her arms. But she was thinking of many things and she whispered a little murmur of content to the child as his brown eyes looked up quietly into hers.

So many strange things had happened to her. It was hard to believe them all. Her people would think her a big liar, or maybe a big medicine woman if they could hear all she had to tell.

Out in the barren country beyond the mountains, where her Shoshoni people lived, they would think this land of the Mandan, Aricara, and Sioux a country of great plenty. Life was not easy for the Shoshoni; it was hard to capture game with only club and arrow. And when other tribes disputed their right to hunt and the men spent most of their days upon the warpath, life was harder still for those who were left and hunting poorer indeed.

She had been very unhappy to leave her native mountains, though. She would never forget the terrors of the fight with the Minnetaree and how she and another little girl had been captured and carried far away toward the rising sun. How afraid they were among those strange people! And when her companion had escaped, how lonely she had been with the women and girls of the Minnetaree laughing at her strange ways and strange talk! Ah! that had been a hard time indeed.

Her people, the Shoshoni, knew that there were strange men living far to the east, men with pale faces, not of the Indian race. But only the far-travelled ones had seen such folk. They would find it hard to believe that the little captive not only saw such people but had one of them for a husband.

To sixteen-year-old Sacajawea her French *voyageur* husband Charbonneau seemed very old indeed — but no older than the Shoshoni to whom she had been promised by her parents when she should become of marriageable age. Charbonneau had other wives, that is true; but that is the way of man, and the Shoshoni had two others when he bought from her father the right to add her to his household later on. She had to work hard, but that was the lot of women. An Indian girl was always proud to have one of these strange folk for her mate. Sacajawea felt that, after all her captivity and hardship, fate had been good to her.

And this winter in the country of the Mandan had been such a season of marvels. She could scarcely count them all as she sat softly crooning to little Toussaint in her arms.

The Mandan themselves were a very strange people who stayed closer by their odd huts and their clustered villages than any Indian tribe she had heard about. And there were many of lighter face among them — not lighter because they were *métis,* like her own little papoose, but for some older reason, far back, which tradition failed to tell. And some even had eyes like the eyes of a rabbit and a coarse heavy white hair that looked like old snow on the twigs of a dead bush. *Cheveux grises* was the name Charbonneau gave them. None of the women could tell why these people were set aside from the others by their strange appearance. They chattered about it often when they were alone at their tasks. Of course they did not talk when the men were close at hand.

But there were really white people here too — not the more familiar *voyageur* sort to which Charbonneau belonged, for these had come so closely into Indian life here that they were accepted as brothers. There were " King George's men," much more to be held in awe. There were visitors who travelled afar and brought tales of lands far to the east where people lived in houses built

STATUE OF SACAJAWEA
Bismarck, North Dakota

close together in great villages that would shelter a hundred tribes. She would never dare tell her Shoshoni people such stories as that. They would think she had gone mad.

And now all winter there had been these even stranger folk who had come up the river just as the cold weather was settling down. These "Long Knives" were going on farther as soon as spring set the streams to flowing. They were going from one tribe to another, telling the warriors to make peace with one another. That was a queer idea — that men should live without warfare. No doubt these Long Knives were a little mad.

They had made the Mandan smoke the pipe of peace with the Ricara, and it was told around the campfire that they had held council all the way up the river, giving presents and flags. They believed in peace, these two tall captains who led the party; but they could be stern, too, and they were not easily deceived.

She herself would always think of them as kind. On that cold day of last month when she was in such dreadful pain, one of the captains had given Jessaume the interpreter some medicine which had helped her. The women all told her it was harder because she was young and this was her first baby. Well — here he was, and a fine quiet little fellow, and the tall captain with the red hair already liked to play with his little brown hands or talk to him, even as she was doing. They would be good friends on the long journey.

For, most wonderful of all, better than the warm fire and the abundant food and the *voyageur* husband and the fine baby, was the good fortune that she, little Sacajawea, was to travel on with the captains and their party. Charbonneau was to go as interpreter; but she, his last and youngest wife, was the one who knew the languages farther to the west than any of them. She would go with them and help them to talk with the tribes as they went. Even beyond her own people they would go — perhaps to the great salt water far to the west of which she had heard people talk. Perhaps that was only a dream, though. They should see.

These white men were making ready now to travel. For them it was to be a long hard journey. But she was used to rough travel in the wilderness, to rocky pathless steeps and to forest perils. They would have to leave the stream behind and travel afoot before they would reach her own people. What a surprise there would be when they saw her !

"And you, my little man," said Sacajawea to wondering little Toussaint, "you are going to have a journey such as few babies have. Six weeks old you will be, perhaps seven, when we start away. Ah ! you will grow to a great legend, little one, in the lodges of the Shoshoni ! "

IV

CAMEAHWAIT was a young chief of the Shoshoni tribe. His people knew, as all the Indians knew far and wide, that a party of white men were coming across the country. And like all the others his people feared greatly and stayed quite out of the way of the strangers, though all the time they kept close watch to see what they did and where they went. When the party was at a place where the river is too small for canoes, four of the men left the main body and travelled off by themselves. Cameahwait knew by the trail how many had gone and how far. They seemed to be searching for something.

As they were so few Cameahwait thought that he and

his warriors might venture out to observe them more closely. They had never seen such people before; they had heard of the Long Knives from far-away tribes, but none had ever before come to this mountain country. The leader of the four made the sign of peace, and, to an old woman who had not been able to run away fast enough when they came unexpectedly upon a group of her people, they made a present of some bright beads. So the Shoshoni men came forward and began to exchange signs, and such talk as they could, with the newcomers.

It made them very suspicious that the leader seemed desirous of having the Shoshoni go back with him to the main party. This might be an ambush, the Indians said to one another. They very strongly suspected these men of being in league with the Pahki, as they called the Minnetaree. There was a great deal of reluctance. Many of the men and women slipped away into the woods and rocks and would not go along.

But these white men shared some strange and very pleasing foods with the Shoshoni. Then their men went out to hunt deer. This too caused anxiety for it might mean a plot, also. But the Shoshoni who still stayed by, held by faith or curiosity, were richly rewarded in getting the better part of three deer that were killed. That was a feast indeed; they could never hunt as these men did with their long smoking sticks.

So Cameahwait went back, reluctantly indeed, to the whole big party of white-faced men. A council tepee was made ready, and the two white chiefs entered with Cameahwait and his leading warriors. They all took off their moccasins, for this was the sign of peace and conference. Cameahwait put on his shell ornaments and seated himself upon a white robe. After much ceremony the pipe of peace was smoked and it was time for the council.

There had been a woman with them whom Cameah-wait had seen talking to some of the women of his party; but he had not noticed her except at a distance. There was too much that was interesting among the white men for him to observe an Indian woman. Now, it seemed, she was to be the interpreter. The head man spoke in his strange language to the Frenchman; the French-man spoke to his Indian woman in his own tongue; and then she was to talk to them in the words of the Shoshoni.

She was beginning now; and there was something that he could almost recognize in her voice. He looked at her closely for the first time. She, too, raised her eyes and looked at him. Then with a loud cry of surprise and happiness she rushed up to him. It was his little sister, stolen so long ago by the Minnetaree. He did not sob and cry out as Sacajawea did; that was beneath the dignity of a chief and a warrior. But he could not be quite calm when the little sister he had lost came so sud-denly to life again; for it was as if she had been dead.

Sacajawea told him many things besides the mes-sages she interpreted for the white men. She told how one of their leaders had saved her life and the baby's when a sudden freshet or cloudburst had come upon them. She told him of their kindness to everyone and how they wished all men to be peaceful. Of course, brother and sister agreed, they were a trifle mad; but they meant no harm and they brought most useful presents with promises of more. So they were not to be feared so long as they were not made angry. They could do dreadful things with those smoking sticks which brought down the deer so quickly.

Now they wanted horses to go farther to the west be-

yond the river up which they had come so far. They
wanted to travel across the mountains to reach another
river and there make more canoes to float down to the
big salt water. The Shoshoni knew of this salt water
but had not seen it. Cameahwait's much prized beads
had come from there, so said the Indians who sold them.

Cameahwait listened to the talk of the white men and
promised to help them carry over the hills the goods which
they had unloaded from their canoes. But he quickly
repented of this; for his people were about to start away
to the hunt. It was getting late in the summer and they
must go soon if they would keep from starvation in the
winter. Winters were hard enough at best. They had
to turn the older people out. Even then it was hard for
the young and strong to keep alive through the bitter
weather.

So he planned they would forget their promise and
slip away. But that sister of his was too clever for him.
She must have learned much in her travels. She told the
white chief; and the white chief argued with Cameahwait
until the Indian was quite ashamed of his change of
purpose.

Reluctantly he helped the white men onward until
they reached another Shoshoni band. Now Cameahwait
could turn back to the buffalo hunt. With good fortune
they would return before the stream was locked with
ice and bring enough buffalo meat to keep them alive
through another season.

Cameahwait said good-bye to Sacajawea with some
surprise that she did not wish to stay among her own
people. She seemed, instead, pleased with the prospect
of going on.

The party had directions, now, how to reach the Indians who lived where the waters join on their way to

the big salt water. The white men called these people by the strange name of Nez Percé, or Choppunnish.

V

IN THE Northwest, where the Snake, the Clearwater, the Salmon, and their smaller tributaries girdle a land of deep ravines and sudden rounded slopes, nature is somewhat more liberal than on the highlands where the Shoshoni dwell. From afar this country looks like huge eggs piled together, so sharply defined are the little valleys, so smoothly rounded the hillsides. Today rich golden wheat fields alternate with darker squares where the ploughed ground lies fallow.

No such promise lay upon it in 1805 when Lewis and Clark came down from the hard Lo-lo pass into more open country; the only harvest these strangers interrupted was that of three little boys gathering camas roots in the Weippe meadow which furnished the tribe its winter store of that delicacy. The lads fled in affright. Most of the strong men of the tribe were away on the buffalo hunt, and those who were left with the women and children consulted hastily with one another. It might be best, they thought, to kill these strangers. No one could tell what evil might come of letting them remain in the country.

One of the women of the Nez Percé had been, like Sacajawea of the Shoshoni, carried away a prisoner to the east. She too had gone far, to the settlements on the Red River, where she had seen many white men. She had learned to call them So-yap-po, or the crowned ones, from their custom of wearing coverings upon their heads.

She had escaped from her captors and with hard toil,

her baby on her back, had made her way toward the west and her own people. But the baby had died on the journey and had been buried in the land of the Flatheads. Now she herself was dying in her tent, coughing and growing feebler every day.

Wat-ku-ese, from the skin upon which she lay suffering, heard the talk about the white men. With all the strength she could muster she urged her people to welcome these newcomers. They were the crowned ones who had been kind to her whenever she met them. The Nez Percé listened and tried to overcome their fears.

The So-yap-po stayed here some time and built canoes so that they might float down the river to the bigger waters beyond. They were coming back in the spring, but Wat-ku-ese did not live to see them return. When she had coughed her last, her word was remembered by the Nez Percé. It had been a good saying.

The Nez Percé watched for the coming of the white men and sent out delegates to greet them and bring them in. To this day they tell stories of the month's sojourn of the explorers while they waited for the snow to grow less forbidding upon the Lo-lo pass. It is one of the two great events of Nez Percé history.

Lewis and Clark had learned from the Indians that they might see white men when they reached the falls of the Columbia. But they saw no trace of them, even down at the coast where they spent the winter among the Clatsop and the Chinook. The explorers heard of vessels that had visited the coast in other seasons. The Indians had learned such words as musket, powder, and damned rascal, which argued that the comers by sea spoke the common or garden variety of English. But this was not the time of year for ships.

Charbonneau felt that his youngest squaw would

never be the same after this journey. It made him disgruntled at times to see the importance she had attained. She was aware, shrewdly enough, that among these coast tribes her very presence meant safety to the whites; for it was good evidence that the strangers were not on a war party. Then the women among these coast folk were much more independent, as they could gather roots and catch fish, and did not need to depend upon the skill of their hunters, as was the case in the interior. So they would actually speak in the presence of men and in general behaved in a way that would be quite scandalous to a squaw of the Missouri. Sacajawea had been so infected by their bad example that she actually implored the captains to let her see the ocean; and what is worse, they had given in to her. Charbonneau would see that she learned something different when they got back to the Mandan villages.

It was easy to see that white men had already been among these Indians. There were plenty of babies with light skin and even blue eyes. These men were as liberal in offering their wives as all the other tribes. Next year no doubt there would be a lot of youngsters, all along the way, with kinky black hair; for the women seemed to like that big black York, servant to the captains, best of all. He was sure of a clustering crowd wherever he appeared. Funny men, these captains, to refuse the Indian squaws, no matter how persistent they were. Their followers were not so squeamish.

VI

THE ONLY unfriendly encounter of the white men was on the return, when the party was divided in exploring the upper reaches of the Missouri. Captain Lewis was victorious in a duel with an Indian, saving his own life at the expense of the red man's. This was held by the vague tradition of the times to have led to a general war of the Blackfoot or Siksika upon white men as a whole, and to have forced, later on, the Astorian party to take a lower route to the Pacific with consequent suffering and disaster.

Nearer the truth of the matter appears to be the naturally restless and predatory nature of the Blackfoot tribes. They were three in number: Blackfoot, Blood, and Piegan. They had been later in getting the horse and gun than many of the other tribes and they were thus newly fortified for a career of aggression. They roamed from away up in the Canadian Rockies down to the buffalo grounds of northern Montana, which were a meeting place for many tribes. Here they hunted the buffalo and one another.

Like their western Algonquian cousins, the Cheyenne and the Arapaho, the Blackfoot were strong, tireless hunters and warriors. They had no agricultural leanings. They were Indians of the hills and the plains, dependent upon the buffalo in large measure, with such additional supplies as they could get by raiding the villages of other nations. Their reputation for valor and ruthlessness antedates the coming of the Lewis and Clark party. The encounter of Captain Lewis with a group of their men illustrated the tribal character admirably but was not responsible for their mode of life or their disposition toward warfare.

Beyond this incident it was a peaceful and productive journey. It brought to the United States a great body of simple and useful observation about tribes and regions whose names had not before been heard. It acquainted eastern America with the vastness of its new purchase and the richness of the unclaimed Oregon country which lay beyond.

Not at this time, nor for thirty years later, did anyone imagine that settlement would penetrate very far into this country. The Indians and the buffalo would always roam there, and the chief interest of the white men would be in trading with them for the skins of the wild creatures. American fur companies were eager to start in and take the place of the old Spanish and French connections. St. Louis heard with excitement and satisfaction the report of the captains' return. A law had been passed establishing on the Missouri two or three government trading posts. This policy was to last until the growing power of the private traders proved too much for it, fifteen years or so later.

In the meantime the field was wide and men awoke year by year to the fact that there were opportunities in this western wilderness. It was, however, on barter and trade that they based their hopes.

Neither the red man nor the white could in wildest surmise contemplate the coming of white women and children and white men's homes to this trans-Mississippi empire of the beaver and the buffalo.

·CHAPTER V
Tecumseh

I

THE INDIAN TRIBES of the Northwest Territory did not calm down sufficiently to make peace with the Americans for a dozen years after the official close of the Revolution. Then, when Little Turtle of the Miami had been defeated by General Anthony Wayne at Fallen Timbers, they came together and signed at Greenville a treaty which gave a period of respite for the settlers along the Ohio. About the same time the British reluctantly yielded possession of the forts along the Great Lakes, which had been nominally relinquished at the close of the war, and retired to Fort Malden just across the river from Detroit. It was felt that the coincidence of Indian submission and British retreat was by no means accidental.

From the British Fort Malden on the north, away down to the Spanish settlements of Pensacola in West Florida, ran a well-travelled trail. It passed through the lands of the different tribes that lived and roamed along the Mississippi and its eastern tributaries. These tribes were many, from the Chippewa in the forests about Lake Superior down to the lower Creek who were just beginning to bear the name of Seminole.

The American settlers looked with apprehension upon this trail as the passing moccasins beat it harder and harder. They felt assured that the stream of furs going to Fort Malden and the stream of arms and ammunition, guns and knives and hatchets, coming south from that place of supply, meant no good to young America. Equally did the Indian feel certain that the nearer and nearer approach of the white man was a menace to his freedom and happiness.

As a matter of sober fact, in these early days of the nineteenth century the settlers beyond the Alleghanies were not sufficient in number to crowd the natives very much. Ohio, it is true, had just become a state; but her population was not large, and it was chiefly gathered along the Ohio River. Indiana, the land beyond, of which William Henry Harrison was governor since its erection as a territory in 1801, was very sparsely settled indeed. For years to come there would be fewer than six inhabitants per square mile. There was plenty of elbow-room.

Nature offered her bounty to the Indians as she had ever done. Why, then, this growing feeling that they were being crowded from the face of the earth, driven ruthlessly and irresistibly to the land of the setting sun?

Several elements combined in this dissatisfaction. There was first the unhappy example of the eastern tribes, many of which had either succumbed entirely to the power of the white man or had fled before it. Then there was constant antagonism with the more turbulent element among the border settlers who persisted in roving and hunting where the Indians wished to rove and hunt. And undoubtedly the Indian listened with eager ear to " the talking of evil birds " — to use his own picturesque phrase.

Perhaps most of all he resented his own growing dependence upon the white man. But this sharing of the country had become a necessity. The red man wanted the gun and the knife, the cloth and the beads, the flour and sugar and whiskey. He wanted, fiercely indeed, his old independence and untrammelled range; but he by no means wished to go back to the Stone Age as the price of the ancient freedom.

The white man, then, was the source of gifts too useful to be refused. But the price the white man wished for these gifts was a matter difficult to understand. Always, when the council was assembled and the presents were offered, the chiefs were ready, after much discussion of their desires and needs, to make a speech of assent. Always they were ready, at last, to put their marks upon a piece of paper as a preliminary to the distribution of goods. Always, when the goods were used and the feasting forgotten, they resented bitterly the fact that the white man held those marks and that paper as a license to come nearer and nearer to the heart of the Indian land.

With no matter what circumspection and good faith the white man might make treaty, the result was bound to be the same. The minds of the two races never met; they never could meet. To this day the Indian has but a vague conception of what is meant by land ownership. He may have learned to use the words but the idea is far from his comprehension. The earth was to him like the air and the water — the possession of anyone who wanted it and had power enough to keep the others away.

The idea of being bound by the thumb mark of his chiefs was another notion the Indian could not entertain. Of government, in the sense in which the white man used the word, he knew very little.

This intense individualism is something which the white man has never understood. Seeing the tribe banded together, travelling together, sharing together the resources of food, the outsider has jumped to the conclu-

sion that here is a community of interest, making a
government much more closely welded than his own.

Nothing could be further from the truth. Public
opinion, tribal custom, and traditional taboos are very
powerful among the Indians, but of actual authority by
one person over another there is scarcely a trace, save in
a few exceptional groups.

The white man interpreted the tribal relationship as
a fixed and formal government, the chief as a high magistrate with power to promulgate and enforce laws, the
warriors as a council whose word would be binding upon
all the tribe. Believing in this interpretation, they made
treaties and received cessions of land. It was a theory
the Indians had never accepted or even comprehended.

But more and more treaties were made. With the
Americans, the old policy which had been followed
vaguely by Spanish and French and English was becoming fixed by statute and decision. Only the government
of the United States could acquire Indian lands, and that
by cession from the government of the tribe. At Fort
Wayne in 1809, Governor Harrison induced the Indians
to cede three million acres. The frontier of the invaders
was coming perilously near to the Shawnee villages on
the Wabash, and the Shawnee were the most warlike of
all the tribes of the region.

Tecumseh was now a man of forty years. He had seen
much in the course of his life. He had planned — and
had not been alone in his planning. The time was coming to carry his ideas into execution.

The Indian yields readily to oratory, and the race has
had many who can justly be termed orators. Within
the scope of his knowledge and ideas, the red man is not
unaccomplished in diplomacy. Indian diplomats are
not as rare as might be imagined. Statesmanship, how-

TECUMSEH

By Courtesy of the Smithsonian Institute

OSCEOLA

By Courtesy of the Smithsonian Institute

ever, is not a common attribute anywhere. The man of
vision and power and persevering achievement does not
often appear. Tecumseh has been fairly acclaimed as
the statesman of his race.

He was not, however, without allies. . .

II

TECUMSEH came of a fighting family. His father had
been killed in the Point Pleasant affair in 1774. An
older brother who seems to have been the lad's mentor
fell in one of the border raids of the Revolutionary era.
Tecumseh himself made his acquaintance with warfare
during this post-Revolutionary period. It is recorded
that at his first battle he turned tail and fled. If this be
more than legendary, he certainly profited by the scorn
this action must have brought upon him from a warlike
clan. There was no fear in his later years. He put his
white allies to shame more than once by his daunt-
lessness.

But fighting is the natural heritage of the race. Tecumseh had gifts that were much less usual among his
people than courage and daring. He had intelligence and
foresight. He had a plan which looked ahead for years,
and he was willing to work steadily through the years to
advance it. His ambition was no less than the federation
of all the Indian tribes into a single state that should
resist the advance of the Americans as a unit, and should
hold the Mississippi Valley forever as its domain.

To this end he taught that no Indian chiefs had the
right to dispose of the land by treaty. He went further
and declared that no whole tribe, even, had that right.
The land belonged to all the tribes, to the race as a whole,

and only by the assent of every one of them could it be conveyed. Such an assent being manifestly unobtainable, it followed as a matter of course that the Indian country could never pass into the hands of the white man.

"The Great Spirit," was his teaching, "gave this great island to his red children; he placed the whites on the other side of the big water; they were not contented with their own, but came to take ours from us. They have driven us from the sea to the lakes; we can go no farther. They have taken upon them to say, this tract belongs to the Miami, this to the Delaware, and so on; but the Great Spirit intended it as the common property of us all."

This theory assumed the degree of unity which he wished to bring about, but which was far from being a fact. Getting all the members of even one tribe to agree perfectly upon a course of action is an impossible task. The existence of faction or of political party goes back as far as we can trace the history of man. Study of primitive folk brings the belief that political division is one of the natural instincts like self-defence and hunger. Where two or three are gathered together, faction is in the midst of them.

This assumption of the need of universal assent to land cession, if accepted, would block all negotiations between the races. The practice of the "Seventeen Council Fires" had by this time settled down to a fixed form, which the courts were duly approving. It was based, as we have seen, on fundamental misconceptions of the Indian nature and mind; but it was not so entirely the conscienceless and wholesale grabbing of property from the innocent and defenceless that is frequently portrayed for us. We like to dramatize ourselves, and if we condemn must do so with a sweeping gesture that makes

Satan by comparison a mere trifler. Life is not really
so simple as all that.

Tecumseh naturally took Pontiac as his model. The
young warriors of Pontiac's assembling who fought and
ran away were forty years later the old men of counsel.
In the meantime, the progress of the " Thirteen Council
Fires " which by now had grown into seventeen, was
before them as a potent example of the value of union.
Tecumseh planned something more than a mere agreement upon war. He was to create an Indian state, one
which should be supreme from the lakes on the north to
the southern swamps. Perhaps it would be wiser to say,
from Fort Malden on the north to Pensacola on the
south, since it was undeniably from those two sources
of arms and counsel that Tecumseh drew much of his
inspiration.

However strongly the white man influenced his plans,
we must give credit for the execution of them to Tecumseh himself. He was tireless in carrying the news from
one tribe to another; diplomatic in gaining their agreement; and above all, able to hold them back from
sporadic aggression until he was ready for a master
stroke, with an influence no other Indian leader has
attained.

Every Indian uprising has its prophet. Tecumseh's
list of brothers was still unexhausted, and from one of
these he drew the high priest of his new movement. This
functionary is known widely and simply as the Prophet
—less, we surmise, because of the superiority of his
supernatural gifts than because his several Shawnee
names were all tediously long and difficult to the tongue
of the white man.

The Prophet was not so admirable, either in appearance
or in character, as his farseeing brother. In his early

years he had gained a reputation for stupidity and drunkenness, and in some unrecorded encounter he had lost an eye. In a trance which lasted long enough for his friends to assemble for his funeral, he went to the spirit world and had the doors of revelation opened to him. Returning, he set Indian hearts aflame with his preaching of a new order.

It was in reality the old order revived. These waves of religious emotionalism which sweep the tribes from time to time call as a rule for the return of the ancient days before the coming of the white man. The conjurer who helped drive home the message of Pontiac had exhorted his hearers to reject the food and drink and weapons of the newcomers. In his wisdom the Great Spirit said to him:

"Why do you suffer the white men to dwell among you ? My children, you have forgotten the customs and traditions of your forefathers. Why do you not clothe yourselves in skins, as they did, and use the bows and arrows, and the stone-pointed lances, which they used ? You have bought guns, knives, kettles, and blankets from the white man, until you can no longer do without them; and what is worse, you have drunk the poison fire-water which turns you into fools. Fling all these things away; live as your wise forefathers lived before you."

More than a century later, Chief Joseph's Dreamers were spreading the same gospel. In the last wild excitement of the ghost dance the vision was even yet of a continent made clear of farms and of white faces, of the beaver and the buffalo thick again upon the land, of the old freedom to rove and hunt at will.

The Prophet, after his visit to the promised land in 1805, told his people that they should reject all the gifts of the white man. Above all, he condemned the use of the fire-water of which he himself had had such sorry experience. The two races should thereafter remain separate. His people should return to buckskin clothing and stone arrowheads; refuse the flesh of sheep and cattle and eat only of the meat of the wild creatures of the forest. Only those tools which they themselves could make and had invented, should be used. When they had learned to do all this the old happy days would dawn again.

Consistency, however, does not always dwell in the lodge of the soothsayer. The Prophet finished his exposition of the new faith to Governor Harrison with an appeal which showed a willingness to make use, still, of the white man's weapons.

" We are all well pleased with the attention you have shown us; also with the good intentions of our Father, the President. If you give us a few articles, such as needles, flint, hoes, powder, etc., we will take the animals that afford us meat, with powder and ball." The red Prophet was not the first man who wanted to eat his cake and keep it too.

Among the benefits the Prophet had received from his sojourn among the spirits was the power to cure all ills. He could promise his fellows immunity from the white man's weapons. Under his incantations they would go into battle invulnerable.

Before long Indians were coming in from the tribes far and wide to Greenville, where the Prophet had set up his headquarters. When, the following year, the dusky soothsayer predicted an eclipse of the sun and brought it off on schedule time there was no longer any doubt of his supernatural powers and authority. The Prophet was emboldened to break off a council with the declaration that the deputy sent by the governor was not sufficiently important for his notice.

"Why does not the President send to us the greatest man in his nation? I can talk to him—I can bring darkness between him and me—nay more, I can bring the sun under my feet, and what white man can do this?"

To the apprehensive settlers, this growing crowd of red warriors could mean only that trouble was brewing. It was the prestige and ability of Tecumseh that kept the peace as months and even years went on. It was his convincing eloquence that more than half persuaded Governor Harrison that his intent was not a warlike one. Nevertheless the white man kept on his guard and did not fail to observe what the red leader was doing.

This is Harrison's estimate of Tecumseh:

"He was one of those uncommon geniuses which spring up occasionally to produce revolutions and overturn the established order of things. If it were not for the vicinity of the United States he would perhaps be the founder of an empire that would rival in glory Mexico or Peru. No difficulties deter him. For four years he has been in constant motion. You see him today on the Wabash and in a short time hear of him on the shores of Lake Erie or Michigan, or on the banks of the Mississippi; and wherever he goes he makes an impression favorable to his purposes."

III

THE PRESENCE of a greater and greater number of warriors at Greenville was an increasing source of alarm to the settlers. To the Indians, also, it became apparent that they could pursue their objects better without observation. They withdrew to a site near the junction of the Tippecanoe and the Wabash, in the heart of the Indian country. From a strategic point of view it was an admirable choice as a center of either hostility or communication. Here the Prophet's Town waxed ever larger and more powerful. The assembled red men indulged in warlike exercises as well as religious ceremonies; they refused to buy ammunition from the traders about, declaring haughtily that they could get all the arms and ammunition they needed without having to make any payment for it.

By a treaty with the various Indian tribes at Fort Wayne in 1809, Governor Harrison had obtained cession of the Indian land east of the Wabash. He had bidden to the council all the tribes that could claim any interest whatever in the lands to which he sought to extinguish the Indian title. But on Tecumseh's theory it would have been necessary, to make the transfer binding, to gain the consent of every tribe and each individual member.

The following year Tecumseh and four hundred gaudily painted warriors swept down the Wabash in their canoes to confer with Governor Harrison at his little capital, Vincennes. Tecumseh's professed purpose was to assure the Governor that he had not allied himself with the British forces in the war which all felt now to be imminent. His actual discourse was an eloquent recital of the wrongs of his people, of the succession of treaties which had year by year diminished their lands and deprived them of their hunting grounds. He ended with an appeal that the treaty of Fort Wayne be set aside. Governor Harrison promised to report his request to the great chief at Washington.

"Well," replied Tecumseh, "as the great chief is

to determine the matter, I hope the Great Spirit will put sense enough into his head to induce him to give up this land; it is true, he is so far off he will not be injured by this war; he may sit still in his town and drink his wine whilst you and I will have to fight it out." The appearance and manner of the handsome chief and his bedizened braves spoke eloquently of the warpath.

He had brought all the northern tribes into his confederation, Tecumseh declared; and now it was time to unite the southern bands with them. They were following the example of the white man with his many council fires.

True to his intent, a few days after this spectacular council, Tecumseh was off with a party of braves to visit the Creek and the Choctaw. Of the results of that visit we shall have ample evidence in the later story of the southern conflicts.

Tecumseh had enjoined his followers at Prophet's Town to keep the peace during his absence and to make ready for the great day when the signal should go forth for all the tribes at one moment to take up the hatchet. While his own commanding voice could be heard, the eager warriors were kept back from depredations. But the Prophet, for all his religious fervor and his control over the forces of nature, had not the same sway over his devotees. He had a marvellous success in arousing men but not the genius to make their zeal serve a destined end. His messages had gone out, it was said, to the lodges of Indians even across the great western mountains; and certain it is that many strange costumes and faces had been seen, and many a strange tongue heard, in this great town upon the Tippecanoe.

But the man who could make this assemblage into a nation or an effective army was Tecumseh; and Tecumseh was down in the deep southern forests, proclaiming to the listening Creek his message of a union of all the red men against the white.

"Do you not believe that the Great Spirit has sent me?" he demanded of Big Warrior, the Creek chief. "You shall know. I leave Tuckhabatchee directly and shall go straight to Detroit; when I arrive there, I shall stamp on the ground with my foot and shake down every house in Tuckhabatchee."

He proved himself an even better soothsayer than his brother. The Prophet might easily have had from the whites advance information of the eclipse which confounded those who doubted his powers. But in Tecumseh's case it was sheer good fortune that an earthquake shook the lower Mississippi region and shattered the huts of the little village of Tuckhabatchee about the time the watching Creek thought he must have reached Detroit. What wonder that they knew, then, that the time was ripe for action?

But Tecumseh came back to find that things had not gone so well in the North. His guiding hand removed, the warriors had enjoyed all too well their raiding upon the border farms and settlements. The white men, more and more anxious, memorialized the President of the United States, who placed a regiment of infantry at the disposal of their Governor.

With the soldiers there came a most fervent recommendation that hostilities should be avoided. War was drawing nearer, but the inhabitants of the eastern part of the United States were desirous not to precipitate it.

Those in the West, however, looked upon it as a matter of self defence. Governor Harrison felt that the safety of his people required him to demand that the Indians give up those among them who had been active in the murder of white families. He sent messages to all the tribes urging them to remain friendly to the United States. The Prophet countered with his own group of messages urging them to stand firm against the intruder.

To the Delaware, who had remained friendly to the settlers, the Prophet announced that they must make a decision between them at once. They went to him counselling peace and a cessation of depredations; but returned to tell of the insult with which they had been received. Governor Harrison sent a delegation of Miami on a similar errand. They listened and remained with the Prophet. Evidently they believed his great town would prevail against the scattered settlers.

Governor Harrison decided that a show of force was the only way in which to keep the Indians even nominally under control. With his little army he marched onward into the Indian country toward the headquarters of the Prophet on the banks of the Tippecanoe.

It was now late in the autumn of 1811. Hostile eyes were watching from every side. Nearer and nearer came the white soldiers. It looked as if a conflict would come at any moment. The Prophet proposed a council and Harrison agreed — though without much belief in the sincerity of the proposal. That night, the sixth of November, he did not relax guard at his encampment not more than a mile from the Indian stronghold.

The night was moonless and rainy. At four o'clock a sentinel saw the foremost of a line of warriors who had stealthily encircled the camp. His shot called the white soldiers into instant action.

It was not a long fight; later, in the heat of the campaign which made Harrison President, the "battle of Tippecanoe" was a target for many sneers. But the Governor fought in the thick of it, grazed by more than one bullet, while the Prophet sang his war-song and performed his religious rites at a safe distance. He did not care to test in his own person the truth of his prediction that the white man's bullets would fall harmless.

Soon his warriors were in a position to reproach him with the failure of his prophecy. Bullets laid many of them low; but the survivors were urged to go on while the war-song was chanted for their encouragement.

Adam-like, the Prophet declared that his wife had approached the fire while he was brewing his charms. This of course had rendered his medicine ineffective. His defence did not soothe the spirit of his braves nor call to life those whom they left upon the field of battle.

Before the late November dawn had fully come, the sharp conflict was over and the Indians were in flight. Thereafter, Harrison and his men withdrew, not without difficulty, to their starting point. Following up the engagement would have meant forcing a state of war.

Tecumseh returned from the South to find Prophet's Town deserted. His hope of an Indian federation was in ruin like the charred tepees. It is said that he was so enraged by his brother's failure and the pitiful excuses by which he attempted to justify it that he seized the Prophet by the hair and shook him until his teeth rattled.

It looked like complete failure. Tecumseh mused gloomily beside the blackened ruins. Where now should he turn?

Well, there to the north was Fort Malden.

IV

BEFORE going down into the country of the Creek Tecumseh had intimated to Governor Harrison his willingness to go to Washington and confer with the President about matters of state. He now sent word that he was ready to carry out his intention. This was agreeable to Harrison; but he demurred when he found that he was expected to furnish conveyance and supplies for a large body of warriors. Tecumseh refused to go otherwise than in state and at the head of his retinue. There the matter rested.

With all his undoubted cleverness and power the great chief had not had, like Joseph Brant, close acquaintance with the white man's world. Far-off Washington was probably to his mind much like the other towns, red and white, he had met in his wide wanderings. He pictured no doubt another little Vincennes to be overawed and silenced by the sight of his hundreds of painted and feathered warriors. He, Tecumseh, was the great ruler of an empire as wide as that of the Seventeen Council Fires. He would deal on equal terms with Great Britain or America as best suited his purpose.

About this time he came to the Indian agent of the United States at Fort Wayne with a request for ammunition, ostensibly for the hunt. In view of the depredations which had not slackened during the winter this official did not deem it a proper time to be issuing such supplies.

"My British Father," Tecumseh averred haughtily, "will not deny me."

To his British Father he went and the result was his commission as Brigadier-General in the Army of His Majesty King George. Indian stock was rising in the British market; the accomplished and debonair Brant had achieved no more than a colonelcy.

Tecumseh paid for his commission with the power of the high standing he had won among his people, with the

more than two thousand naked warriors he brought to
the aid of the Canadian troops, with his knowledge of the
country and his keenness in strategy. He paid for it with
his resourcefulness, his daring, his hardihood. In the
end he paid for it with his life.

" Tecumseh was very prepossessing," wrote a British
officer who was present when the Indian leader joined
his forces with those of the King; " his figure light and
finely proportioned, his height five feet nine or ten inches,
his complexion light copper, his countenance oval, with
bright hazel eyes beaming cheerfulness, energy, and decision. Three small crowns or coronets were suspended
from the lower cartilage of his aquiline nose, and a large
silver medallion of George the Third, which I believe his
ancestor had received from Lord Dorchester when Governor General of Canada, was attached to a mixed colored wampum string which hung around his neck."

Bois Blanc was a little island opposite Fort Malden,
where the Detroit River merges into Lake Erie. Here
the Indian warriors gathered. Far tribes came to the
rendezvous. Even the Sioux from the far off Missouri
were part of the alliance. Potawatomi, Ottawa, Miami,
Wyandot, Sauk, and Fox, and the various tribes of the
Illinois grouping were joined with Tecumseh's own
Shawnee. Among the lesser chiefs there was Black
Hawk, a subchief of the Sauk, who was to retain his
reliance upon the British for twenty years longer.

Some bands who still wished for neutrality in the war
met in council at Brownsville on the United States side
of the river and sent to Tecumseh an appeal to meet and
parley with them. He replied with indignation:

" I have taken sides with the King my Father, and I
will suffer my bones to bleach upon this shore, before I
will recross that stream for any council of neutrality."

He recrossed it not long after at the head of a body of warriors and won at the little town of Brownsville the opening engagement of the western war.

Tecumseh was master of all the Indian troops, though each band had its own chiefs. To his credit be it said that when his eye was upon them, mutilation of the dead and torture of the wounded and prisoners did not follow an engagement. It was otherwise when his restraining influence was not felt. Unmodified Indian warfare was seen at Fort Dearborn and following the battle of the River Raisin. Tecumseh did not love slaughter for slaughter's sake.

Because he knew his Indians, and because he knew his country, Tecumseh made a better general than the British who commanded beside him. The first success at Brownsville seemed a small matter; but Tecumseh knew that the earliest breeze of success or failure often turns the Indian weather-vane. The capture of Hull's mailbag was to the Indians an omen of success. To the British, who could read its contents, it was a revelation of the weakness of the American forces.

Hull surrendered Detroit without a blow, and at almost the same moment, on the southwestern shore of Lake Michigan, the little garrison at Fort Dearborn, obeying the order to destroy their stores and retreat, marched out to face murder or capture. A few were taken as prisoners to various British commanders; but most fell to the tomahawks of the many Indians who had been camped about the little fort waiting to see how the fortunes of war would turn.

In a year of warfare Tecumseh was a tower of strength to his allies. General Sir Isaac Brock wrote: "The conduct of the Indians, joined to that of the gallant and brave chiefs of their respective tribes, has since the commencement of the war been marked with acts of true heroism." Brock gave Tecumseh much of the credit for the success at Detroit; the Indian had etched upon bark with his scalping-knife an intelligent map of the fort and its surroundings; and by his influence over the various Indian tribes had led them first across the river, to the dismay of the American garrison.

In recognition of his aid, Brock decorated the blushing Tecumseh with his own sash and pistols. Then the English general went to meet his fate at Queenstown, leaving Colonel Proctor in command of the western forts, now all in British hands once more.

The defeat of the Americans at Frenchtown and the massacre at the River Raisin were not to be entered to Tecumseh's glory or discredit. He was away at the time inspiring new recruits to the British cause. Round Head, the old chief of the Wyandot, to whom Tecumseh had generously given Brock's sash in recognition of the chief's years and valiant service, was the one who dominated that bloody field. Tecumseh withheld his approval. " I conquer to save, and you to murder," he told Colonel Proctor.

With all Tecumseh's generalship, however, the sieges of Fort Meigs and Fort Stephenson proved unavailing. The Indian forces went again into encampment on Bois Blanc island. Here they awaited the outcome of a naval engagement which the British assured them would be a decisive one.

It was indeed decisive; but it is the American, not the Englishman, who commemorates the day of September 10, 1813, as Perry's victory on Lake Erie. Proctor made preparations to retreat from Fort Malden, to the intense disgust of his Indian allies.

Indian interest in the contest had been waning as British power seemed to wane. Before this the lower tribes had wished to go back to their own land and assure the Americans of their neutrality. It is said that Tecumseh himself had all but made up his mind to leave but had been dissuaded by the persuasions of the Sioux and the Chippewa — old foes who oddly found themselves for the first time on the same side of a conflict.

But if he were to stay Tecumseh wished to fight in earnest. Remaining in camp had no attractions for him; still less did he relish Proctor's idea of retreat.

" In the old war," he said to Proctor, " our Father was thrown on his back by the Americans; and our Father took them by the hand without our knowledge; and we are afraid our Father will do so again at this time." Events had shaken the confidence of the red children.

Eloquently he reminded the British general of his promise never to draw his foot off British ground.

" You are like a fat dog, that carries his tail on his back, but when affrighted, drops it between his legs and runs off."

In vain he harangued the harried Proctor. The British general felt that the endurance of insolence and abuse was a high price to pay for the Indian alliance. Not all Tecumseh's eloquence could induce him to make a stand at Amherstburg. They fired the town and continued eastward. The retreating garrison from Detroit joined them. All along the way Tecumseh urged Proctor to resistance.

Beyond Chatham, on the Thames, at last they made a stand. It was an unequal contest. Tecumseh went into the fight, this morning of the fifth of October, with the conviction that it would be his last. He was a true prophet.

So long as his voice was heard above the din, urging on

his men, the Indians gave him that obedience which he had always been able to command. But the voice was heard no more; and the red men speedily scattered afar. The British had been even readier to give up the contest.

Harrison, in his official report of the engagement, did not state that Tecumseh had been killed on the field of battle. But before long it became known that this must have been the case. Great dispute arose among various claimants for the honor of having finished this notable career; but the question is still an open one.

Tecumseh was gone, and gone was the hope of Indian unity in the Northwest. The British government pensioned his family and the Prince Regent sent his seventeen-year-old son a sword; but Tecumseh's dream of a great Indian nation had faded away even as his voice died out that day upon the little Thames.

The more discreet Prophet lived to draw his half-pay for a quarter of a century after that day of disaster for his mighty brother. For a long time he lived in Canada, but in 1832 the artist Catlin found him with a small group of Shawnee in Kansas and delighted in painting a representation of him in all the paraphernalia of a great medicine man. He was still the Prophet but his incantations no longer called men forth to battle.

No doubt, in the long years, he reflected more than once that it is better to be a living dog than a dead lion.

CHAPTER VI
Creek Country

I

IN THE Choctaw chief, Pushmataha, Tecumseh had found an adversary of his own mettle — courageous, resourceful, eloquent. Pushmataha, at the time when the Shawnee chief came south in 1811, was a man of middle age, who from youth had been famous for his exploits in war. But it had been in the west that his laurels had been won. The black locks of the drying scalps that dangled from the poles of his wigwams had been wrested from the head of Osage or Comanche far out on the plains. It was Pushmataha's boast that he had never raised his hand against the white man.

Tecumseh had tarried but briefly in the country of the Chickasaw north of the Choctaw. Their half-breed leader William Colbert had served America in the Revolution and later under General St. Clair. He was to do equal service in the war to come, first as a part of the regular army, and later as leader of a band of his own people against the hostile Creek. He had no ear for Tecumseh's song of battle. Hoping for better things, the Shawnee and his warriors pushed on downward to the towns of the Choctaw nation.

The long feather of white that dangled from Tecumseh's headdress was the symbol of peace among all Indian peoples. The red feather that hung beside it was an emblem of the war against the whites to which he was summoning his race. Arrayed in beads and buckskin,

bands of silver on their arms, rings and lockets pendent
from nose and ears, he and his braves made an impressive picture.

Through Seekaboo, a southern interpreter and prophet,
he made an equally impressive talk. Tecumseh knew
well the long list of treaties which marked the retreat of his people to the west. He would tell with
eloquent sincerity the story of their diminishing hunting
grounds and the steady onward march of the farmsteads
of the white man. His vision of a united red race upheld by the troops and the treasury of the English King
was a promise that this tide of settlement should be
stemmed forever. And to his credit is recorded a plea
that in their warfare the women and children be held
inviolate.

Union the Choctaw did not scorn and the new rule of
warfare suited them well enough. But the proposition
to aid the British held no appeal for them. At Tecumseh's first council Pushmataha rose to answer. He knew
his hearers as Tecumseh could not know them; and his
gift in speaking was not inferior.

He reminded his hearers of their long and unbroken
friendship with the whites. He warned them that from
a conflict with their old friends they had nothing to hope
and everything to lose. His judgment prevailed. Tecumseh went on to the next town without having gained
any converts for his cause.

From village to village he went, and just as faithfully
Pushmataha followed him. When Tecumseh concluded
his appeal Pushmataha was ready with his reply. From
Hoentubbee to Yazoo, from Mokalusha to Chunky
Town, went these forerunners of the Chautauqua and
Redpath. Finally all gathered for a great decisive council at one of the residences of the chief Moshulitubbee.

In the course of a two-weeks' conference all the Choctaw chiefs were heard. Indian etiquette requires that
everyone have his say, that each speaker duly recount
all the previous proceedings, and that an impressive interval elapse between speeches and replies. Time is not
of the essence.

Pushmataha's eloquence had won. Tecumseh was
not to teach his northern ceremony, the Dance of the
Lakes, to these southern people. One and all, the Choctaw refused to take up arms against the Americans.

They went still further. They gave Tecumseh his
choice of leaving their country or being put to death. To
insure his departure, David Folsom, one of their number, with a party of warriors escorted the Shawnee leader
across the Tombigbee River into the land of the Creek.

II

AMONG the people of the Muskhogean confederacy
dwelling in the well-watered country between the Tombigbee and the Chattahoochee Rivers Tecumseh met
with better fortune. Yet the disturbance which he succeeded in fomenting among them was at the outset much
more like a civil war than a union against the troops of
the United States.

Various reasons have been given for calling this conflict the " Red Sticks War." One old story represents
Tecumseh as having given to each group of his allies a
bundle of small sticks painted red in token of warfare.
Each day one of these was to be thrown away and when
the last one was discarded the war would be begun.

This would seem a rather elementary form of calcula-
tion for the Creek, who by this period were pretty well
accustomed to the ways of the white man and pretty well

mixed with his blood. A more plausible theory recalls the fact that in the public square about which every Creek town was clustered it was the custom to erect a pole, painted red, when a war was declared. About their red poles Tecumseh taught the Creek to join in his Dance of the Lakes. It had not been the habit of the Creek to dance before a sortie; they waited until after the victory for a celebration.

But by no means all the Creek danced at Tecumseh's bidding. From beginning to end there was sharpest division among them. There were Creek leaders like Highhead Jim and Francis, who made trips to Pensacola for the ammunition supplied by the English and cheerfully handled by the Spanish. There were Creek leaders like McIntosh and Big Warrior who brought contingents of fighters to aid the American militia and regular troops. And there were Creek leaders like Weatherford who appeared on different sides of the contest at different times.

Billy Weatherford, more picturesquely called Red Eagle, was not the dominant figure in this war that his uncle Alexander McGillivray had been in the earlier one. He was no emperor nor were his people united under any single individual in this turbulent day. But legend has made him one of the romantic figures of the time, portraying him as far more Indian than his small quantum of red blood would seem to justify.

Billy Weatherford is said to have boasted that he "had not a drop of Yankee blood in his veins"; which meant simply that all of his white forbears — Spanish, French, English, and Scotch — had been born on the farther side of the Atlantic. His father was a well-to-do Scotch trader and his mother a sister of McGillivray. In spite of the tuition of this ruling uncle and of another uncle even more notable, the French General LeClerc Milfort, he had not absorbed much of the white man's education and was not a master of the arts of reading and penmanship. As woodsman, horseman, and planter, however, he was pre-eminent. He was wealthy, intelligent, active. At this time he was about thirty years of age, at the height of his powers. Tecumseh wisely fixed on him as an ally worth the winning.

Ten years before this time the Creek had made treaties ceding lands to the United States and receiving in return annuities and goods. Colonel Benjamin Hawkins, appointed agent to administer the terms of this and other treaties, had dwelt long among the Creek and had the friendship of many. He saw the trouble brewing and did all one man might to allay the dissatisfaction.

While he was present at the great Creek council called to receive Tecumseh's message, no incitement to battle was offered. Tecumseh offered his tobacco in token of friendship and made no revelation of his warlike designs. Each day they would speak and as the afternoon came Tecumseh would say:

"The sun has gone too far today; we shall talk to-morrow."

Colonel Hawkins finally withdrew, and the wily chief delivered his message of war. Tradition states that the Shawnee took north with him a delegation of Creek chiefs who visited Fort Malden some months before the opening of hostilities between England and the United States. There they received written orders for guns and powder to be delivered to them by the commandant at Pensacola. But in this whole story Dame History seems to have lost her head altogether and tells so many conflicting tales that it is well not to place too implicit faith in any of them.

There was plenty of fighting among the Creek in the spring of 1812, but it kept up the appearance of civil warfare until some time after the declaration of war with England in June. The next month Peter McQueen, Highhead Jim, and the Prophet Francis, having collected a good supply of booty from raided homes and farms, went down to Pensacola to trade for more munitions of war. On their return they were met at Burnt Corn by a body of volunteers, white in sympathies but in many cases Creek in blood. The volunteer party at first put the Indians to rout; and believing themselves victorious, fell upon the abandoned plunder. McQueen seized the opportunity to return; with the result that his Indian party was completely master of the field.

The victory in itself was a small one but it inspired the rebellious Creek with the idea Tecumseh had already implanted in their minds. They felt themselves invincible. The civil war had now merged into a wider conflict.

The settlers, taking alarm, began erecting a series of so-called " forts " — rough little stockades in which they were to take refuge from the storm. At little Fort Mims, a rude stockade upon a Creek plantation near the junction of the Alabama and the Tombigbee, five hundred men, women, and children were gathered. But because as yet there had been no open attack from Indian parties in any force, they believed too easily in the security of their numbers and position.

After much wavering Weatherford had decided to join in with the Creek, though his brother and other relatives had sided with the white party. He assembled a thousand warriors for his descent upon the little fort.

Major Beasley, in command there, had been culpably careless. The attackers found the gates open and the inmates forgetful of danger. Weatherford waited until the sound of the dinner bell — it was a hot August noonday — assured him the thoughts of all would be the greatest possible remove from watchfulness. Then at a signal the attackers were within the gates and the fight was on.

Beasley and his untried soldiers, the refugee settlers — all paid dearly for their carelessness. Of the five hundred within the walls barely a dozen had managed to creep away to the shelter of the woods when the afternoon's fierce fighting came to an end. Not half of the five hundred Tensaw people were to be considered as combatants, but everyone — old women and little children, red, black, and white — had been slaughtered.

This was war in earnest. The Creek had men and munitions and strong leadership. The settlers would need help from without if this were not to be a war of extermination.

III

HELP was coming from more than one source. Not all the Indians applauded Weatherford and the victors of Fort Mims. The friendlies were increasing in number. And up in Tennessee at The Hermitage there was a man whose name was to be forever linked with the story of this southern warfare.

The Choctaw debated much among themselves about the matter. British and Spanish emissaries sang a seductive song. The Choctaw had a tradition of remaining quiet until attacked and reserving their forces for defence. They did not wish to give active support to the British party, but they felt that by remaining neutral they might be able to reap benefits from both sides.

Not so Pushmataha.

FT. SNELLING

FT. CRAWFORD
(Prairie du Chien)

ST. LOUIS
(Jefferson
Barracks)

GALENA

FT. HOWARD
(Green Bay)

FT. ARMSTRONG
(Rock Island)

CHICAGO

Hagstrom Map Company, Inc., N. Y.

VI. SCENE OF CREEK WAR

1. CAMP JACKSON
2. TOHOPEKA

Yazoo R.

FT. MIMS

Tombigbee R.

Alabama

PENSACOLA

Coosa R.

Tallapoosa R.

Chattahoochee R.

Hagstrom Map Company, Inc., N. Y.

"You know the Tensaw people," he said to the council. "They were our friends. They played ball with us. They sheltered and fed us when we went to Pensacola. Where are they now? Their bones are rotting at Sam Mims's place.

"The people at St. Stephen's are also our friends. The Muscogee intend to kill them, too. They want soldiers to defend them.

"You can all do as you please. You are free men. I dictate to none of you; but I shall join the St. Stephen's people. If you have a mind to follow me, I will lead you to glory and to victory."

He had finished; and for a moment the warriors were silent. But the words echoed in their hearts. Then one by one they solemnly arose. Each one, striking his breast with his open hand, gave the ritual response of their people:

"I am a man! I will follow you."

So came Pushmataha with his four companies of Choctaw to offer aid to the white forces. Very proudly he bore his rank of lieutenant colonel, and very careful was he to discipline his red troops as rigidly as the other officers about him. There were smiles, sometimes, for his punctilio and his naïve imitation of the manners of his fellow officers in matters trifling as well as important. But for his accomplishments as a leader there was sincere approbation.

Meanwhile the neighboring states were warned by the disaster at Fort Mims, and Tennessee was authorizing troops which Andrew Jackson would alternately lead and drive southward. Hungry and ill-supplied in every way, they were more than once to be in open mutiny against their gaunt indomitable leader. Of the oddly assorted troops — half-hearted militia, half-starved volunteers, terrified settlers, Pushmataha and his Choctaw braves, McIntosh and Big Warrior with their friendly Creek, Richard Brown and his Cherokee allies — somehow in the end an army was made and a victory won.

Weatherford, too, had his troubles as a commander; but he did not have to encourage his men to battle. Rather the difficulty was in keeping them together for formal attack. Every Creek warrior wanted to go out and prosecute a little war on his own account against any settler whose home and family he encountered. It was the Indian method of warfare; but Weatherford was not thoroughly enough the primitive fighter to adopt it. He tried to keep his people gathered at least in substantial bands, and fight the foe in force rather than by sporadic depredations.

Since Fort Mims a central place for Weatherford and his unruly followers had been at the Holy Ground not far from the present capital of Alabama. It was a spot so ringed about with ravines and bluffs that the prophets readily persuaded the Creek that it could not be conquered. Pushmataha and his Choctaw force aided General Claiborne of the Mississippi troops to put this prophecy to the test. After hard fighting they drove the Creek from the stronghold.

Weatherford was the last to leave the field of battle. Legend, busy with his name, has attached to "Weatherford's Bluff" the tale of a quite impossible horseback leap to safety as he fled before the victors.

The bluff that is pointed out as the scene of this exploit is fully a hundred feet high. Some stories reduce the height to fifty by permitting Weatherford to ride his horse down a ravine before attempting the leap. The hero himself, telling the story in later years to an historian of the period, thought himself fortunate enough to have jumped his horse from a bluff "ten or fifteen feet high" into the river and to have come up again, still in the saddle, grasping the mane of his horse with one hand and still holding his rifle in the other.

Pushmataha and his Choctaw were less concerned with this exploit than with the rich booty of corn and clothing which they found upon the abandoned Holy Ground. Indians and whites alike shuddered when, hanging from the tall pine pole in the center of the town square, the three hundred scalps brought from Fort Mims met their eyes.

This was late in 1813. Fighting went on for some months longer. It is almost as much the story of Jackson's contest with his men as of warfare against an enemy. The Hillabee Indians were victims of the divided councils among the white men. They had sent messengers to tell Jackson they would surrender and remain at peace. Shortly thereafter General Cocke of the East Tennessee forces, nominally under Jackson but actually a free-lance, fell upon the Hillabee and slaughtered them in great numbers. Those who escaped were active and revengeful additions to the Creek forces.

The fortunes of war swung back and forth. Emuckfau was a drawn battle. It was long a Creek boast that in the course of the fighting they had "whipped Captain Jackson and driven him to the Coosa River." They had even greater reason to maintain that at Calebee Creek they had defeated Captain Floyd, although he held the ground against their assault. But whatever their victories at this field or that, the Creek knew they could not prevail in the end against the United States. Only by English or Spanish aid could they be really successful. And by this time it became apparent that this aid was not to be expected.

The decisive engagement was at Tohopeka — the Horse Shoe — in March 1814. A large bend in the Tallapoosa River gave the name to the place and was supposed to give the protection of a fortress to the thousand Creek warriors entrenched there. Surrounded on three sides by the river, the field of a hundred acres had for its only land approach a narrow isthmus across which Weatherford had thrown a strong breastwork of logs, arranged with holes through which the defenders might pour forth shot upon an advancing enemy. Within the stockade the houses and walls had been arranged as fortifications; while on the river bank a fleet of canoes was the final resource if flight became necessary. Indians do not as a rule provide thus thoroughly for warfare; but Weatherford was Indian in only a small degree. He had learned much from McGillivray and Milfort in his boyhood days.

Jackson looked upon this stout fortress. " They have penned themselves up for slaughter," was his comment.

It was a bloody day. Coffee attacked from the water side and Jackson on land. There was desperate fighting before the first defences were passed; then fierce hand-to-hand combats as foe grappled with foe within the walls. Refusing quarter, the Creek fought almost to the last man. Only a small number escaped from the field.

Now that the power of the enemy was broken, Jackson received the support he had so sorely needed. A month or two later, to the Camp Jackson he had established at the junction of the Coosa and Tallapoosa Rivers, where now the Creek were flocking to surrender, came the news that he had been commissioned a Major-General in the Army of the United States.

IV

THE WAR in the Creek country proper was over. Later in this year of 1814 General Jackson was to pursue even into Florida those still embattled Creek who fled to the protection of British and Spanish at Pensacola. But for the present treaty-making was the order of the day.

After the usual fashion the loser was called upon to pay the costs of warfare. The treaty of Camp Jackson opened to white settlement a goodly portion of the land of the Creek. Thirty-nine chiefs of the nation affixed their signs-manual to this document and promised to remain forever at peace with the tribes about them, refusing audience to foreign emissaries. And inasmuch as this year of warfare had laid waste all the rich land of the nation the United States government agreed to subsist the surrendered tribesmen until another season of harvest.

One by one the Creek warriors came in to Fort Jackson and surrendered. The story had gone forth that General Jackson would not consider the war at an end until Billy Weatherford had been captured and hanged. His slaughter of women and children at Fort Mims, in Jackson's stern judgment, called for the punishment due a criminal rather than the treatment accorded a soldier.

Weatherford had no taste for exile in the swamps of Florida, whither Josiah Francis and Peter McQueen, with some of their followers, had betaken themselves. It had been a losing game from the beginning, and he was wise enough to know this. Now his life was doubly forfeit. If he should escape General Jackson there was Big Warrior, leader of the friendly Creek, who had vowed to dispatch him. There were many Creek on the

watch to exact vengeance for Fort Mims. Weatherford
decided to take his chance with the white man.

Hazarding all on a single stroke, he rode alone and all
but unarmed into the camp of General Jackson. He was
" mounted on the veritable black horse," as his grandson, three quarters of a century later, wrote in response
to the request of a historian.

" I believe it is a recognized fact," said Charles Weatherford, grandson of the renowned Bill, " that all warriors
of note ride either a milk-white or a raven-black steed.
Now sir, I, being a man of peace and altogether unlike
my grandsire, ride an old sorrel mare."

Tradition has it that Weatherford, on his raven steed,
slung behind him on his saddle the carcass of a deer he
had killed on his way. Ignoring the taunts and threats
of Big Warrior, he made his way to Jackson himself and
offered his surrender.

> *My brave ones I'd rally,*
> *And fight at their head;*
> *But where is the warrior*
> *Can rally the dead?*

> *At red Talledega,*
> *Emuckfau they stood;*
> *Thou knowest that our valleys*
> *Are black with their blood.*

> *By the wailing Savannah*
> *Unburied they lie;*
> *Spare, warrior, the remnant,*
> *Let Weatherford die!*

Struck by the boldness of the man, and believing in his sincerity, Jackson recalled his invitation to the gallows. He took Weatherford under his personal protection. It was needed. Big Warrior was not the only Creek who thirsted for Weatherford's blood.

Even after the treaty was signed and peace at least nominally restored, there was little chance of peace for Weatherford. It was a year or more before he found it safe to return to his southern plantation. A tall, fair man, with light brown hair and mild black eyes, there was little of the Indian about him. Few in Tennessee surmised that the retiring guest at The Hermitage was the former adversary of his host.

When he turned south again it was to the life of a white man among white men, of a planter in a land of plantations. The Indian Red Eagle was forgotten; wars and alarums did not again call him forth. He had but a decade longer in which to enjoy the life which Jackson had spared him and had preserved for him. To his many descendants he left the status of white farmers, with the Indian warrior all but forgotten.

The same year — 1824 — that saw his passing marked also the end of the story for old Pushmataha of the Choctaw. Weatherford, the white man's enemy, ended his life as a white. Pushmataha, who gloried in his title of the white man's friend, was Indian to the last.

During this decade the Choctaw chief was the signer of a number of treaties. In his sixtieth year he was one of a delegation visiting Washington, treaty-making once more. It was a noteworthy year, and the return of Lafayette, coming as an old man to revisit the nation he had loved and aided in his youth, was the occasion of gatherings and demonstrations innumerable. Pushmataha was one of those who greeted the French veteran.

He spoke with all his native eloquence of Lafayette's services of which they had heard in their far-off Indian villages.

"Our hearts longed to see you. We have come, we have taken you by the hand, and we are satisfied. This is the first time we have seen you and it will probably be the last. We have no more to say. The earth will part us forever."

Pushmataha was already ill. His throat was in bad condition. David Folsom, interpreter for the party, writing to friends back in the Choctaw country, was of the opinion that the chief was "completely burned out by hard drinking." Folsom is rather sanctimonious about it, but there is the ring of sincerity in his pronouncement. Even this seems a little more dignified than the official statement on the stone which still stands in the old Congressional cemetery in Washington. It ascribes the death of "the Indian general" to croup.

"When I am gone," the dying chief requested, "let the big guns be fired over me." His request was granted; there was a military funeral with cannon and bands and banners, with a long parade, with the President himself in attendance. It would have delighted his Choctaw soul. One of the younger warriors envied him next morning saying: "I wish it might have been for me."

Today one may still read, on the grey shaft which has marked his grave for more than a century, the words which John Randolph repeated in the Senate:

"Pushmataha was a warrior of great distinction. . . He was wise in council, eloquent in an extraordinary degree, and on all occasions, and under all circumstances, the white man's friend."

V

THE Red Sticks War among the Creek had its sequel in the Florida swamps a year or two later. Fighting went on intermittently across the Spanish border in those days, and in 1817 it assumed sufficient importance to be designated as the First Seminole War.

Colonel Hawkins, the veteran agent to the Creek, wrote of this southern offshoot of the Muskhogean confederacy:

"The towns of the Seminole deserve a place here, as they are Creek. They inhabit the country bordering on the Gulf of Mexico, from Apalachicola, including Little St. Johns and the Florida Point. They have seven towns. They are called wild people because they left their old towns and made irregular settlements in this country to which they were invited by the plenty of game, the mildness of the climate, the richness of the soil, and the abundance of food for cattle and horses." But some of the earlier writers voice the suspicion that the Creek gave these folk the name of wild people because of the tribal feuds that separated them from the parent confederation.

During the eighteenth century they were considered simply an offshoot of the Creek; but with their determination to be treated as a separate tribe the troubles between the factions increased. Creek turmoil did not subside even when the British ships sailed away from Pensacola.

The numbers of these southern refugees had been swelled for generations by runaway slaves. The Spanish settlers had called them Maroons, a West Indian term applied to freedmen. This name was often used to designate those who had lived long among the Indians,

while only those of recent acquisition were spoken of as
runaway slaves.

To the Indians the distinction was not a grave matter.
Where no man works very hard, if at all, forced labor,
the particular indignity of slavery, does not exist.
Where no man cares for material possession the ownership of another human being means little. Where
there are no social classes there are no social stigmata.
The distinction, to an Indian tribe, between slavery and
adoption, was never a sharp one. Intermarriage took
place freely in either case; and before long, the mixture
was quite sufficient to justify the Seminole contention that they were a different tribe from their Creek
forbears.

Naturally, when called upon to give up fugitive slaves,
the Seminole people saw no reason for doing so. In
general they could see little reason for acceding to the
wishes of either the white men or the red who lived to
the north of their peninsula. Nor had their Spanish and
English associations helped to inspire any love or respect
for the Americans.

The Prophet Francis, fleeing south after the battle at
Tohopeka, set up for a Seminole ruler under the name
of Hillis Hadjo. That he found a welcome there among
whites as well as Indians is attested by a visit he made
in state to England.

" The sound of trumpets," an English publication set
forth, " announced the approach of the patriot Francis,
who fought so gloriously in our cause in America during
the late war. Being dressed in a most splendid suit of
red and gold, and wearing a tomahawk set with gold,
gave him a highly imposing appearance." Brant's silver
ornaments pale beside this magnificence. But Brant's
diplomacy and address brought back from England a

grant of land for his Mohawk, while Francis had less to offer his people when he returned to the New World.

A year or two later, in the Seminole town of Mikasuki where Francis was supreme, his daughter Milly emulated the clemency of Pocahontas, saving the life of an American named McKrimmon, who had fallen into the hands of the savages and was about to be burned at the stake. Milly appealed to her father in vain. Francis, or Hillis Hadjo, was unwilling to forego his revenge for former defeats.

The girl — she was but sixteen — next pleaded with the warriors who stood around waiting for the application of the torch. They too, at first, shook their heads; but when Milly declared that she would stand, if they persisted, beside the captive and be burned with him, they relented. McKrimmon was given his life on condition that he adopt Indian clothing and remain as one of the tribe.

There was no hidden romance in this story. Two years later her father fell in the warfare against the whites and his family were captured. At St. Marks Milly was the subject of much attention from the whites who heard the story of her compassion. But to McKrimmon's offer of marriage the girl turned a deaf ear, preferring to become the wife of one of her own people. Years later Milly, widowed and poor, out in the western lands to which the Creek had migrated, was the recipient of a pension voted her by Congress as a reward for her brave deed.

The affair of Fowltown has been called the cause of the first Seminole War. More properly it was the culmination of two or three years of desultory warfare. Just what series of demands and recriminations finally led General Gaines to march against this little Seminole village on November 20, 1817, history does not make clear. He professed that his intent was not to make war; but as his troops of friendly Indians approached the village in the grey dawn of a winter morning the dwellers inside the grass huts had no doubt whatever of his unfriendly purpose. They had their guns ready and they put them to use.

The approaching party had their own weapons ready and returned the fire. Thereupon the Seminole fled leaving behind four of their number who had fallen in the skirmish.

General Jackson was then called upon to take command and reduce the rebellious Indians to submission. He did it in about five months of fighting. It was a most remarkable war from all standpoints. Most of the participants on both sides were Indian. The fighting was largely carried on in a country to which neither of the parties to the war laid claim. Jackson hanged his two Creek captives, Francis and another of his band, instead of giving them the status of soldiers. In his inimitable manner he likewise hanged an Englishman or two whom he suspected of giving aid and comfort to the Indians. Ultimately he so embroiled the Spanish and American governments that Spain, already finding her hands too full with her new world dependencies, was willing to sell the peninsula to the United States. Jackson seemed to use his sword to hack away at Gordian knots all over the place.

For a very little war this had vast results. It was but one stone in the structure of Jackson's presidency, of course; but years later it was to disrupt a cabinet and shatter the presidential aspirations of the great South Carolinian, John C. Calhoun. Billy Boleck, or Bowlegs, the Seminole chief, ancestor of today's chief of the same name, knew nothing of this. Probably he knew as little of the change from Spanish to American rule which was to be the source of more trouble to his people later on.

For the present, at least, there was something approximating peace in the southern lowlands.

CHAPTER VII
The Western Frontier

I

ENTER the United States Army in a new character — scientist now instead of soldier. At least that was supposed to be a scientific expedition which Major Stephen H. Long led across the plains in the summer of 1820. With much fanfaronade the Yellowstone Expedition had set out the year before, designing to show the power of the United States to the dwellers along the upper Missouri and to affirm that power by the establishment of a military post at the mouth of the Yellowstone River. In America, and even in Europe, the newspapers heralded the enterprise as a momentous one.

"It will add to the security of the western country, particularly the frontier settlements; it will keep in check the Indians and prevent their depredations; it will tend to destroy in some measure the influence that our British neighbors possess over the minds of the natives — " and so forth, in brightest anticipation.

Alas for hopes ! The expedition started in part in the autumn of 1818 but promptly went into winter quarters at the mouth of the Kansas. Setting out with high hopes and greater numbers the next spring, they spent the entire summer struggling up the river to the point where Lewis and Clark had held their first big meeting and had left the name of Council Bluffs. Another winter stand was made and called Camp Missouri.

"It proved," writes Chittenden, "to be one of the

most disastrous winter encampments in the history of the army. The troops suffered terribly from the scurvy. Over three hundred were attacked and of these about one hundred died. The disease prevailed to some extent all winter, and by spring the situation had become ' truly deplorable.' "

" Thus far," continues the historian, " the Yellowstone Expedition had been an unqualified failure if not a huge fiasco." The title was dropped; and to future years the trip bore the name of Long, who with a smaller party and a less military purpose, did actually succeed in getting a part of the distance for which he had planned.

No doubt his steam-snorting *Western Engineer,* puffing its way up the Missouri, accomplished in some measure its purpose of impressing the Indians, for it was the first steamboat in western waters. But the failures of the larger group had, it appeared, soured the spirits both of those adventuring across the plains, and of those in authority who supplied the sinews of war. Dr. James, who made the final report of the expedition, declared the outfit " very inadequate."

They were instructed, when they had left the river and struck out across the plains, to direct their efforts toward discovering the sources of the Platte and the Arkansas; but this proved to be too hard a task. They did not penetrate beyond the first barrier of the Rockies, leaving to the trapper those lovely parks that lie just within the range.

Long was to bring back to the States a report on the nature and resources of the western plains between the Missouri and the Rockies; and this was his sage conclusion:

" In regard to this extensive section of the country, it is almost wholly unfit for cultivation, and of course uninhabitable by a people depending upon agriculture for their subsistence." Apparently it did not occur to him that the abundant grass which supported innumerable hordes of buffalo might feed domestic cattle equally well, or that the ground which sent forth this grass might afford equal opportunity to wheat and corn.

Had he been a man of such vision as that with which Frémont viewed the country, twenty years later, the whole history of the relations of the United States with its Indian wards might have been very different. For it was this idea that the western plains could not support civilized life, but were suitable only for the buffalo and the hunters of the buffalo, that dictated Indian policy at this time and for a generation to come.

"This region, however, viewed as a *frontier,* may prove of infinite importance to the United States, inasmuch as it is calculated to serve as a barrier to prevent too great an extension of our population westward, and secure us against the machinations or incursions of an enemy that might otherwise be disposed to annoy us in that quarter."

This policy of creating a western domain where the Indian might roam unmolested, and where white settlement and entry would be prohibited, had been faintly foreshadowed by England's Proclamation Line in colonial days. Her attempt to confine the white settlers east of the Alleghanies had died almost as soon as it was born. Now any such proclamation must range far to the westward; in places even beyond the Missouri itself.

At the mouth of the Mississippi, Louisiana had already been admitted to statehood; and around the junction of the Missouri, the state named for that stream was organized and begging for the admission that would come the following year. Between these two states the Territory of Arkansas had been erected. North of these for a vast stretch of land the country was populated only by roving bands of the plains and roving herds of buffalo. In the extreme north the forests were as yet untouched by the white man, eastward as far as the Great Lakes.

Green Bay, in Wisconsin, had in Pontiac's time been the westernmost of the forts in the wilderness. Now on this inland bay, in 1816, Fort Howard had been built. It was to be the farthest east of a string of forts projected, whose building was to extend over a period of a dozen years. This line of fortifications was designed to serve as a defence against Indian warfare and a delimitation of what was then fully believed to be the permanent western frontier of the United States.

The same year had seen the establishment of Fort Crawford on the Mississippi, in the heart of the old French traders' village Prairie du Chien. Between and around these two forts might be found Potawatomi, Menominee, Chippewa, Sauk and Fox, and Winnebago. To the westward were the many bands of the Sioux.

Already the migration of these tribes southward was a notable fact. Governor Harrison had written in 1814:

" It is a fact, that for many years the current of emigration, as to the tribes east of the Mississippi, has been from north to south. This is owing to two causes; the diminution of those animals from which the Indians procure their support; and the pressure of the two great tribes, the Chippewa and the Sioux, to the north and west."

Two or three years after the establishment of Forts Howard and Crawford, Fort Snelling was set in the midst of the Sioux country to mark the confluence of the St. Peter's with the Mississippi. Here, as elsewhere, trading posts had preceded the military. Southern forts came later; and latest and westernmost of them all, Fort Leavenworth in 1827 took its place at the big bend of the Missouri.

Beyond the line roughly sketched by these outposts, it was felt that the white man would never want to live. There was no place for civilized life on these grassy plains. The buffalo would roam there forever, and the Indians would roam in quest of the buffalo. Let the land, then, be devoted to the red man. Here could be found a home for the hard-pressed tribes east of the Mississippi. White settlement would never crowd them from this region.

It was an admirable plan if the underlying premises had only been sound.

II

WHERE the Army had failed to go, traders did not fail. The tribes of the upper Missouri and beyond made their first real acquaintance with the white race through those hardy trappers and travellers who themselves lived a life not unlike the red man's. It was parties of fur hunters who followed the Indian trails over the mountains and across the deserts beyond. And of their countless meetings with Indian bands large and small, peaceful and warlike, there are at best but brief and fragmentary narratives.

In 1823 the traders had an unusual series of Indian encounters. A party of the Missouri Fur Company, under Immel and Jones, met with disaster in the Blackfoot country. Their leaders and five others were slain and all their stores taken from them. The survivors escaped almost as by miracle, and Joshua Pilcher, president of the company, wrote to Major Benjamin O'Fallon, Indian agent at Council Bluffs:

"The flower of my business is gone; my mountaineers have been defeated, and the chiefs of the party both slain."

That same summer General Ashley's party of trappers was meeting with a serious reverse on the Missouri, before the villages of the Aricara. Ashley had stopped to trade for horses but the fickle savage folk opened fire upon his men before dawn on a June morning and in an incredibly short time had killed fourteen and wounded nine others.

Dropping down the river to a spot where he could make preparations for defence, Ashley too sent word to O'Fallon. Colonel Henry Leavenworth was at hand with his troops; and on hearing of the encounter the soldier determined to act without waiting to send down the river to St. Louis for orders from his superior officers. Pilcher, smarting from his own losses, was not far off. He equipped two boats and hastened to join Colonel Leavenworth. He brought with him a body of Sioux who were only too glad of a chance to fight their ancient enemies the Aricara.

Indians, mountaineers, and soldiers, they numbered about eleven hundred when, on August 9, they faced the Aricara villages in martial array. There were fewer warriors among the Aricara — no more, probably, than eight hundred, with women and children bringing their numbers up above three thousand. But the villages had the advantage of position and of rude palisades which had been set up. The two parties seemed about evenly matched.

The Sioux started in fighting. They had come out for war and plunder, and when they had worsted a group of Aricara they turned upon the cornfields of the enemy and proceeded to wax fat thereon.

It was the second day before the army was in action; and a shot from one of the cannon penetrated the Aricara village, killed Grey Eyes, the chief, and shattered the medicine pole in the middle of the town. It became apparent, in spite of this, that the village could be reduced only by actual assault. There was great reluctance to do this. Parleying ensued instead.

The Sioux, disgusted, withdrew to a distance to observe the course of events. It might prove more profitable to forsake the whites and join with the Aricara in plundering the invader. Pilcher was about as disgusted as the Sioux he had brought. He was keenly conscious of the unreliability of the Aricara profession of contrition and refused to smoke the peace pipe. This brought about a quarrel between him and Leavenworth which reverberated long after their return to the settlements.

The upshot of several days of shillyshallying was that the Aricara, refusing to restore the goods stolen from Ashley's party, under cover of peace promises stole away and left their villages deserted. Thereupon the only thing Colonel Leavenworth could do was to start his boats down the river once more,

and ten score martial clowns
Turned from the unwhipped Aricara towns
Earning the scornful laughter of the Sioux.

Leavenworth's errors seem to have been of judgment; there is little question of his courage. But the whole comedy of errors had many untoward results. The wind was sowed, and many a whirlwind remained for later

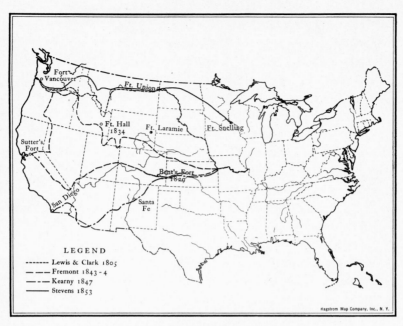

VII. SOME WESTWARD TRAILS

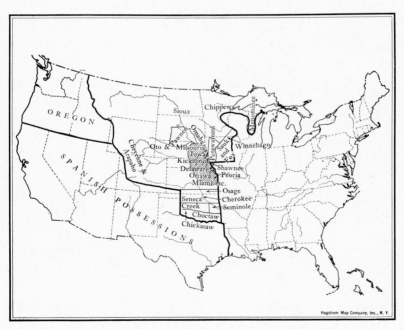

VIII. DISPOSITION OF TRIBES AFTER
WESTWARD MIGRATION

reaping. There was food for bitter reflection in the letter which Pilcher wrote to Leavenworth, when the abortive campaign was over:

"You came to restore peace and tranquillity to the country and to leave an impression which would ensure its continuance. Your operations have been such as to produce the contrary effect, and to impress the different Indian tribes with the greatest possible contempt for the military character. You came (to use your own language) to 'open and make good this great road'; instead of which you have, by the imbecility of your character and operations, created and left impassable barriers."

III

ALL GOVERNMENTAL dealings with the Indians in these days were under the jurisdiction of the War Department. The building of the frontier forts was a part of a wide survey and study of Indian affairs in general. It was the forerunner of a plan which should embrace all the tribes and make proper disposition of them. John C. Calhoun, Secretary of War, presented the plan to President Monroe during his second administration. Monroe, approving, submitted it to Congress as one of his last official acts. Succeeding administrations for sixteen years — Presidents Adams, Jackson, and Van Buren — were to accede and to further the scheme, until the forties wrought their magical transformation in minds and maps.

Briefly, the land between the Missouri and the Rockies was to be "Indian country" forever. Given the necessary authority of law, the Army was to make treaty with the different tribes. Those of the West would be

induced to set limits to their lands and to assign sections
for the use of incoming tribes. Those of the East would
relinquish their lands and accept western areas in their
stead. When the treaties had been duly approved, the
removal of the eastern Indians to their new homes would
take place. So many and so different were the peoples
and places involved in the change, that it could not be
other than a long and intricate business.

Of course these treaties implied payments of all sorts
to the different tribes for land cessions. These would
take the form of yearly distributions of moneys and
goods and implements. Indian agents would be appointed to administer the terms of the agreements.
There would be stipulations for the teaching of the mechanical arts. Farmers and blacksmiths would be sent
to aid and instruct. Schools too would be a part of the
programme; but for a half century to come they would
be more the business of the missionary than of the government.

Here is the genesis of the reservation system. The
beginning had been made long before, whenever treaties
had been made, with their usual accompaniment of payments and annuities. But this meant the introduction
of the system on a widespread scale.

"The care of the Indian tribes within our limits,"
wrote President Monroe in his second inaugural address, "has long been an essential part of our system;
but, unfortunately, it has not been executed in a manner to accomplish all the objects intended by it. We
have treated them as independent nations without their
having any substantial pretensions to that rank. The
distinction has flattered their pride, retarded their im-
provement, and in many instances paved the way for
their destruction. . . They have claims on the magna-

nimity, and I may add, on the justice of this nation, which we all must feel. We should become their real benefactors; we should perform the office of their Great Father, the endearing title which they emphatically give to the Chief Magistrate of our Union."

And the President foreshadowed the allotment policy of sixty years later by this judgment:

"Their sovereignty over territories should cease, in lieu of which the right of soil should be secured to each individual and his posterity, in competent portions, and, for the territory thus ceded by each tribe, some reasonable equivalent should be granted, to be vested in permanent funds, for the support of civil government over them, and for the education of their children; for their instruction in the arts of husbandry, and to provide sustenance for them until they could provide it for themselves."

In spite of his expressed hope that Congress would digest such a plan and carry it into effect, the second administration of Monroe almost passed into history without Congressional action. Three years later Mr. Monroe was still emphasizing the need:

"Experience has shown, that unless the tribes be civilized, they can never be incorporated into our system in any form whatever. . . Their situation will become deplorable, if their existence is not menaced. Some well digested plan, which will rescue them from such calamities, is due to their rights, to the rights of humanity, and to the honor of the nation. . . Between the limits of our present States and Territories, and the Rocky Mountains and Mexico, there is a vast territory, to which they might be invited, with inducements that might be successful."

So, almost as the last act of his administration, the

President submitted Calhoun's plan, Senate and House adopted it — the former unanimously — and the creation of a permanent Indian frontier was begun.

IV

An era of treaty-making followed. Presumably so large an undertaking as this would affect to some extent all the tribes within the borders of the United States, both those who would move and those who would welcome — more or less heartily — new neighbors to their hunting grounds. Hundreds of villages, from the Tallahassee River to the Fox, from the Ohio to the Upper Missouri, must be visited. There must be talks and smokes, councils and gifts and promises. Not quickly nor easily was to be inaugurated this " boldest experiment upon human life and happiness that is to be found in the history of the world."

At St. Louis the Superintendent of Indian Affairs was William Clark, the same who twenty years before had struck out with Meriwether Lewis across the unknown West. In this French-American town, headquarters of the fur trade, the veteran of that dauntless journey was representative of the Great Father at Washington to the red men of many tribes that came and went along the Missouri and the Mississippi.

It was westward of the new State of Missouri that the policy would have its greatest effect; for here it was designed to locate the populous tribes of the southeastern country — Cherokee and Creek, Choctaw, Chickasaw, and Seminole. A goodly number of them had already found their way to the western wilderness.

Most important, therefore, were the treaties which

Superintendent Clark made early in 1825 with the Osage and the Kansa tribes. Lands were ceded which should later become the habitation of the eastern bands. Limits were set for the roaming of the western Indians. Annuities and instruction were duly promised, and the United States agreed to meet claims against these Indians for their depredations upon other tribes and upon the neighboring whites. Peace and amity were promised for all time to come.

Up the Missouri again went a delegation of the United States Army, a real Yellowstone Expedition this time instead of the abortive attempt of six years before. Brigadier General Henry Atkinson and Major Benjamin O'Fallon, Indian agent, were authorized to make treaties with the many tribes along the Missouri. They travelled to the Ponca and exchanged assurances of peace and good conduct; to the Teton, Yankton, and Yanktonai bands of Sioux; to the roving Cheyenne; to the Huncpapa Sioux who were later to produce so many wild warriors; to the Minnetaree; to the Aricara, who had not abated in hauteur since they outgeneralled Leavenworth two years before; and even to the Mandan villages, where treaties were made with the Mandan and with none other than the Crow, far east, here, of their usual haunts.

With the Crow there was some promise of disaster which happily was averted. Edward Rose, the interpreter of the party, was as much Crow as white man in his sympathies, and at times was recognized as chief of the Crow Indians, as later was the well known trapper Jim Beckwourth. To this day the Crow are noteworthy for their hospitable admission of aliens into their councils and ceremonies.

Beyond the Mandan villages the expedition looked in

vain for Blackfoot or Assiniboin chiefs. They achieved the mouth of the Yellowstone River this time and made a safe return with a sheaf of agreements.

In August of this treaty-making year there was a great assembly at old Prairie du Chien on the Mississippi. Tribes that had been at war for generations gathered here as on a neutral ground to meet the commissioners of the United States. Sioux from the upper Mississippi, Chippewa from Sault Ste Marie, Menominee from Green Bay; Ottawa and Potawatomi from the Lake Michigan country; Fox and Winnebago, Sauk and Iowa, all were come to listen to the council of the Great Father. General Clark, the "Red Head Chief" known to all the Indians of the plains and of the West, directed the proceedings. For years he had not been so far into the heart of the Indian country as this.

Governor Cass of Michigan Territory was at his right hand. He was ruler over a vast dominion of forest and water-ways. Indian Agents Taliaferro, Forsyth, Schoolcraft, each represented a large contingent of braves and a large stretch of territory. Captain McCabe of Fort Crawford represented the military power.

It was as dramatic a scene as Prairie du Chien was ever to see. The plain, the green islands in the broad Mississippi, the lovely bluffs beyond, all gleamed with the color of savage finery, moved with the tossing of plumes, resounded to the Babel of a dozen different tongues. The distribution of rations was an essential part of any conference; and on the last day of this long council more than a thousand Indians ate at the feast spread for them by the Great White Father and grumbled at the stingy ration of fire-water provided for them. Nor were they better pleased when the Long Knives, explaining that kindness and not illiberality stinted the portion, poured forth upon the ground several kettles of the coveted drink.

A hundred and thirty-five dusky chiefs signed the great treaty which crowned the labor of many days. It was a treaty by which the white man neither asked nor received a foot of land. Its aims were the pacifying of the different tribes and the setting of boundaries between them. In the first articles the tribes promised one another " a firm and perpetual peace."

Long discussion among the native chiefs had preceded the setting forth of limits to their hunting grounds. The idea of refraining from warfare and of granting rights in the soil by treaty were alike alien to many of them. Wind, a Chippewa chief, was incredulous.

" I wish to live in peace," he averred, " but in running marks round our country or in giving it to our enemies it may make new disturbances and breed wars."

Curly Head, war chief of the Chippewa, died on his way home from this conference and was succeeded by Hole-in-the-Day, who carried on both his friendship to the whites and his enmity to the Sioux. The Chippewa admitted that the Sioux had formerly lived east of the Mississippi but would not submit to their return. The right of superior prowess had given the Chippewa the eastern domain and they fully intended to keep it. Between the Sioux and the Sauk and Fox there was equally long discussion before a boundary line could be fixed. But at length an agreement was reached by them all and promises made of mutual forbearance and amity.

The second war with England, the possible future wars with other European countries, were vivid enough in the minds of men to call for a provision in these treaties renouncing " all dependence upon and connection with another power." In many of the treaties of this year there is a specific promise not to furnish arms and ammunition to any enemies of the United States.

In another year Oto and Missouria, Pawnee and Shawnee, who for one reason or another had failed to attend the grand gathering, made treaty in their turn. The boundaries of the permanent Indian country were now fairly outlined.

In the north, the Chippewa extended across the northern half of what is now the State of Wisconsin, to the Great Lakes, with the Menominee just below them in the Green Bay region. Both tribes are to be found in this location today.

The country that is now Iowa was the home of Sauk and Fox, Winnebago and Potawatomi. Along the Platte were the Omaha and the Pawnee. North and west of all these were the limitless prairies where the hordes of restless Sioux ranged and hunted.

Below Iowa the frontier lay westward of Missouri and Arkansas. Between the Platte and the Arkansas were various tribes already at home on the plains; to these were to be added a number of others, colonized there from the east. Some had already begun their migration, like the Delaware.

From the Arkansas down to the Red River of the South lay the country which was to be the home of the Five Civilized Tribes, the Indians of the South Atlantic States. The promise of removal made in 1802 was about to be redeemed.

Much water would flow down the stream before all these changes would be brought about.

CHIPPEWA "PAGAN" CEMETERY
in Northern Minnesota

CHIPPEWA BARK HOUSES
on the Wild Rice River, Minnesota

V

Nor can such governmental changes as these be made without an increase of governmental machinery. Before this time dealings with the tribes had always borne something of a temporary air. For the making of treaties special commissioners had been sent, or Army officers might be detailed. For the administration of them agents were appointed as the need required. Congress was the treaty-making power, while to the Army fell the actual contact with the tribes, whether in war or peace. Even in this early period there was growing up an assumption that an Indian agent was to be addressed as "Major" — a title once as surely attached to the reservation administration officer as "Colonel" to an adult Kentuckian.

But heretofore the administration of a few treaties and of a few "factories" or government fur-trading houses had been the sole concern. Now there were many treaties, and many tribes that had never before felt the paternal hand of the Great White Father at Washington were to receive the doles that would inevitably change their status and their spirit.

After some years of half-hearted trial the government trading posts had been abolished. They too had partaken, always, of the temporary character which prevented effectiveness. They were established with the design of weaning the Indians from the British and Spanish traders who had proved such powerful political agents as well as men of business. It was at President Washington's suggestion that the act of 1796 was passed, and under his immediate direction that the first trading houses were set up. Jefferson had been equally an advocate of this governmental enterprise as designed to further the civilization of the Indian and discourage foreign traders:

" And thus with the good will of the Indians rid ourselves of a description of men who are constantly endeavoring to excite in the Indian mind suspicion, fears, and irritation toward us."

In 1806 the position of Superintendent of Indian Trade was created. At this period the factories numbered fourteen. Chicago on Lake Michigan, in Indiana Territory, had been added to the list in 1805, and thus the early history of one of the world's largest cities begins in an Indian trading post. Farthest west of them all was Fort Osage on the Missouri, founded in 1808.

The law establishing these was not a permanent one but was extended by two-year periods, from Congress to Congress. There was great pressure brought to bear against them at each renewal. The usual arguments against government enterprise were more potent in men's minds in that day than at the present time. Private firms naturally wished an opportunity for lucrative business, speculative though it must always be. To these considerations was added the fact that the trading posts were run at a loss, goods being supplied practically at cost and the employees paid from the public treasury.

On the other hand the prestige and will of George Washington were still strong and the feeling against foreign traders still a valid argument. When one two-year period expired there would be another extension. It was not until 1822 that the advocates of private enterprise had their way and the government factories were abolished.

Thomas Hart Benton, then beginning his long career as Senator from Missouri and spokesman for the West, said that the system had been " no benefit to the Indian, no counteraction to British trade, an injury to our own fur trade, and a loss to the United States." Thomas L. McKenney, who lost his position as Superintendent of Indian Trade by the abolition of the factories, was convinced that the Missouri Fur Company, all-powerful in Benton's home town St. Louis, was the moving cause and a sinister one.

At any rate the gates were now open for private traders and at once there was a great new impetus in the fur business throughout the West. Superintendent McKenney did not remain long unconsoled, for Secretary Calhoun created in the War Department a tiny Bureau of Indian Affairs and placed the former superintendent at its head.

It was a small beginning indeed, with Superintendent McKenney, one clerk, and one assistant. But a hundred years ago the Federal Government was everywhere a matter of small beginnings. The total clerical force of the War Department at this time numbered twenty-two. Apparently it was devoting nearly a seventh of its total endeavor to the care of the Indian.

Out of this little acorn a fair-sized oak was to spring. It began to sprout at once. In 1832 Congress authorized the President to appoint a Commissioner of Indian Affairs. Two years later came into being the laws which are today practically the organic act of the Indian Service. Its regulations as to the licensing of Indian traders, the entrance of whites upon Indian land, and the sale of intoxicating liquors to Indians, were in fulfilment of the authorization of the Constitution to " regulate trade and intercourse with the Indians."

The Department of the Interior had not yet come into being. When it was created in 1849, the Indian Office and the Land Office, twin services created by the divorcing of the Indian from his lands, were its first charges. But for the present the Indian Office remained under the direction of the Secretary of War.

Already the big task of speeding the eastern tribes on their journey to the West was moving on apace.

VI

A CENTURY ago, when this plan was maturing and the Indian country taking shape, men felt as sure of the boundaries of the United States as they do today. The Rockies were an insurmountable barrier; the plains an unfruitful wilderness. There would be forever reserved for the Indians " all that part of the United States west of the Mississippi, and not within the States of Missouri and Louisiana or the Territory of Arkansas, and also that part of the United States east of the Mississippi River and not within any State, to which the Indian title has not been extinguished."

Here the white man could enter only under special license from the United States government. Traders were to be licensed for a seven year period. Intruders were to be summarily ejected. Here the laws of the white man were for the most part in abeyance and the law of the tribe was supreme. In fact, it was to be quite the happy hunting ground tradition credited to native aspiration.

While the treaty was being made at Prairie du Chien, Alexander Stephenson and Company were building the earliest of those iron horses which were to revolutionize men's ideas of distance. While the Army scientists contented themselves with a look at the eastern slope of the Rockies, the mountain men of St. Louis and " old Touse " were penetrating far into the fastnesses of the hills. And while the wiseacres of Congress decided that the number of states would in a few years be completely filled out, and neatly balanced as between slave states and free, there were growing up on the eastern seaboard boys who while still young men would lead the way far to the sunset and plant the flag of the United States upon the shores of the Pacific, the symbol of a land bounded east and west by no barrier less than that of the mighty ocean.

CHAPTER VIII
Forest Folk

I

THE GREAT Prairie du Chien treaty did not bring immediate peace to the northern lakes and woods. Hole-in-the-Day, succeeding to the position of Chippewa war chief, actively maintained the traditional warfare against the Sioux for twenty years to come; and dying in 1846, bequeathed the heritage of hate to his son, Hole-in-the-Day the Second. But he remained friendly, during all that period, to the white man. He even listened with tolerance to the teachers of the white man's religion and more than once promised to embrace Christianity " after just one more good fight with the Sioux."

It was not from Chippewa and Sioux, however, but from Winnebago and Sauk, that the more serious difficulties arose. The second summer after the big council the Winnebago were leading figures in a picturesque outbreak.

The Winnebago were Siouan by linguistic affiliation, but by their dwelling place were in closer contact with Sauk and Fox, Menominee and Potawatomi. The French first found them at Green Bay, and between that harbor and the Mississippi River was still their range. They were by no means pleased that this territory was being more and more invaded by the white man.

The Canadians called them Puan; and it was a band known by this name that had endeavored to assassinate George Rogers Clark at Cahokia. They were ever a warlike people and had espoused the cause of the British in both of the American wars. Their old chief Carimine, also known as Nawkaw, had been beside Tecumseh as he fell on the field of the Thames. He was an old man then; and now, if the seasons had been reckoned correctly, he had attained more than ninety years. But he was still erect, still powerful, still proud of his rank and authority and the brilliant trappings he wore as insignia.

Red Bird was one of the younger warriors of the tribe, so called because of his fondness for wearing a British uniform, it was said, with a preserved red bird on each shoulder in place of an epaulet. However great his early fondness for the British, at this period he was known well and favorably to the inhabitants of Prairie du Chien, and his relations with the whites there had been uniformly friendly.

The tribe as a whole was somewhat disgruntled at the approach of the whites and their working of mines at Galena. In the spring of 1827 a family from Prairie du Chien had gone out into the woods to make sugar. They did not return when the season was over, but friends found their burned camp and their scorched and mangled bodies.

Fort Crawford's garrison had been withdrawn in spite of the Winnebago ill temper. The soldiers who marched to Fort Snelling had taken with them two Winnebago prisoners. Evil birds now began to whisper in the ears of all the tribe. Rumor had it that up at Fort Snelling the Winnebago captives had been made to run the gauntlet of the white men and had been clubbed to death.

This report was as effective as if it had been truthful. The Indians in council decided to exact blood vengeance for the crime. Red Bird must go out and " take meat " to satisfy the demands of tribal honor.

Red Bird went unwillingly. He made a circle around the country and returned without a scalp, hoping the anger of his people might have abated. Instead they taunted him with his empty hands. He must find them a victim or be himself disgraced.

With We Kau and a third Indian whose name did not impress itself upon the historians of the day he went forth to Prairie du Chien. At the home of Lockwood, a trader whom the Winnebago had long known and liked, the warlike intention of the party became apparent. Through the intercession of a British trader there Red Bird's purpose was diverted, and the three went on to the home of a French-Indian, Registre Gagnier.

After the Indian fashion the visitors entered the kitchen and asked for food. Mrs. Gagnier turned to the stove to provide it. A sound behind her was a warning; she turned to see her husband fall by a shot from Red Bird's gun. The third Indian a moment later slew the hired man, a discharged soldier by the name of Lipcap. We Kau was less successful; Mrs. Gagnier struggled with him over his gun and then succeeded in running away to alarm the settlement, taking her three-year-old boy with her. We Kau consoled himself by scalping the baby she had left behind; but even this was not a complete triumph. Rescued by the relief party of settlers, the little girl, in spite of mutilations, eventually recovered and grew to womanhood.

On the same day two keel boats came down the Mississippi on their return from a trip to Fort Snelling with provisions. They had been cautious in passing the Sioux village on the west bank of the river but anticipated no harm from the Winnebago on the eastern shore. They were widely separated when they reached the mouth of the Bad Axe River.

From an island in the middle of the stream the ambushed Winnebago poured forth a rain of shot across the decks of the first keel boat. After their first shock the crew prepared for defence; and although the boat grounded upon a sandbar, the Indians who darted forth in their canoes failed to board her. A return fire sent them back to the shelter of the island.

Firing went on until nightfall. If dark found the boat still aground, it would be easy for the Winnebago to finish the work they had begun. But to their disappointment several of the crew braved a storm of bullets to push the boat off the sandbar and it was able to make its way down the river carrying its dead and wounded to Prairie du Chien. The second boat coming along at midnight escaped with but the exchange of a few shots.

Terror now spread all over the country. Not the Winnebago only, but all the northwestern tribes were said to be in arms. The fear of the scalping knife lay on every heart.

II

AT THIS very time Governor Cass and Colonel McKenney were on the way to negotiate supplementary treaties of boundary adjustment with the Winnebago and their neighbors. Reaching the Fox River, they found that their prospective councillors were on the war path.

Cass acted with a promptness characteristic of the man. He left McKenney in charge of the council camp at Butte des Morts — " Betty More " in the parlance of the time — while he took canoe for the Mississippi. On his way he must paddle or portage through the heart of the Winnebago country. One encampment he met, and on them he enjoined peace with some good effect. A young brave tried to shoot him, but an older man averted the attack.

At Prairie du Chien he enrolled the local militia and promised to see that they were speedily reinforced. Hurrying down to Galena he enrolled a rifle regiment and sent them up the stream while he kept on down to Jefferson Barracks, at St. Louis, where General Atkinson with five hundred men was soon pressing on for the Prairie as fast as a steamboat could take them.

Cass now turned northeastward, up the Illinois and across to the Des Plaines, to warn the little village of Chicago to be on its guard. When he had followed up the western shore of Lake Michigan to Green Bay and the Fox once more he had been gone less than a month and had travelled sixteen hundred miles. He had set in motion all the military force of the entire section.

Faster than Cass could travel, news travelled in the Indian country. Before the lines of soldiers reached their point of junction at the portage of the Fox and the Wisconsin Rivers the Winnebago warriors knew they were sadly outnumbered. The counsel of old Nawkaw told them there was but one thing to do. They must give up the perpetrators of the deed which had so roused the white man. They must surrender at once before the great chief of the soldiers arrived. The Indian Father would be more inclined to leniency than the man of war.

The Winnebago were ready to listen. One of their number came to the camp of McKenney and Cass.

"Do not strike!" he warned. "When the sun is up there —" pointing upward — "they will come in!"

"Who will come in?"

"Red Bird and We Kau." The messenger wrapped his blanket about him and vanished again into the woods.

At three another Indian brought the same message; at sundown came a third. Next morning the camp awaited the fulfilment of the triple promise. It was the first day of September 1827.

About noon a body of Indians solemnly and slowly approached the camp. At the head and at the foot of their mournful column floated the American flag. A third banner was the white emblem that told they were bent on peace. As they crossed the stream the waiting camp heard the voice of Red Bird raised in the wailing of the death song.

Then came two fierce yells. The friendly Menominee recognized the sound all too well; they were scalp yells. They might mean two scalps to be given up; but on the other hand they might indicate an intention to take two trophies. The Menominee decided to be on the safe side. They got themselves and their guns in fighting order on the moment.

Old Nawkaw led the line and made the speech of surrender. He asked only that the surrendered men should not be put in irons. This promise was readily made.

Red Bird, tall, commanding, fine of feature and bearing, won instant admiration from the whites.

"There was just the manner and appearance," wrote the enthusiastic McKenney, "you would expect to see in a nobly built man of the finest intelligence who had just been escorted by his armies to a throne where the diadem was to be placed on his head."

For his comrade We Kau the Indian superintendent had no such praise. This culprit "looked as if he were born to be hanged. Meagre, cold, dirty in his dress and person, and crooked in form — like the starved wolf, gaunt and hungry and bloodthirsty — his whole appearance indicates the existence of a spirit wary, cruel,

and treacherous; and there is no room left, after looking
at him, for pity. This is the man who could scalp a child
not more than eleven months old, and cut it across the
back of the neck to the bone, and leave it, bearing off its
fine locks, to suffer and die upon the floor, near its murdered father ! But his hands, and crooked and miser-
able-looking fingers, had been wet, often, with blood
before." McKenney seems momentarily to have forgotten that it was Red Bird who murdered and scalped the
father.

The two stood up; a moving contrast.

" I have given away my life — it is gone — " said Red
Bird. He stooped for a pinch of dust and blew it from
his fingers. " It is gone — like that ! I would not take
it back."

Indian law would have called for the execution of
these two who had been brought in. The American law
was hard for the red man to understand. When General
Atkinson arrived a few days later the prisoners were
turned over to him and taken to Prairie du Chien, where,
in captivity, they awaited trial and punishment.

To the Winnebago this was far worse than death.
Two years passed. Old Nawkaw visited Washington
and begged the President for the pardon of the two. His
plea was successful.

He returned to his people with pardon for the two
offenders; but while he had been away visiting the cities
of the East the life of Red Bird had ended in the prison
at Prairie du Chien. One writer of the day says that
" he committed suicide in consequence of chagrin and
the irksomeness of confinement." The less scrupulous
We Kau survived to profit by Nawkaw's intercession.

That sturdy old chief, still erect and dignified, had told
the President ninety-four winters had passed over his

head. Four more he was to see; and as a parting service
to the whites he was to restrain the Winnebago from
joining Black Hawk in his uprising in 1832.

III

THERE had long been rivalry and dissension between
the two leaders of the Sauk. Black Hawk was the older
man, the braver warrior, the son of more distinguished
forbears in the tribal annals. But Keokuk was the
shrewder, the more politic, the more farseeing.

Nor was Keokuk by any means lacking in valor. As a
youth he had won his first renown in a single-handed
combat with a Sioux, whom he had run through with his
weapon, leaning forward from his seat on the back of his
horse. His admiring fellow braves accorded him thereafter the right to appear on horseback on occasions when
others were required by primitive etiquette to be on foot.
Black Hawk was still less pleased by this signal mark of
honor.

Keokuk had made the wiser choice when the Long
Knives and the Red Coats were at war around the lakes.
Great was Black Hawk's disappointment when the
British Father at Fort Malden advised them that he
could no longer promise them soldiers in case of war
with the whites. Black Hawk always hoped trustingly
that times would change; that the Great Father across
the waters would again send his men and guns. But the
years went on and Black Hawk was getting older. Keokuk grew more and more powerful among the Sauk. His
band, which went to St. Louis to trade with the Long
Knives, was by far the majority of the Sauk and Fox.
Black Hawk's "British Band" dwindled from year to
year.

Black Hawk thought that the first treaty which a group of Sauk had made with Governor William Henry Harrison at St. Louis in 1804 was the source of all the trouble. It had given the white men an immense territory and had brought very little to the Indians by way of recompense. In fact it was not until years after that many of the Sauk understood that the yearly presents which the agent of the White Father in Washington distributed, had any relation to the treaty. They thought they were simply the usual gifts.

But since they were to be permitted to roam and hunt upon the ground they had ceded until it should be needed by white settlers, none of the Sauk complained of the treaty. In fact they reaffirmed it, in a way, by agreeing to subsequent treaties in the years between its making and the great council at Prairie du Chien. Even Black Hawk, tardily promising peace to the United States in 1816, made no reference to the cession.

But now that settlers were coming that was another matter. These were still only on the eastern fringe of the great territory where the Sauk roved; but they were beginning to cast covetous eyes at the lands around Fort Armstrong on Rock Island. Here the Sauk had their fields where the squaws cultivated corn and beans and pumpkins each summer. Soon there were white men here, disturbing the crops of the Indian women and planting crops of their own. All the Sauk were aroused. Black Hawk ordered the settlers to leave the country.

Meanwhile the troubles with their wilder neighbors had continued as of old despite the promises made in 1825 at Prairie du Chien. Four years after that great conference another council had been held. The Sauk and Fox refused to attend until assuaged by gifts and presents from General Clark. The Sioux had been equally unwilling to attend. They said the Sauk had recently scalped twelve of their women, and they had no wish to have the affront repeated.

Both parties were brought in under guard, the detachments of white soldiers on watch to keep both from a renewal of hostilities. After a few days they were prevailed upon to sign an agreement to bury the tomahawk. A neutral zone forty miles wide between their territory was established — on paper. The same complaints of mutual slaughter were renewed the next season.

Now the trouble between Sauk and settlers rose to a height and General Gaines in a series of councils forced the Sauk to agree to remain on the west side of the river. The land had now been opened for settlement and the Sauk could claim it no longer. The Sauk promised. The next month, however, they fell upon a Menominee camp on the eastern side of the river and murdered twenty-five before they could rouse themselves from a drunken sleep.

The government demanded that the Sauk give up the murderers. For once Keokuk and Black Hawk stood together in refusing to do so.

" If what they did and what we have now done was put in scales it would balance," Keokuk stoutly declared to the emissaries of the government in council.

That winter Black Hawk schemed and waited on the western side of the big river. Neapope, the medicine man on whom he relied, went on an errand of state to Fort Malden. He came back with reassurances that gladdened the heart of the old warrior. To be sure the British agent at Fort Malden had said no more than that the Sauk could not properly be removed from their lands unless they had duly sold them. But Black Hawk felt that the lands had never been sold and the removal had no justification. Potawatomi, Chippewa, and Winne-

bago had all been turbulent of late; Neapope assured
Black Hawk that they would be ready to join as soon as
the signal for an uprising should be given.

But not all the Sauk were ready for such a signal.
Keokuk the wily had ingratiated himself with the white
chiefs by asking that one of them make his residence
with the tribe for the winter as a restraint upon any
warlike enthusiasm that might arise among his young
men. Black Hawk thought those young men could be
induced to join in his enterprise. With several hundred
of his warriors he came to Keokuk's village.

In an impassioned speech Black Hawk reminded the
Sauk of the happy days before the white men entered
their country. The palefaces were the cause of all their
unhappinesses. "Even now," he told the assembled
braves, "they are running their ploughs through our
graveyards, turning up the bones and ashes of our
sacred dead."

He ended with an appeal to them all to come with him
at once across the Mississippi to their old haunts. Neapope followed, promising them aid from the British and
from the northern tribes. The camp was in commotion;
many were for joining the old warrior at once.

Keokuk felt that it was a crucial moment for him. He
could not stand out against the demands of his own
warriors. Yet he did not wish to give up his friendship
for the whites. He, at least, could see what a losing game
any resistance would be. But he rose to speak to the
frenzied assemblage.

"I am your father," he reminded them, "and I must
lead you in war if you decide upon it. The cabins of the
whites are as plenty as the trees in the forest and their
soldiers are springing up like grass in the prairies.

"But once across the Mississippi, let no one think of

returning while there is a foe to strike or a scalp to take. I will lead you to victory, or if the Bad Spirit prevails I shall perish at my post of duty.

"But what shall we do with our old and sick, our women and children ? We dare not leave them behind us to perish of hunger or fall captive to the enemy. I will lead you forth on this condition: Let us first put them to sleep in that slumber which knows no awakening and then lay their bodies away by the side of our sacred dead. We cannot take them with us and we dare not leave them behind us."

Keokuk's oratory turned the tide. His hearers began to realize upon what a hopeless quest they were to start. But it was in vain that Keokuk appealed to Black Hawk. The old chief and his warriors rode away determined as before.

In April 1832 they crossed the Mississippi and started up the Rock River toward the land of the Winnebago.

Alarm spread rapidly over the entire country though Black Hawk's band gave no hint of fighting as they passed along. General Atkinson, "the White Beaver" of Indian parlance, sent word to Black Hawk bidding him go back to the Iowa country. Black Hawk refused.

Preparations were made for war. Reinforcements for Fort Armstrong, at Rock Island, came from Fort Crawford, which had been regarrisoned after the Winnebago difficulties of five years before. Keokuk came to Rock Island with a band of friendly Indians. The governor of Illinois called for volunteers and an unruly mob of sixteen hundred were speedily enrolled.

It was a body of these volunteers that precipitated actual warfare by ignoring a flag of truce Black Hawk sent toward their line and taking the bearers of the message prisoners.

" In a little while," Black Hawk tells the story, " we discovered the whole army coming towards us in full gallop ! I ordered my brave warriors to charge upon them expecting that we would all be killed. Every man rushed and fired and the enemy retreated in the utmost confusion and consternation before my little, but brave, band of warriors ! "

This encounter at Stillman's Run fired the spirits of Black Hawk and his warriors. If they could put whites ten times their number to flight with scarcely a blow there was every hope to recover their lost lands. They divided now into small parties and scoured the country-side bringing terror everywhere. Every little foray was magnified many times in the rumors that flew about the state.

This situation could not last long. Three weeks after the Stillman defeat there was a force in the field that was bound to spell disaster for the old Indian. Gone now were his hopes of help from the Potawatomi, the Chippewa, the Winnebago, from his British father at Fort Malden. There was nothing to do but stand and be beaten, or retreat and postpone the bitter day of defeat. Black Hawk and his warriors began retreating to the northwest hoping to be able again to put the Mississippi between themselves and their pursuers.

At the Wisconsin fifty braves made a stand on the bluffs to cover the retreat across that river. It was heroic and brilliant in the opinion of one of the advancing officers ; " had it been performed by white men it would have been immortalized."

That night the whites, in camp, heard the voice of Neapope raised in a long harangue to his people. They shivered, thinking it a summons to further battle. There were no Indians in their ranks to interpret the prophet's plea for mercy. At the same time a raft was sent by the Sauk down the river with the hope that as non-combatants their people might find mercy at Fort Crawford. They met instead an attack which dispatched most of them, sending the others off into the woods to meet death by starvation or at the hand of the Menominee. These victims of the warfare were largely women and children.

By the first of August Black Hawk and the remainder of his band had reached the Mississippi at the mouth of the Bad Axe River. It was a last stand indeed. Again the whites ignored an attempt at parley. There were three hours of fighting that meant nothing better than massacre. Scarcely more than one in ten of the thousand followers of Black Hawk lived to return to their village.

Black Hawk with a few followers had gone on toward the Chippewa country. But they were captured by the Winnebago and brought to the Indian agent at Prairie du Chien. The war of a few summer weeks was over.

v

"I AM a man; you are another," said Black Hawk to President Jackson. The old chief had been taken down the river from Fort Crawford to Jefferson Barracks, and was full of admiration for the "young war chief" — Jefferson Davis — who had conducted the party. Now he was being taken on a tour of the East, to be amazed and thrilled by the number and size of the white man's villages.

"We were called upon by many of the people, who treated us well, particularly the squaws ! " Baltimore, Philadelphia, New York; mint and railroad and balloon ascension — wonder grew as the marvels of the white man were unfolded. A grand circle by Detroit and Green Bay brought them around again to Rock Island.

Keokuk had been told beforehand of their return and was prepared to welcome them with all ceremony. While Black Hawk had been in Jefferson Barracks Keokuk had tried to bring about his release but the petition had not prevailed. Now he led a large cavalcade to the camp of the old brave.

"The Great Spirit has sent our brothers back; let us shake hands in friendship." Black Hawk returned the greeting but without enthusiasm. Both remembered in what bitter anger they had parted the year before.

The next day they met in solemn council in one of the rooms of the fort. Major Garland thanked the Sauk for the kindly greeting they had given the returning band. He reminded them of their promises to maintain peace and amity with their fellow red men.

Keokuk made due answer: "We receive our brothers in friendship. Our hearts are good toward them."

The major then went on to tell the Sauk that Keokuk was chief of all the Sauk tribe, and his position was recognized by the United States Government. He wished Black Hawk, also, to acknowledge Keokuk's supremacy.

This was too much for the old warrior. He forgot the grave decorum of an Indian assembly. He rose to his feet shaking with excitement.

" I am a man — an old man ! I will not obey the counsels of anyone. I will act for myself — no one shall govern me ! I am old, my hair is grey. I once gave counsels to young men — am I to be ruled by others ? I shall soon go to the Great Spirit where I shall be at rest. What I said to our Great Father at Washington, I will say again — I will listen to *him* ! I am done."

STATUE OF BLACK HAWK

The Indians were shocked. A murmur of surprise and dissent ran through the assemblage. The officer spoke again, telling Black Hawk it was not a command but advice that he had given. Black Hawk made no answer.

"Why do you speak thus, brother?" Keokuk spoke, for his ear only. "You trembled; you did not say what you meant. Let me speak for you."

He rose and addressed them all: "Our brother has spoken but he spoke in anger. He trembled like a tree whose roots have been washed by many rains. He is old — let us forget what he said. He wishes it forgotten."

Wapello, chief of the Fox and second in command to Keokuk, spoke in his turn: "I am not in the habit of talking — I think — I have been thinking all day. Keokuk has spoken — he spoke for us all. I am glad to see my brothers. I will shake hands with them."

That evening, the formal council over, Major Garland invited the chiefs to his quarters. There were more speeches, the eloquence aided by a much-relished glass of champagne. Black Hawk was still depressed and gloomy but no longer irate.

"I feel I am an old man; once I could speak, but now I have little to say. Our brothers have behaved like Sauk since I left them; they have taken care of my wife and children, who had no wigwam; I thank them for it.

"I told our Great Father in Washington I would listen to his councils; I say so to you. I will listen to Keokuk. What I said in council today I wish forgotten.

"We thank our Great Father for all he has done. We thank you for travelling with us — your path was long and crooked. We never saw so many white men before; but when with you we felt as safe as if among friends. On your road home you will pass where our village once was. No one lives there now — all are gone. The Great Spirit will be with you. I will shake hands with my brothers here, and then I am done."

That autumn Black Hawk dictated his autobiography and dedicated it to General Atkinson, the White Beaver. He was no longer a chief and he felt keenly his loss of prestige.

In 1837, just a year before the old man died, another delegation of chiefs went to Washington to confer with the Great White Father. Black Hawk was not a delegate but he was taken along with the party. He enjoyed all the sights with the others but did not speak in council since the Sauk had not chosen him as a spokesman. But Keokuk could share the feeling of the old man, now frail and broken, shorn of his earlier glory.

At their first conference with the Secretary of War Keokuk said: "There is one here who does not speak with us in council, but he is accustomed to sit with us at home and is our friend. We have brought him with us — we hope he will be welcome."

CHAPTER IX
The Westward Trail

I

GEORGIA had not ceased to remind the Federal Union of the promise made in 1802 when she had ceded her rights in that Territory of Mississippi that was later made into the States of Mississippi and Alabama. The proviso was that the United States would extinguish the Indian title to lands within the borders of the State of Georgia " as early as the same can be effected, on reasonable terms." Ten, twenty, thirty years had passed, and here were the Indians still in her western hills, growing daily more numerous, more intelligent, more prosperous, more mixed with non-Indian blood.

After a quarter of a century's delay, the Creek at last were going westward to the land provided for them beyond the Territory of Arkansas. There had been much dissension among them before emigration was decided upon.

William McIntosh, the chief who had won the title of Major by his leading of the friendly Creek troops during the Red Sticks War, had been instrumental in more than one land cession during the intervening years. An old Indian law punishing with death anyone who should sell their land to the white man, was forgotten during this period. It was maintained that McIntosh himself had introduced this law to the Creek council and brought about its passage.

McIntosh was the leading signer of the Treaty of Indian Springs which in 1825 ceded the entire Creek country and promised that the tribe would migrate at once to the West. The Indian agent felt that the treaty was not representative of the Creek people and transmitted it to Washington with his objections.

The Creek nation was in a ferment. The people of the United States began to shiver in fear of another Indian outbreak. The Red Sticks War of 1813 was still vivid in men's minds. Instead, the opposition to the treaty invoked the old law of the tribal council that any man who ceded land should be punished with death. Menawa was selected to carry out the order and dispatch the offender, McIntosh.

The two had long been rivals, enemies personal as well as political. Both had a liberal mixture of British blood along with their Indian heritage. In the late war Menawa had been as ardent a leader of the Creek party as McIntosh had been of the friendlies. He had all but fallen forever at Tohopeka. Left on the field as one of the dead, he crawled to life again to find that the conflict had destroyed his trading store and his wealth of cattle and horses. Yet he did not seek exile in the Florida swamps as did so many of the defeated party. Instead, he rebuilt his power and property and faced McIntosh in peace as well as war as a rival.

He demurred at the sentence of the council, preferring that someone else be chosen to make way with the signer of the Indian Springs Treaty. Eventually he accepted the trust and with a hundred braves surrounded Major McIntosh's home. It was on the first of May, eleven weeks to a day from the signing of the treaty.

They called upon the whites within the house to leave; and when the aliens passed out there went with them

Chilly McIntosh, son of the Major. He too had been selected for slaughter as he was one of the signers of the pact. But no one recognized him, and he went out to safety.

The house was now fired. There were now within it but McIntosh and his second in command, Etomie Tustenuggee. They knew the fatal summons was for them: "McIntosh has broken the law made by himself, and we have come to kill him for it."

At last the flames drove them to the door, and a rain of bullets met them. Death came in an instant for them both.

II

MEANWHILE the treaty had been pursuing its way in Washington. Secretary of War John C. Calhoun had expressed himself as opposed to the ratification of the treaty without the signature of both factions among the Creek people. President Monroe, however, sent it to the Senate, protests and all; it was almost the last official act of his administration.

A new Senate came in under President John Quincy Adams, and the treaty was ratified almost immediately — on March 7. It was now the law of the land. It was not a law which was to receive implicit obedience from the aroused Indians. The State of Georgia, however, prepared to take such steps as would insure its effectiveness. President Adams, foreseeing trouble, sent federal troops to the vicinity though not within the borders of the state.

Surprisingly, the object of federal troops was not to execute the provisions of a treaty which had been made under federal authority and ratified by the United States Senate. Instead, their purpose was to prevent the State of Georgia from putting the treaty into effect. It was as involved a quarrel as the Indian nation itself could have provided.

All the neighboring states, as well as Georgia herself, were now inflamed with indignation. To avoid serious trouble with both white man and red, President Adams sent for the chiefs of the Creek confederacy. They came in to Washington, Menawa among the number.

Their leader was Opothleyaholo who, though not nominally chief, exercised great power among his red brethren. He had for his trusted advisers two Cherokee, father and son, known as Major and John Ridge. They possessed a larger proportion of white than Indian blood, had been educated under missionary auspices and, like the white man, could talk on paper.

In January 1826 another treaty was drawn up and signed. This new agreement abrogated the Treaty of Indian Springs and ceded most of the Creek lands in Georgia. Those in Alabama were reserved for tribal use so that the party desiring a western home might go on to the country beyond the Mississippi while the objectors might still have a home not far distant from their original location.

The Senate, which had approved the pact of the year before, now had objections to make. The committee of Indian Affairs, consisting of Benton of Missouri, Van Buren of New York, and Berrien of Georgia, made protest, with the result that a supplemental article was added and signed by the chiefs. By this stipulation all the lands in Georgia were relinquished as had been promised years before.

The investigations and debates brought out the interesting fact that of $247,000 to be paid under the treaty, $160,000 was to go to the individual chiefs, a rather

undue proportion of the reward. The objection to the
Indian Springs Treaty of the year before, that it had
been engineered by McIntosh under pay from the United
States, would seem to apply equally here. It is probably
an objection which would apply to any such agreement
— the chiefs would always demand special payment for
themselves, else why were they chiefs? Less reason
appears, however, why three Cherokee — Vann and the
two Ridges — should receive forty thousand dollars,
ostensibly in payment for Creek lands to which they
had no claim. But they had come along with the delegation and had signed the agreement as witnesses. No
doubt they had taken an active part in the negotiations.

The best of Indian treaties must always have involved
much misunderstanding; and a great portion of them
involved much misrepresentation. The negotiations on
behalf of the government were always at the mercy of
the interpreters who were allied to both nations by blood
and were usually glad to profit at the expense of either.
As tribes became more and more mixed with white blood
the situation often grew worse instead of better. Inter-
ests became more conflicting, faction more determined.
These southern tribes had long since given over the
leadership to men whose proportion of Indian blood was
small. Wherever a few clever leaders sway a mass of
the illiterate and unaspiring, political corruption is
inevitable.

At any rate, the Creek were now fairly started on their
westward journey. Opothleyaholo and Menawa and
their followers were to linger in Alabama for a decade
longer. They did not care to go out to the newer lands
and meet the vengeance of the McIntosh party which
had preceded them.

But in the northwestern part of Georgia the Cherokee

still occupied some five or six millions of acres of good land. It was even suspected that in the hills gold might be hidden away.

This was the unfailing precursor of contention.

III

THE CHEROKEE nation was unusually rich in factions. They were a numerous people, more numerous perhaps than was realized, since they lived in their mountain homes quite away from the observation of the white man. But many of them had been open to European influences for generation upon generation. Even the party least fond of the white man's ways had leaders who were of well-mixed ancestry.

It was in President Jefferson's time that a body of Cherokee chieftains came to Washington praying that a division be recognized between the upper and the lower towns of the Cherokee. Those of the upper towns wished to set limits for their country and to establish within it a definite government of their own.

Those of the lower towns were inclined to cling as closely as they might to the ways of their Indian forebears. They complained that game was becoming so scarce they could no longer follow the chase for a livelihood. They asked permission to explore the western country; where, along the Arkansas River, they hoped to find an unclaimed tract of land suitable for their dwelling place.

Permission was given and the plan carried out. The second war with England was one cause of delay, and violent dissension between different parties of Cherokee was an even more fruitful source. Even of these early migrators to the West the leaders were but partly Indian.

Tah-chee, or Dutch, who went among the first, is depicted by Catlin with a flowing sandy moustache and a countenance as little suggesting the Cherokee as his name.

Various treaties punctuated the course of this westward movement; a final pact in 1828 marked its conclusion. There were now more than six thousand of the tribe in the Arkansas country not far from Fort Gibson. In this 1828 treaty they are designated as the Western Cherokee; later, when other groups from the East joined them, these earlier emigrants were known as the Old Settlers' Party.

Meanwhile those remaining in the northwestern section of Georgia had been claiming to be the entire tribe. As such, they maintained, they were entitled to all the annuities and benefits that in earlier treaties had been promised to the Cherokee people. They had also been busy carrying out their plans for a government.

The Cherokee were the first Indian tribe to have a written language and a newspaper published in their own tongue. Sequoyah, or George Guess, to whom we owe the Cherokee characters, was a man of possibly one-fourth Indian blood. His training, however, had been wholly Indian; and his native gift for manufacture and invention, which had shown itself in the work of a silversmith and metal worker, had received no cultivation from outside sources. It was the occasion of great mirth and contempt when his fellow tribesmen saw him set to work, averring that he believed he could enable the Cherokee to "talk on paper like the white man."

He worked on his Cherokee alphabet for a dozen years, derided by those who saw him diligently making little marks upon paper or bits of bark. He was sixty when he submitted to the council the results of his labors and began teaching those about him the eighty-six characters he had evolved.

The council gave approval now instead of ridicule and so heartily did they all enter into the spirit of the endeavor that in a few months thousands were able to read and write in their own language. Soon the missionaries were printing Bible and hymn-book in Sequoyah's characters, and a newspaper was started to carry the news of the nation from one village to another.

The year after he completed his alphabet, Guess went to the West to spread his new learning to the Cherokee beyond the Arkansas. The liking between him and the early emigrants was evidently mutual for he settled down in the western country. He was one of the leaders who came to Washington to negotiate the treaty of 1828.

About this time the Cherokee still in the East made good their claim to be the Cherokee nation pure and simple by adopting a constitution. It was modelled on that of the United States, but it embodied as well many ideas that were the outgrowth of primitive life and customs.

John Ross, who presided over the Cherokee constitutional convention and was for many years the principal chief of the nation, possessed but one-eighth Indian blood. His father was a Scotch trader, and his mother was but a quarter-blood Cherokee. But his ascendancy over the tribe was to be a notable factor in its history until his death forty years later than this.

Ross and the elder Ridge had fought side by side against the Creek party at Tohopeka, leading a brave attack by canoe against the water side of the Creek stronghold. But in these later years they were opposed in tribal matters.

With New Echota as their capital, with the *Cherokee*

SEQUOYA

By Courtesy of the Smithsonian Institute

JOHN ROSS

By Courtesy of the Smithsonian Institute

Phœnix as their official organ, with officials in whom the white blood was decidedly in the preponderance, the Cherokee people were making a fairly effective demonstration of a nation within a nation. Here was a professedly sovereign commonwealth set up within the borders of a sovereign state.

Georgia was quick to retaliate. By legislation passed in 1829 she extended the operation of all her laws to everyone dwelling within the borders of the state. The Federal Government likewise, by a long series of enactments, claimed jurisdiction over the Indian people and the Indian country. Here were three sets of laws contending for power over a single section.

Committees of the House and Senate investigated the new Cherokee government. The House report commented:

" The only tendency yet perceivable in the new institutions, has been to enable those who control them to appropriate the whole resources of the tribe to themselves. . . The committee have not been able to learn that the common Indians have shared any part of the annuities of the tribe for many years. The numbers of those who control the government are understood not to exceed twenty-five or thirty persons."

Besides this ruling class, the committees found a small body of mixed bloods and whites with Indian families, who " make a sufficiency to support themselves and their families." The third class, the " mass of the population," said the Senate report, " are as poor and degraded as can well be imagined. They are without industry, without information, unlettered, and subsisting chiefly upon what they can beg, and upon the birds and fish they can procure. . . It may then be asked, why do those people refuse to emigrate; the answer is, those who have influence over them, use every means in their power to prevent them. They misrepresent the country offered west of the Mississippi. They use persuasion while it answers the purpose, and threats when persuasion is likely to fail."

Matters were in this critical state when the administration of John Quincy Adams was drawing to a close. When Congress convened in December 1828 the President sent a message in which the situation of the Cherokee was discussed:

" At the establishment of the Federal Government the principle was adopted of considering them (the Indians) as foreign and independent powers; and also as proprietors of lands. They were, moreover, considered as savages, whom it was our policy and duty to use our influence in converting to Christianity and bringing within the pale of civilization.

" As independent powers, we negotiated with them by treaties; as proprietors, we purchased of them all the land which we could prevail upon them to sell; as brethren of the human race, rude and ignorant, we endeavored to bring them to the knowledge of religion and of letters. The net design was to incorporate in our own institutions that portion of them which could be converted to the state of civilization. In the practice of European states before our Revolution, they had been considered as children to be governed, as tenants at discretion, to be dispossessed as occasion might require, as hunters to be indemnified by trifling concessions for removal from the grounds upon which their game was extirpated.

" In changing the system, it would seem as if a full contemplation of the consequences had not been taken. We have been far more successful in the acquisition of their lands than in imparting to them the principles or inspiring them with the spirit of civilization. But in appropriating to ourselves their hunting grounds we have brought upon ourselves the obligation of providing them with subsistence; and when we have had the rare good fortune of teaching them the arts of civilization and the doctrines of Christianity, we have unexpectedly found them forming, in the midst of ours, communities claiming to be independent of ours, and rivals of sovereignty within the territories of members of our Union.

"This state of things requires that a remedy should be provided. A remedy which, while it shall do justice to these unfortunate children of nature, may assure to the members of our confederation their rights of sovereignty and soil."

IV

JUST why Andrew Jackson, who succeeded to this problem along with many others when he came into the White House in 1829, is supposed to be the man chiefly responsible for the wrongs of the Cherokee, is a puzzle for the student of history. The trend west was as old as the story of settlement. It had been definitely broached in the case of this particular tribe as early as Jefferson's time. It had been made a settled policy by President Monroe. Matters had risen to a crisis in the time of John Quincy Adams. And the actual removal of the Cherokee did not take place until the administration of Jackson's successor.

But storms always centred about Old Hickory's furrowed brow and this was one of the most devastating. Party feeling was never more violent than during this period. With the mingling of Cherokee faction and white partisanship there was a series of explosions.

The Cherokee grew more and more independent; Georgia more and more menacing. Jackson in his first annual message pointed out the underlying inconsistencies of the government's attitude toward the Indians:

" It has long been the policy of the government to introduce among them the arts of civilization, in the hope of gradually reclaiming them from a wandering life. This policy has, however, been coupled with another, wholly incompatible with its success. Professing a desire to civilize and settle them we have, at the same time, lost no opportunity to purchase their lands and thrust them further into the wilderness. By this means they have not only been kept in a wandering state, but have been led to look upon us as unjust and indifferent to their fate. Thus, though lavish in its expenditures upon the subject, government has constantly defeated its own policy, and the Indians in general, receding further and further to the west, have retained their savage habits."

To this condition the Cherokee presented an exception; but it was an exception which only made the difficulty greater. They had "attempted to erect an independent government within the limits of Georgia and Alabama." The Constitution guarantees that no new state shall be erected within the jurisdiction of a state without the consent of its legislature.

" Much less," said President Jackson, " could it allow a foreign and independent government to establish itself there.

" Actuated by this view of the subject, I informed the Indians inhabiting parts of Georgia and Alabama that their attempt to establish an independent government would not be countenanced by the Executive of the United States; and advised them to emigrate beyond the Mississippi, or submit to the laws of those States."

He did not contemplate using force to remove them.

"This emigration," he wrote, "should be voluntary; for it would be as cruel as unjust to compel the aborigines to abandon the graves of their fathers and seek a home in a distant land. But they should be distinctly informed that if they remain within the limits of the States they must be subject to their laws."

After long discussion and division Congress supported this view. A bill authorizing emigration to the West was passed in 1831. Force was not anticipated. Western lands were to be purchased for the tribe, and those who had improvements upon their eastern lands were to be paid for them. The cost of emigration was also provided for.

Under this authorization more of the Cherokee left for the trans-Mississippi country. But the Cherokee Nation as a whole stood its ground with John Ross standing firm against the removal. They retained as counsel William Wirt, a former Attorney-General of the United States, to seek a legal adjudication.

The matter was now in the thick of partisan politics. Georgia had followed up the Act of Congress with one of her own. She forbade white men to live among the Cherokee and claim immunity from the laws of the state. They must take the oath of allegiance before being permitted to reside among the Indians.

This was a direct attack upon the missionaries who in some quarters had been accused of fomenting trouble. The cause thus became a religious controversy as well. If there were any angles of approach to this difficult question overlooked it was not for lack of the widest airing of the matter. Petitions and remonstrances flooded Congress. The halls of legislation echoed debate and eloquence. The press was all ablaze.

But on all sides there was a notable lack of agreement as to the status of the Indians. Many a presidential message had before this pointed out the inconsistencies in the public theory. These became multiplied in public discussion. It was high time that the situation be clarified.

The Cherokee Nation had applied to the Supreme Court for an injunction to restrain the State of Georgia from applying her laws to the Cherokee. Such an injunction, if granted, would establish the status of the tribe as the independent nation it claimed to be.

But victory was not to be won so speedily. The Supreme Court declined to consider the plea. It held, instead (Cherokee *v.* Georgia, 5 Pet. 1), that the Cherokee Nation was not a foreign state within the meaning of the Constitution. The petition was therefore dismissed.

In passing on the case, Chief Justice Marshall gave a characterization of the status of the Indian which in some measure still prevails after a century of change. It was to govern in Indian matters for a generation and to affect the lives of many in lands that were still under the sway of Spain or England.

" It may well be doubted whether those tribes which reside within the acknowledged boundaries of the United States can with strict accuracy be denominated foreign nations. They may more correctly perhaps be denominated domestic dependent nations. They occupy a country to which we assert a title independent of their will, which must take effect in point of possession when their right of possession ceases. Meanwhile they are in a state of pupilage. Their relation to the United States resembles that of a ward to its guardian."

This decision bore upon the relation of the Indian

tribe to the United States but said nothing of its relation to a State of the Union. Georgia continued the effort to enforce her laws.

Immediately after the enactment of the law requiring white men dwelling among the Cherokee to swear allegiance to Georgia a group of missionaries met and passed resolutions of protest. They felt that the Indians should not be required to obey the laws of the state. Three of the missionaries were arrested. A writ of habeas corpus brought their immediate release on the theory that as dispensers of a government fund for the support and civilization of the Indians they were federal officers.

The Governor looked into the matter and learned that some of the missionaries — and those who were most strongly in opposition — were supported wholly by missionary funds. They could not claim the exemption of a federal officer. They were again arrested and speedily convicted and sentenced under the law.

All but two of them were willing to accept a pardon from the Governor in lieu of a prison sentence and to promise to obey the laws of the state. These two, Worcester and Butler, made a test case of it. It went to the Supreme Court of the United States. The decision was a legal victory for the Indians, declaring that all intercourse with them should be carried on exclusively by the Federal Government.

"The Cherokee Nation, then, is a distinct community, occupying its own territory, with boundaries accurately described, in which the laws of Georgia can have no force, and which the citizens of Georgia have no right to enter." (Worcester v. Georgia, 5 Pet. 357.)

The Governor of Georgia announced boldly that he was "prepared to meet this usurpation of Federal power with the most prompt and determined resistance." But for all his thundering words he pardoned the missionaries, who promptly returned to the New England state from which they had come to make this test case.

This decision is the one of which President Jackson is reported to have said, " John Marshall has made his law; let him enforce it." It was a remark pungent enough to endure to the present time, whether the old fighter actually said it or not. Enforcement was evaded and the question of emigration remained about where it had been these thirty years past.

V

John Ross, one-eighth-blood Cherokee, was the most prominent leader of the nation at this time. There were Bollings and Randolphs in Virginia who had almost as much Indian blood as he.

His power and prestige were all exerted against removal. He was the head of every delegation that came to Washington to protest.

But there was within the nation a party favorable to removal. It was headed by the Ridges and by Elias Boudinot, editor of the *Cherokee Phœnix*. These two made visits to Washington and urged compliance with the wishes of the state and the promise of the nation.

Ross would consent only if the Cherokee were to receive twenty millions of dollars for their eastern lands. This was a staggering sum in those days and a much larger price than Napoleon had asked for the whole great Louisiana country, including New Orleans at the mouth of the Mississippi. One-fourth of that sum with an extra allowance to defray the costs of removal was as far as Congress would go.

This was the amount agreed upon in the treaty which

was drawn up at New Echota, the Cherokee capital, in December 1835. It was the Ridge party, however, which signed this treaty. The Ross faction remained in active opposition.

There was almost enough opposition in the Senate of the United States to refuse confirmation to the treaty. Finally the necessary two-thirds vote was mustered, with one to spare — thirty-one to fifteen. The Treaty of New Echota was now the law of the land both for whites and Cherokee.

It provided and promised that the Indians should remove west within two years. Only a small proportion did so, two thousand possibly. It became necessary to send federal troops to enforce the removal.

The expiration of two years had brought about a change in administration and the hopes of the Anti-Treaty party had risen again. John Ross had been secretly stirring up the Old Settlers or Western Cherokee out on the Arkansas, and brought a delegation of them in to Washington to protest.

President Van Buren listened to them but did not promise to disregard the treaty. Indeed it is difficult to see how he could do otherwise than enforce it so long as the Senate, after full consideration, had given it ratification. Webster, Clay, and Calhoun, the heaviest oratorical guns of the period if not of our country's entire history, fulminated against the procedure but were unable to muster a large enough vote to block it.

Protest there was everywhere; and as the time for the removal drew near, early in 1838, a monster petition from the Cherokee themselves was presented.

" Are we to be hunted through the mountains like wild beasts, and our women, our children, our aged, our sick to be dragged from their homes like culprits, and to be packed on board of loathsome boats for transportation to a sickly clime ? . . Already we are thronged with armed men; forts, camps, and military posts of every grade occupy our entire country. . . Will you shield us from the horror of the threatened storm ? "

Fifteen thousand Cherokee signed this plea — most of them, of course, by mark.

In the spring of 1838 General Winfield Scott began the work of removal. About five thousand were transported down the Tennessee and Ohio Rivers to the Mississippi, the journey beyond that stream being made by land. There was no armed resistance but much suffering and distress. So great was the protest that the task was suspended during the summer.

In the autumn John Ross made a contract to accept the funds provided for removal and to transport his people to their new home. Twelve thousand made the journey under Cherokee guidance, the greater portion of them covering the entire distance by land. It was an undertaking of several months. More than a third of their number died while on the way to the new country.

VI

THE Commissioner of Indian Affairs was evidently a thoroughgoing optimist. The treatment of the Cherokee was declared by him to be " a striking example of the liberality of the government in all its branches."

" A large mass of men," he wrote, "have been conciliated; the hazard of an effusion of human blood has been put by; good feeling has been preserved, and we have quietly and gently transported eighteen thousand friends to the west bank of the Mississippi."

If the Cherokee were friends to the government, ac-

cording to the Commissioner, they certainly were far
from being friends to one another. The years following
the removal were marked by a series of dissensions and
conflicts that practically amounted to a civil war in the
Cherokee Nation. The Old Settlers, and the Ridge and
Ross parties among the newcomers, did not settle down
into a single organization without long and violent dispute as to their respective rights to lands and annuities
and offices in the nation. When the Ridges and Boudinot were murdered the lesser lights in the Treaty party
which they had headed fled for protection to the United
States Army at Fort Gibson. The validity of the union
effected between the differing parties remained in dispute for several years, and by 1845 the murders in a
single year numbered thirty-four.

The following year a treaty was negotiated at Washington in which an effort was made to compose these
difficulties. Delegates from all three parties were in
attendance. Indemnity was paid for the three murdered leaders of the Treaty party. John Ross was recognized as the Principal Chief of the united Cherokee, and
a fair measure of peace was now brought about for this
distracted people.

But about two thousand of the Commissioner's friends
had remained behind after all in the mountains of North
Carolina. It was some time before they ventured to
emerge from the fastnesses in which they had hidden
themselves. Then Colonel William Thomas, a friendly
trader who had long resided among them, interested
himself in their behalf and secured from the government
their share of the annuities and payments which had
been promised to the Cherokee as payment for removal.
With this he purchased land upon which they settled.
Here their descendants may be found today, a half

hundred miles or so distant from Asheville, North Carolina.

Four regiments of them followed Colonel Thomas into the Confederate Army. The disasters of that conflict swept away his holdings and theirs together. The catastrophe was made complete by Thomas's loss of sanity and his death. The Colonel's creditors were about to dispossess the Indians when the Federal Government came to the rescue by instituting suit and making appropriations necessary to a favorable settlement of the matter.

These North Carolina Cherokee are today a simple farming folk, largely mixed with non-Indian blood. The United States maintains a boarding-school for their children, but in other respects they are self-supporting. They have held their land as a band all these years; the Eastern Cherokee Band, Incorporated. Since 1924 a roll has been in progress, compiled for the purpose of allotting the land to individual members of the band. Some six thousand applicants now claim a place on the rolls — about three times as many as were recognized as Eastern Cherokees before a land distribution was contemplated.

The little groups of Iroquois in New York, these North Carolina farmers, and a few dwellers in the Everglades are now the only charges left the Federal Government within the original area of these United States.

CHAPTER X

The Seminole

I

THE SO–CALLED First Seminole War had been
fought chiefly on Spanish territory. Its most noteworthy result had been the addition of that Spanish
territory to the United States. A few years later, in 1823,
the Treaty of Camp Moultrie with "the Florida tribes
of Indians" purported to make division of the peninsula between the red man and the white.

Metes and bounds were set for the Indians' occupation. In consideration of their peaceful retirement to
that area they were to be given the protection of the
United States, rations for a year, implements of husbandry, cattle, hogs, and an annuity of five thousand dollars a year for twenty years to come. So for a time there
was quiet.

The great source of difficulty was the refuge which the
interior of Florida afforded to runaway slaves from the
plantations to the north. There was no disposition to
meddle with the Maroons, with the negroes who had
dwelt long among the Indians and intermarried with
them. It was by such combination that the Seminole
tribe had grown into existence. But their hospitality to
fugitive blacks continued warm as their climate, while
the tempers of the planters who thus lost their slaves
threatened to wax hotter than either.

While the Seminole blood had been largely recruited
from the negro race, for leadership they looked to the

Creek, the main source of their Indian strain. The Red Sticks War had sent many Creek leaders to Florida for refuge. Opposition to the western removal was to send many more. In the coming Second Seminole War there were to be Creek leaders on both sides of the conflict.

Neamathla, who as principal chief of the Seminole was the first Indian signer of the Camp Moultrie Treaty of 1823, later returned to the Creek and assumed a position of leadership among his native people. "He can control his warriors," the Governor of Florida wrote of him, "with as much ease as a Colonel could a regiment of regular soldiers."

Neamathla spoke for the Seminole, however, in rejecting the white man's offer of schools for their children. "We do not wish our children to be taught the ways of your people. The Great Spirit wishes no change in his red children. They are very good as he made them; if the white man attempts to improve them, he will spoil them."

To illustrate his views Neamathla went on to tell how the Great Spirit made the world. He was dissatisfied with his first effort, which proved to be a white man, pale and weak. The second, a black man, pleased him even less. On his third trial he made the red man; "and the red man pleased him."

As yet he had provided no means of subsistence for mankind; but the three men, looking up, saw three large boxes descending from the sky.

"Then," Neamathla went on, "the Great Spirit spoke and said, 'White man, you are pale and weak; but I made you first, and will give you the first choice; go to the boxes, open them and look in, and choose which you will take for your portion.' The white man opened the boxes, and looked in, and said, ' I will take this.' It was filled with pens, and ink, and paper, and compasses, and such things as your people now use.

"The Great Spirit spoke again, and said, ' Black man, I made you next but I do not like you. You may stand aside. The Red Man is my favorite; he shall come forward and take the next choice; Red Man, choose your portion of the things of this world.' The red man stepped boldly up and chose a box filled with tomahawks, knives, war clubs, traps, and such things as are useful in war and hunting.

"The Great Spirit laughed when he saw how well his red son knew how to choose. Then he said to the negro, ' You may have what is left; the third box is for you.' That was filled with axes and hoes, with buckets to carry water in, and long whips for driving oxen, which meant that the negro must work for both the red man and the white man, and so it has been ever since.

"Father, we want no change; we desire no school, and none of the teaching of the white people. The Master of Life knew what was best for all his children. We are satisfied. Let us alone."

II

By 1832 the removal policy of the government had been carried out almost everywhere. The Creek as a rule were going and it was supposed that the Florida Indians, their kinsmen, would not be too unwilling to travel along and join them in the new land. The Treaty of Payne's Landing was negotiated on this basis.

The Seminole were to cede to the United States their Florida lands and receive in return a portion of the Creek territory in the west. A special section was to be procured and added to the Creek land for their benefit.

They were to be incorporated as a part of the Creek nation, " and readmitted to all the privileges as members of the same."

The only proviso was that seven of their confidential chiefs, with their agent, and their " faithful interpreter Abraham," should go at the expense of the United States to examine the Creek country. There they should satisfy themselves of two things: the desirable character of the land, and the favorable disposition of the Creek people toward the reunion.

The " faithful Abraham" was a Maroon, a liberated negro who had once been slave to the Seminole chief Mickenopah. Abraham had lived all his life among the Seminole and occupied a place of great influence among them. "He always smiles and his words flow like oil," wrote one Army officer.

Westward the delegation went, and, after inspecting the country and talking with the Creek leaders, the seven Seminole chiefs met three United States commissioners at Fort Gibson. There, on March 28, 1833, they signed the supplementary treaty which confirmed the Treaty of Payne's Landing and bound the Seminole to a western removal. This emigration was to take place within three years. A third, they promised, would go in 1833; and " the remainder of the tribe, in about equal proportions," during the years of 1834 and 1835.

Dissension and disaster were the result. The Senate was slow to confirm the double treaty. It was not proclaimed as law until April 12, 1834, more than a year after the conclusion of the supplementary articles at Fort Gibson.

Mickenopah had refused to sign the Treaty of Payne's Landing, or rather by remaining away from the meeting had permitted his leadership to pass into the hands of those who were not unwilling to sign. Now he was ranging himself with the younger warriors who were strong in opposition. They panted for battle, but Mickenopah wished to remain on his fertile acres surrounded by his hundred slaves. Most of the Seminole were now refusing to go and declaring that the seven chiefs had not really been authorized to sign the agreement for removal.

Certainly none of them were removing. The year 1833 passed into history, and the Indians of the Big Swamp had made no move toward the emigration that had been agreed upon. Their old place in the Creek councils awaited them in vain. The next year saw no exodus, nor the next.

The end of the three year period was at hand, and it was apparent that if the Seminole were to go the Army would have to escort them.

III

LIKE so many other leaders of these southern Indians, Osceola or Powell, as he was also called, was of mixed Scotch and Indian ancestry. Whether or not he had negro blood as well is not known, but at least one of his wives was a former slave. It is typical of the controversies raging among the whites at this period that some writers derive his Indian name from a root which gives it the meaning of " the rising sun," and refer to him as the glory and hope of a noble race. Others trace the etymology to the " black drink " which it was the happy custom of the Creek to drink as a prelude to ceremonial dance or council. This acted as an emetic and removed from their systems all traces of previous intake. The public square of an Indian village was not a pretty sight when the braves were about to go into council. Adherents of this second linguistic theory found Osceola as uninviting as the recollections inspired by his name.

Osceola was not yet thirty at the time of the treaty at Payne's Landing; and inasmuch as he was not then, nor at any time later, a duly chosen chief of the Seminole, his name is not among those appended to that agreement. Nor was he, at that time, in open opposition.

Two years later, however, he was vehement in his refusal to consent to emigration. It was by his boldness and his planning that he was accounted first among the Seminole in the war which now began.

A dramatic story of the times represents Osceola as attending a meeting at which the chiefs were urged to sign a paper acknowledging the validity of the agreement to migrate. A few were prevailed upon to do so; but Osceola, rising from his place, walked forward to the table where the document lay. Drawing his long knife, he raised it far above his head for a moment; then brought it down vigorously piercing the paper and sinking deep into the wood beneath.

" This," he exclaimed in the piercing tones that were so peculiarly his that they were often, later, to proclaim his presence upon the field of battle, "this is the only way I will sign ! "

The meeting broke up in confusion; Osceola was detained a prisoner at the fort for four days; and on his verbal consent to emigration, was released.

So the story goes. If it does not seem probable that officers of the government would be procuring the signature of one who was not a chief for a treaty which had already been signed by the chiefs of the tribe and ratified by the United States Senate, we must remember the poetic license which is always granted to those who tell a tale of battle.

Winter was the only time in which warfare could well be prosecuted in the Seminole country. November was approaching in this year of 1835 which was, according to the treaty, to have seen the final departure of the tribe to the lands beyond the Mississippi. The war party of the Seminole chiefs met and resolved to resist emigration to the death. They began the procedure with an attack upon Charley Emathla, one of the treaty-signing chiefs. Charley wished to carry out his agreement and with a band of followers was making preparations for the westward journey.

Pressed by Osceola and a group of warriors for a decision, Charley Emathla refused to change his purpose. Osceola raised his rifle to dispatch the chief at once. Abraham, the interpreter, intervened, suggesting a council. So the Seminole retired to consider the matter. Osceola and a few adherents, however, adroitly absented themselves from the council and returned to Emathla. With cool deliberation they shot the old chief.

Now the Seminole were preparing for war in earnest. Soldiers were coming into the country to enforce the removal treaty, though as yet they had taken no steps that looked toward fighting. Osceola, now risen to be war leader, proved himself not unskilled in strategy. The women and children were sent deep into the swamps; the cattle and hogs driven into secret hiding places in the jungle-like depths to which white men had never penetrated; and supplies and weapons of all sorts were made ready.

Osceola now came with a band of seventy followers to the Indian agency and made representations of his readiness to emigrate. So well did he play his part that he received subsistence and supplies for his entire party to carry them on their journey. The unsuspecting agent, General Thompson, reported:

" We closed with the utmost good feeling; and I have never seen Powell and the other chiefs so cheerful and in so fine a humor at the close of a discussion upon the subject of removal."

With the capture of a baggage train coming in under the escort of Florida volunteers, the Seminole leader felt he was well supplied. He was now about ready to begin operations.

On December 28 open warfare began. Osceola reserved the Indian agent for his personal vengeance; for General Thompson had been the cause of his earlier brief imprisonment as well as his more recent source of supplies. Lieutenant Constantine Smith had dined with the Indian official in this holiday week; and the two men were having a quiet afternoon stroll but a few hundred yards from the agency office. This was at Fort King, some hundred and thirty miles north of Tampa Bay.

Suddenly from the brush about them Indians sprang up on every side. Osceola's characteristic piercing warwhoop was recognized by the interpreters and by the friendly Indians within the fort. The two men fell instantly. General Thompson's body was pierced with fourteen bullets.

The Indians went at once to the house of the sutler, Erastus Rogers, whom they surprised at dinner. They killed him and his two clerks and fired the house as they departed with the scalps, speedily and stealthily as they had come. All this happened almost within view of the fort but not within reach of its guns because of an intervening building.

This was but a small part of the afternoon's work, a forerunner of bigger achievement. Two messengers sent

out from the fort to carry to General Clinch the news of
the attack were picked off as they rode. There was now
the greatest apprehension as to the fortunes of Major
Francis Dade and his command. They had started
north from Fort Brooke, on the bay, to reinforce Fort
King.

The apprehension was well founded. Major Dade
and his men, marching through the sparse pine woods,
were suddenly fired upon from all sides. The bodies of
the attacking Seminole and Maroons were quite hidden
as they lay in the thick coarse grass. The soldiers
charged wildly and managed to start a few of their
assailants from cover.

After an hour of this sort of fighting it became apparent
that they could not go on as the wounded were now too
many to carry. At ten the fighting had begun and by
noon their dogged resistance had won a short respite;
but it was impossible either to advance or to retreat. A
small barricade of pine logs was prepared behind which
they continued their resistance during the short winter
afternoon.

As sunset drew on every officer was dead but one, a
desperately wounded lieutenant. Major Dade had
fallen early in the action. Most of the men were dead or
dying; only two had so far escaped being wounded.

With his last breath the lieutenant advised these men
to save themselves by pretending death. All signs of
resistance died down in the rude little fort. The echoes
of the last shot grew faint in the evening air.

The two hundred assailants, forty of whom were
Maroons, crept cautiously toward the pen in which lay
the dead and the dying. As they grew bolder, they
poured over the rough log barricade, stabbing or club-
bing the life out of those in whom some spark still re-

mained. Four of the wounded men managed to conceal all sign of life and to survive this treatment. Under cover of darkness, when the attacking party had withdrawn, they crept away.

One of these four was discovered and shot; but two days later the other three staggered one by one into Fort Brooke and told their story. It was nearly two months before General Gaines with his volunteers from New Orleans reached the spot and buried the victims of this first battle of the war.

Mickenopah, Alligator, and Jumper had led the Indian and negro forces in this encounter. Osceola and his men had been busy earlier in the day at Fort King and had probably suffered some delay in disposing of the messengers sent out after the murders there. But they joined their fellow tribesmen that evening near the scene of slaughter. Probably they were in good time to take part in the dance of rejoicing which follows an Indian victory.

IV

THROUGHOUT the following year there were many engagements, but none with decisive results. The Seminole accomplished no more such complete surprises and victories as this attack upon Dade and his men; but, whenever the fortunes of battle seemed to be turning against them, they were always able to effect their escape into the interior jungle. There they would rest and recruit for the next encounter.

At the close of this year (1836) General Thomas S. Jesup succeeded to the command of the forces which were a combination of regular troops and Florida volunteers. After a minor engagement in which some Indian captives had been taken the General sent one of these to ask for a parley with the Seminole leaders. There was a talk which resulted in a general cessation of hostilities and preparation for a conference with all the chiefs of the nation at Fort Dade early in the spring.

This council, held in March 1837, was apparently successful. The Seminole agreed to emigrate. Articles of capitulation were drawn up and signed and it was arranged that the Seminole and Maroons who were willing to go west should come into the forts and declare their intention of doing so.

Several hundred did come in; men, women, and children. The vessels were at Tampa Bay, ready to convey them westward. Daily the white flag was seen and groups of Seminole would present themselves as prospective emigrants.

Osceola himself, in the month of May, came in to Fort Mellon with a considerable party and surrendered to Lieutenant-Colonel Harney. He said that he and his people were tired of fighting. They were willing now to go to the new country. Harney took the statement at its face value and issued supplies for the entire party. They went off on parole, without a guard, under Osceola's pledge to report at Tampa for embarkation.

Tampa was not to see him at this juncture. Osceola and his people rejoined the hostile forces in the swamps. To them fled the greater portion of the others who had surrendered. They left General Jesup for transportation fewer than a hundred, chiefly fugitive negroes. The General reflected that the truce had proved an excellent means of recuperation for the enemy. He was forced to conclude that his peace-making had been premature.

Osceola was by now confirmed in his plan of offering peace in order to obtain the sinews of further warfare.

It had won him his first supplies from General Thompson, the Indian agent. It had proved equally efficacious in dealing with Colonel Harney. It was too useful to be discarded.

Accordingly in October he came in, again under a white flag, to Saint Augustine. General Jesup gave his men orders to surround the group and the entire number, seventy-two warriors and six women, were quietly taken prisoner. The old Spanish dungeons of Fort Marion were conveniently at hand and to them the Seminole were temporarily consigned to await emigration.

The public protest against the delays of the war, the lack of any decisive victories from a large force operating for two years, had already been vehement and prolonged. This capture roused a storm of protest which was to beat about General Jesup's head for the remainder of his life. He had violated the law of nations, committed an act of treachery which nothing could palliate. No invective could do justice to his evil doing.

"Never," wrote an Englishman in a London magazine of the day, "never was a more disgraceful piece of villainy perpetrated in a civilized land."

Osceola, at the beginning of the year transferred with his fellow warriors to Sullivan's Island, opposite Charleston, South Carolina, became the hero of the day. Visitors thronged to the island to see the chief and talk with him. When he and a party of braves visited the theatre in Charleston, they vied with the actors in holding the attention and admiration of the audience.

To Fort Moultrie came George Catlin, the artist, fresh from the painting of Keokuk, Black Hawk, and other Sauk notables, eager to add to his gallery the Seminole chiefs before they should be sent on their journey to

Oklahoma. Osceola arrayed himself in his best and stood, accoutred for war, while the painting was done.

"I have painted him," wrote the artist, "in precisely the costume in which he stood for his picture, even to a string and a trinket. He wore three ostrich feathers in his head and a turban made of a varicolored cotton shawl — and his dress was chiefly of calicoes, with a handsome bead sash or belt around his waist, and his rifle in his hand." Osceola is a rather fine-looking young man as Catlin has delineated him for us.

The elder — and fatter — Mickenopah was especially desirous of having proper presentation made of his legs incased in a pair of red leggings of which he was particularly proud. The artist obliged him by a portrait in which the old chief sits cross-legged, bedecked with bows, beruffled, beaded, with a rose-tinted mantle as large as a bedspread draped about one shoulder.

Neither of these two was to reach the western lands to which the party was destined. Mickenopah died on the journey; Osceola before they embarked. Shortly after his portrait was finished he became ill with "a quinsy or putrid sore throat," as the artist records it. The physicians of Charleston held consultation over him; but he refused their ministrations preferring the incantations of the medicine man of his tribe. These availed him little.

A half hour before his death he called for his costumes of war and donned them. At his request the officers of the post were summoned to see him arrayed for battle. Before their gaze he painted one side of his face with vermilion as one going into the fight. In silence, then, he shook hands with all the onlookers; he let himself be lowered again upon his bed and drew his scalping knife. Grasping it in his right hand he folded his arms across his breast; and so, without a struggle, died.

Two of his wives were by his side. Their piercing wails told that the end had come.

v

THE WAR went on. General Jesup remained in command a few months longer. He had been sent to Florida because in his criticism of his predecessor he had intimated that with proper management the conflict in Florida could be speedily ended. After a year and a half he had reversed his opinion and tried to convince the War Department that the war was not worth the further expenditure of blood and bullion. He advised retreating and leaving lower Florida in the possession of the Seminole.

In reply the Secretary reminded the General that the policy of western removal was a settled one which neither of them had the power to alter; but he suggested that an armistice be arranged. A somewhat quieter period ensued and when Jesup was succeeded by General Zachary Taylor, the more or less voluntary removal of groups went on until there were seventeen hundred of the Seminole who had emigrated.

In the spring of 1839 the Commander-in-Chief, General Macomb, came to negotiate a " lasting peace." At the conclusion of a council at Fort King he announced that he had " this day terminated the war with the Seminole Indians by an agreement entered into with Chitto Tustenuggee, Principal Chief."

One of the newspapers that had been most critical of the conduct of affairs, and most distant from the scene of strife, carried this comment:

And yet 'tis not an endless war,
As facts will plainly show,
Having been ended forty times
In twenty months or so.

This particular ending prevailed for but the briefest of periods. Chikika, said to be the largest Indian in the state, with a band of two hundred and fifty warriors attacked, in this summer of peace, Harney and a small party of soldiers and citizens who had gone peaceably to establish a trading post for the Seminole as provided in the Macomb agreement. The party was without any defence; ten of the twenty-six managed to escape in night attire.

A year passed; General Armistead succeeded General Taylor. In the summer of 1840 Chikika with seventeen canoe-loads of Indians attacked, sacked, and burned the village and trading post of Indian Key. A half dozen inhabitants were killed; the rest escaped to a neighboring island.

It seemed time for the Army to resume operations. Harney with a hundred soldiers penetrated into the Everglades and attacked one of the camps of the Seminole. Four Indians were killed, five more captured and hanged. Chikika was one of the victims. A great quantity of loot from Indian Key was found at this rendezvous.

A new idea was evolved. The Florida Legislature authorized the purchase of Cuban bloodhounds and a pack of them was brought to the state. It was supposed that they would trail the Seminole to their remotest retreats. Instead, the creatures showed no enthusiasm at all for the pursuit of the Indian. They sat down on their haunches and howled. The readers of newspapers howled likewise in derision.

Presidents had come and gone while the Seminole defied the order of removal. Jackson had been President when Osceola shot General Thompson; Van Buren's four years had been punctuated with the varying fortunes of the lingering warfare. The hero of Tippecanoe enjoyed his brief month in the Presidency and Vice-President Tyler succeeded to his office and responsibilities, not least of which was the Seminole imbroglio. In May 1841 General William J. Worth took charge of the Florida situation.

He was able to make friends with Wildcat, who since the death of Osceola had become one of the most influential of the Seminole warriors. Wildcat had been among those taken prisoner at Saint Augustine but had made his escape by squeezing through a narrow embrasure in the deep stone wall of old Fort Marion.

By this time he had realized the futility of resistance; and he came with a hundred and eighty followers and gave himself up for emigration. He continued his persuasion of his fellows until three hundred Seminole and Maroons were assembled at Tampa. In due time they all took passage for the West.

There was fighting throughout the winter, and on the ninth of April 1842 General Worth commanded in the last actual battle of this long-drawn-out war. Haleck Tustenuggee, one of the most determined opponents of emigration, was encamped at Chief Mickenopah's old town near the Great Wahoo swamp not far from the place where Dade had fallen nearly seven years before. There was a long fight in which but two Indians were killed and three wounded.

But the warriors who escaped realized by this time that there was little hope of success for them. Before long, hungry and spent, the chief and his band came into camp and surrendered.

In this long struggle nearly four thousand Seminole and negroes had been finally sent away to their western home. It had cost the lives of more than fifteen hundred soldiers to accomplish this end. It had taken seven years and many millions of dollars. The conduct of the war had aroused constant criticism and vituperation from one end of the country to another, and even in foreign lands. It ended without a treaty. But it did at last come to an end.

Shortly before this final engagement, General Worth had reported to the War Department that so far as he could estimate, there were now only about three hundred Seminole left in Florida. These were hiding in remote and inaccessible places scattered over a vast territory into which it was all but impossible for an army to penetrate. He recommended that so small a number be disregarded, that the greater part of the troops be withdrawn from the territory.

The War Department was reluctant to confess defeat even in so small a proportion as this. But the citizens of Florida were in agreement with General Worth. The Indians left were not strong enough in numbers to cause alarm, and there was an endless stretch of country where none but the Seminole would wish to live. The Governor of Florida seconded General Worth's suggestion, and in the end the Department consented.

A parley was held with such representatives of the Seminole remnant as could be induced to issue forth from their hiding places. They were assigned a location in the extreme south of the peninsula and were told they could remain as long as they refrained from hostilities. General Worth lingered in Florida with a small force for another year to establish the new reservation. The peace that was made then has been generally kept.

The descendants of this Seminole remnant, two tiny bands of them, live in the same section today. Not until within the past few years have they emerged from their swamps sufficiently to make the white man aware of their presence. For a generation they have had a government agent to whom they could apply for aid in times of destitution and a large tract of land has been formally set aside for them. But they have not yet overcome their distrust of all strangers even of their own race. The Creek in Oklahoma send missionaries to them with little effect. They have little more fondness for the white man's schools than Neamathla had years ago.

The tourist in Florida becomes aware of them by reason of "villages" set up outside Miami and Palm Beach where a few of the Seminole have been induced to make themselves into a sort of side-show for commercial purposes. Aside from these exhibitions their contact with the white man is still almost negligible.

CHAPTER XI
Oregon Country

I

PEOPLE who have no written language must carry their records in their heads and on their tongues. Although he was only eight years old, little Ku-ku-loo-ya of the Chopunnish had decided that he wanted to be a record keeper for his people. He had " finished his mind," as the Nez Percé saying has it.

The lad's father shook his head over his son's small stature; it was evident he would not grow into a great hunter or warrior. But his mother's big brown eyes glowed with pride when she watched her boy, all the dearer to her because of his smallness. And when she heard him repeat to his little sister every word of the long story he had heard the night before by the fire when they thought him asleep, she felt that her boy would be known among his people for something more individual than the slaying of the buffalo.

Already Ku-ku-loo-ya had a storehouse of memories to think about each night before he fell asleep by the campfire. First there were the tales of the great monster that once lay snorting fire, his huge body taking up the whole length and breadth of the Kamiah Valley. He swallowed all the animals of the forest till the world was all but empty; for this was before the days of man.

But the brave little coyote had taken pitch-pine and flint with him when he went within the jaws of the monster, and so was able to blaze a way out for himself and

205

his fellow creatures. When the monster had been suffocated with the fire and lay dying, the coyote and his friend the fox cut the great body up and made the various tribes: the Blackfoot from the feet, the Crow and Flathead from the head and neck. So they sent tribe after tribe to people the world till the great body was all gone and no members left to make the people to live in this beautiful Kamiah valley.

But the coyote bethought himself of the few drops of the best heart's blood that remained upon his paws; and with clear water from the sparkling river he washed it away. And as the drops fell upon the ground, the Chopunnish people sprang to life before them.

This was a marvellous story; but Ku-ku-loo-ya knew it must be true, for had he not seen the big stone in the middle of the Kamiah valley, and was not that stone the last remnant of the monster's great heart?

The story did not tell who made the white men; all this had happened long before these men with pale faces had come to the valley. But before Ku-ku-loo-ya was born, when his father was only a little boy, the So-yap-po had come and had tarried long among them. What tales the older people told of that sojourn! At length they had vanished over the Lo-lo pass.

More summers had passed while the Chopunnish danced about the sun-pole in worship and awe dreading to go near the sacred staff. "The sun is our father and the earth our mother," went the saying of the *tooats*, the medicine man whose word was holy to them all. Ku-ku-loo-ya feared almost to look toward that pole.

Yet he listened to the talk that went on about the other newcomers who had scouted the idea of fearing the pole or the sun itself. These newer people were King George's men and they came across the northern mountains. Far down on the way to the big western water, on the banks of the big river which this stream of theirs joined on its journey, the great old white-headed chief of the red-coated men had established a place where one might trade and see and hear many wonders. This was Fort Vancouver; and now, down at Walla Walla, there was a nearer, smaller fort.

To these trading posts many men came and went. There were strange Indian folk from afar off to the east who told of a land of great lakes and trees so thick one could scarcely pierce his way through. And these people said to them:

"There is One greater than the sun and the earth. You should sing and dance for him, not for this pole set up before you." The Chopunnish heard and wondered much.

Other traders came to them too; "Bostons," the men of the big Company called them. Of these the Chopunnish asked many things; but they shook their heads or laughed when asked to tell about the Greatest Spirit, greater than the sun himself. These fur-hunting folk came sometimes to the Chopunnish for wives; and the young women were always willing to go with them. Sometimes they would come back years later; the strange trapper husband had been killed in fight or hunt. But the Chopunnish widow and perhaps a brown baby or two would ride back on a good pony, leading others laden with the lodge and the trappings, the "fofurraw" her mountain husband had given her.

Not long ago a Boston had come to them who was different from the rest. When the elder folk asked him about the right way to worship he had shown them a book he carried always with him. That book, he said, told them all about the Great Spirit who was the father of both white man and red. But it was written in a language no Chopunnish could understand.

In the towns far to the east, this strange trapper had said, were white men who could translate the words of the Book and make them plain. Then he went his way and they saw him no more. Ku-ku-loo-ya remembered this man well; he had been a quiet and kind man. He had always been drawing lines and pictures to show which way the streams ran and where the mountains would rise high above the plains. Ku-ku-loo-ya listened with eagerness when the talk was of this man and his Book.

In a town many weeks' journey to the east, he had told them, there still lived the Red Head Chief of the Long Knives who had visited them so long before. He was the good friend of all Indians and many from the tribes on the plains came to see him and tell him their complaints and their needs. Perhaps he could help them to find the Book.

Long, long had been the talks the Chopunnish held before their council fires. Ku-ku-loo-ya had kept ears and eyes wide open, and knew many things his mother and father could not guess a boy of eight had found out. He knew almost as soon as the decision was made of the plan to send a party far across the mountains and the plains to learn more of what the trapper had told them. How he longed to be older and larger and stronger, that he too might go on the journey !

One of the younger men was his own cousin, No-Horns. No-Horns had thought much about the teachings of the different white men who had come their way and he felt very sure that dancing around the sun-pole was a mistake. Ku-ku-loo-ya wondered that No-Horns dared to say such a thing but in his secret thoughts it sometimes seemed to him that the young man might be wise as well as brave. He was certainly full of courage, both to speak and to act, and now he was going out into the unknown country to carry out a great search for his Chopunnish people.

Three others were going with him. Two of the men were older, for wisdom and council. Black Eagle had been a chief when the captains had visited the tribe. Man of the Morning was one whom they all trusted and liked, though his mother had come from the Salish country to the north, from those people whom the incomprehensible white man, for no good reason, called Flathead.

The other young man, Rabbit-Skin-Leggings, was a nephew of Black Eagle. He had always liked the white men and he was very happy to have this chance to know them better. Ku-ku-loo-ya knew just how Rabbit-Skin-Leggings felt about it.

All the Chopunnish rode out with the four messengers when they started on their long journey. Ku-ku-loo-ya on his little pony rode farther than any of them. His mother and father turned back; he heard, far off, his mother's voice calling him. But he could not bear to turn his face back to the west.

"Come now, little cousin," said No-Horns, "now it is time for you, too, to say good-bye."

Ku-ku-loo-ya nodded but he could not speak. He pulled his pony back. There was a lump in the little boy's throat as he watched the four men ride steadily on their way. Soon they were out of his sight. Ku-ku-loo-ya rode back to camp with his little face overcast.

"Next year, when we go to the buffalo hunting," said his mother, "we shall see them again and wonderful things they will have to tell us."

II

NEXT summer at the buffalo ground Ku-ku-loo-ya looked in vain for his cousin No-Horns, for Black Eagle, for Man of the Morning. Of the four who had gone out only Rabbit-Skin-Leggings had come back into the mountains. Sadly and yet eagerly the Chopunnish listened to his story.

It had been a long hard journey to the home of the Red Head Captain, who was a white-haired captain now. He had welcomed them to the Indian council house which stood behind his great wooden home on the banks of the river. But though he gave them food and friendliness and kind words of promise he could give them no Book to carry back with them.

Here in the white man's village Black Eagle had sickened and died; and just as they were about to start away Man of the Morning, too, had found the strange food and water and the strange country too much for his poor old frame. The two younger men had started back in sadness. At the mouth of the Yellowstone No-Horns had said good-bye to his companion. He had helped to bring his people a message but he could not live to carry it all the way.

"The Red Head Captain promised," said Rabbit-Skin-Leggings as he finished his sorrowful story, " that men would come to us. Not now, but in another year, or another, they will come. Look for them each year where the white men gather. As for me, I shall stay with the white men hereafter. They have been very kind, and I like their ways."

So only the horses that Rabbit-Skin-Leggings had brought went back with the Chopunnish to their country on the Clearwater. But the promise they carried in their hearts.

Another summer found them again at the trappers' rendezvous. Great travellers, these Nez Percé folk. They wondered why the white men should call them "Pierced Noses" instead of Chopunnish. They did not have any nose-piercing custom. But these Bostons were funny folk. They called the Salish Flathead and when they met Indians they gave them odd names of their own like John and Silas and William.

Away over on the Snake River in the valley where the Portneuf River joins the larger stream, a young Boston by the name of Wyeth was building great thick walls of earth for a trading post this summer of 1834. And with the party that came to his place was a man who had heard of the visit of the four to St. Louis and had come to give the Indians the message they asked for.

But the Nez Percé people sadly saw themselves passed by. Jason Lee and his companions went on down to the big fort on the Columbia and the old White Headed Eagle down there told him to stay nearer the coast. It must be that King George's men were more powerful than the Bostons.

The Nez Percé did not lose hope. Another summer found them at the rendezvous, and marvellous things rewarded their search. Two men had come, a man of the book, Dr. Samuel Parker; and a man of magic, Dr. Marcus Whitman.

Old Jim Bridger had borne for years in his shoulder a barbed arrowhead. The Nez Percé stood amazed to see the strange man skillfully probe the flesh and bring out at last the Blackfoot arrow. A low murmur of admiration went around. Patients thronged to the clinic.

"I have heard a little of the white man's talk," said

the Nez Percé chief to Dr. Parker; "but only enough to
go down into my ears. I want to hear more, to go down
into my heart all the way and stay there."

But still another year the Nez Percé must wait. Dr.
Parker would go on to the West and visit the many tribes
of the land; then return to the United States to tell the
people there about the Indians. Dr. Whitman was going
to turn back eastward at once to carry the same message.
He would return the next year with a party of teachers
of the Book.

The Nez Percé gladly sent with him two boys, Ites and
Tueka-kas. The jolly doctor quickly gave them the
names of John and Richard, and they were quite proud.
Ku-ku-loo-ya, too, was proud of his Boston name of
Billy, which he carried throughout his life. He longed
to go with Dr. Whitman, but though he was a big enough
boy now to feel quite grown up he was considered too
small to attempt the long journey. "Remember No-
Horns," his mother said to him.

With Dr. Parker on his journey west the Nez Percé
sent one of their young men, Kentuc, as guide. Charley
Compo went along as interpreter. Charley Compo was
a French-Canadian who had come with the Hudson's
Bay folk, had married a wife among the Cayuse and had
learned the talk of several of the tribes. Many of the
Cayuse, who lived just to the west of the Nez Percé, were
married into one band of their neighbors. But they were
a wilder folk and less friendly to new ways.

Each year the journey for the buffalo took the Nez
Percé farther and farther from the Salmon River and
Clearwater country which they called their home. But
from all their hunting and fishing trips, their journeys to
the buffalo grounds or the trading places of the white
man, or their searching for roots or berries, they would

always come back to the home land. It was here that Dr. Parker met the head chief of the tribe who was called Charley.

" I have been like a little child, uneasy," said Charley, " feeling about in the dark after something, not knowing what. Now I hope to learn."

Here on a bright Sunday morning the Nez Percé set their lodge poles and made a great canopy for shade. They dressed in their best and knelt upon a carpet of their finest dressed skins while the white man talked to them of the commandments the Book held for their living. Very earnestly they listened to every word from him and from Compo who put the English phrases into their own tongue.

" They gave the utmost attention, and entire stillness prevailed, excepting, when some truth arrested their minds forcibly, a little humming sound passed through the whole assembly, occupying two or three seconds."

These were earnest folk, these Nez Percé; a strange seeking people. One might question much of this as the dream of an ardent missionary spirit were it not borne out by the same people today. They are still capable of deep devotion to an ideal, still more earnest, more intense, than the Indian world about them.

Dr. Parker went on — on to the forts of the Hudson's Bay Company, to the Methodist Mission where Jason Lee and his two helpers had already a school of fourteen children, on to the coast tribes, Clatsop and Chinook, to the tribes of the upper Columbia and the mountains beyond. His *Journal of a Tour to the Rocky Mountains*, published after his return to the States, was the first authentic information of this far land since Lewis and Clark had written their journal more than thirty years before.

Before leaving the Nez Percé he had intrusted to them a letter which they were to deliver to Dr. Whitman and his party the following year at the trappers' rendezvous on the Green River.

III

MEANWHILE John and Richard had had a wonderful year indeed. They had not dreamed the world could be so large. Thousands of miles they travelled by land and by water.

The lodges of the white man were of wood or stone or brick and were set firmly upon the ground not to be removed. They were set closely, side by side, rows upon rows of them. The Bostons must be almost as many in number as the buffalo.

From the town of the Red Head Captain they had gone far, far to the east and north to a land where the winter was colder than any they had known and where the people rode about in queer carts without wheels that slid on top of the close-packed snow and ice. Here, through the short winter days, the two boys sat daily in a lodge of the Bostons and learned the meaning of black marks on white paper.

In a lodge built for worship and prayer they saw, one winter evening, a golden-haired young woman stand beside their doctor friend. They heard the words repeated which meant that these two were now husband and wife. John and Richard rejoiced and wondered. They knew that this meant that Mrs. Whitman would go with them when they returned home in the spring. And before the long cold winter was over another husband and wife, Henry and Eliza Spalding, had decided to go with the party to the Oregon country.

White women in the country beyond the mountains !
John and Richard knew that this would be the most wonderful of all the wonderful things the Nez Percé would
hear.

Their hearts failed them more than once on the long
westward journey. Mrs. Spalding was very ill, they
could see as they rode beside the wagon in which she was
often lying. But she was as brave as any warrior and
as long as she could sit up would stay in the saddle and
press onward with the rest toward her new home.

On the great summer holiday of the white man they
were coming to the crossing place, the pass where the
eastern rivers are left behind and the little streams all
turn their way toward the setting sun. Mrs. Spalding
fainted, and the boys knew from the grave faces of them
all that fear was upon them. John and Richard grieved
to think they might have to leave this good friend to a
lonely resting place in the mountains.

But before long breath returned to her and she could
go on with the rest and kneel at the crest of the pass to
give thanks for the sight of the world beyond over which
they shook out the folds of the flag they loved. Just
beyond the pass was the place appointed for the rendezvous.

Word had gone ahead that the missionary party was
coming with the caravan of the American Fur Company.
The Nez Percé were waiting. This time they were not to
be disappointed.

A tempestuous cavalcade rushed out to meet the newcomers. There were Indians who had never seen the
face of a white woman. There were rough trappers and
voyageurs, hardly less wild, who had not been within
the settlements of the whites for many a year. They
gave all the appearance of a war-party as they tore

madly along to the meeting. It was a strange welcome indeed for these two women of quiet piety.

"They are friends," John and Richard assured the mission party. "There is the chief Lawyer; King George's men gave him that name. Here are the Nez Percé women too, coming to make you welcome."

The Indian women liked Mrs. Spalding from the first. The boys had felt sure they would. She was quiet, gentle, and sympathetic; yet cool and composed in times of stress. Best of all she was quick to learn their names and ways. Many years afterward, Mrs. Lawyer said with pride: "Why, she could talk quite well with us before we reached our own land !"

IV

THE INDIANS were of course unaware of all the undercurrents beneath the events that made such impression on their minds. The Treaty of Joint Occupation, by which England and America were to waive the question of the ultimate ownership of the country, meant nothing to the red man who dwelt there. But the time was coming when the question could be waived no longer.

The true significance of the journey of these two courageous missionary women across the Rockies lay not so much in the religious message they brought as in the object lesson they gave. The eastern half of the continent had been settled by a series of waves coming like the tide each a bit farther. Now the water was rising for another western sweep.

The barriers that had held it back before this time were less than nothing — Long's dictum that the prairies were uninhabitable, the unfounded belief that the mountains could never be crossed. Now two young women from central New York had proved that belief untenable. They had made the journey safely enough. The letters that came back to the States were proof enough that here was a land of promise. One had but to cross over.

While America had listened to Long and similar theorists, England had wisely confided her growth in the northwest to that remarkable organization, the Hudson's Bay Company. Emerging victor from a life and death struggle with the Nor'westers, the Company swayed an empire in the fur country. It opposed an autocratic rule, a close-knit government, a single firm purpose to the scattered efforts of the carelessly independent free traders and trappers of the United States.

England might nominally have no more power than America in the Oregon country. In actual fact the Hudson's Bay Company was supreme. And now that supremacy was challenged by a handful of idealists, men and women who tilled the soil and sang psalms and clothed themselves from boxes and barrels sent out by the congregations of little rural churches in the East.

Every one of these homes menaced the fur empire none the less. Every missionary who wrote home in glowing terms of the country in which he dwelt helped to bring more of these questing Bostons. They were in the way in this land of the hunter and the trapper.

Dr. Elijah White, who had come to act as physician to Jason Lee's mission on the Willamette, returned to the States. A season or two later he turned up again in the Oregon country with a hundred settlers, men, women, and children, and with his own commission as an agent appointed by the United States for the Indian tribes of Oregon. This was not to be brooked. Another such party, and the Canadians colonized by the Company to maintain British supremacy would be outnumbered. England must have her title confirmed with all speed.

But the authorities in Washington and London were not so keenly aware of these needs as the dwellers on the Columbia. In the far-off capitals long diplomatic conversations were held over a tiny section of boundary and some cod-fishing in Maine; but this western empire received little notice.

Dr. White visited the different northwestern tribes in pursuance of his new duties and got them to agree to a code of laws which made the Mosaic regulations seem mild by comparison. To most of the Indians it made little difference since the worthy agent did not stay to see the decrees enforced.

The Nez Percé took them more seriously. Since 1839 their mission had owned a printing press brought by the missionary board from the Sandwich Islands. The code was printed and studied beside the Bible in their school. Dr. White presided over the Nez Percé council which elected as chief Ellis who had gone in boyhood to the Red River settlements. He complimented the tribe on the noteworthy fact that no one had begged from him during his visit. There was no other tribe that had shown this forbearance.

Each year brought more people, hungry for land, hungry for the prosperity that is always to be found a little farther along the sunset trail. Dr. and Mrs. Whitman, in their mission station at Waiilatpu among the turbulent Cayuse, were in the path of the newcomers and gave them hearty welcome. Everyone who came was another stroke of the hammer that was building an American commonwealth.

In the summer of 1844 Dr. Whitman, returning from a mission to the States, was guide and convoy to a party of settlers who numbered nearly a thousand. This meant a clear majority in the country for the people of the States.

What it meant to the Indians was not yet apparent.

v

THIS same year of 1844 there came along the Oregon Trail a young lieutenant with a party of exploration. He had with him French *voyageurs* and a group of old time mountain men. Kit Carson, most celebrated of them all, was with him. Delaware Indians were in his party.

Lieutenant Frémont had been in the West the summer before as far as the Wind River Mountains from which the rivers flow away in four different directions to reach the Atlantic and the Pacific. But he had not gone on. This summer he was going all the way to the Columbia River and from there to the south on his way back to St. Louis. It would be a winter trip, the return; for the year was old when he reached the Jason Lee mission at The Dalles.

The teacher at the mission brought to Frémont's notice a Chinook boy who had learned a little English. Chinook, as they called him, had proved an agreeable and adaptable member of the mission household. Now he " wanted to see the whites." Lieutenant Frémont engaged to take the lad under his special care for the journey back to the States and to see that he returned in safety another year.

It was a long hard journey upon which Chinook embarked. For a short distance they had Indian guides; then they must make their way unaided. Their route first led them to the country of the Klamath or Tlamath Indians. These people, dwelling about the lake that bears their name, had a wide reputation among the other tribes for cruelty and treachery.

They talked no language which those familiar with the tribes of the other regions could understand; so it was by signs that they made known the fact that they were at war with the equally wild Modoc to the east of them. For this or for some other reason they refused to send a guide along with the party.

They were now in country nominally Spanish, but actually all but uninhabited save by an occasional wretched group of the Digger type, that had never before seen the face of a white man. As their language was basically not unlike that of the Shoshoni, it was possible to communicate with them when their first fright was diminished. In that desert country on the barren eastern slopes of the Sierras they were a pitiable people.

"Eight or ten appeared to live together, under the same little shelter; and they seemed to have no other subsistence than the roots or seeds they might have stored up, and the hares which live in the sage, and which they are enabled to track through the snow, and are very skillful in killing. Their skins afford them a little scanty covering. Herding together among bushes, and crouching almost naked over a little sage fire, using their instinct only to procure food, these may be considered, among human beings, the nearest approach to the mere animal creation. We have reason to believe that these had never before seen a white man."

The increasing severity of the season warned the party not to cross the barren Great Basin. Instead they turned westward to cross the Sierras and find shelter at Sutter's fort in California. Around Pyramid Lake and in the vicinity of the Salmon Trout River (now known as the Truckee) they found Washoe Indians now and then

ROCK OF ACOMA

From Frémont's Report

PYRAMID LAKE

From Frémont's Report

Piute. Occasionally they could get some information about the road that lay ahead of them. More often they struggled on up the steeps, through the snow and ice, in hardship and danger. This was not like Chinook's mild country of the northwest.

It was a surprise to the party when they mounted a Washoe Indian upon one of their horses only to find that he did not know how to ride. Even horses had not penetrated to these fastnesses.

It was in February, after weeks of struggle through the icy mountains, that they met two Indians the older of whom tried to dissuade them from attempting the last hard crossing that would take them over the heights to the western slopes that fell away to the valley of the Sacramento. It was too hard, the old man said.

By signs and by words whose repetition forced their meaning into the minds of the travellers, he made them comprehend that they must meet " rock upon rock, snow upon snow; " that the precipices and the treacherous gulfs of ice would prove their undoing.

Chinook, who understood better than the white men what the old Indian meant, covered his head with his blanket and began to lament.

" I wanted to see the whites," he cried. " I came away from my own people to see the whites and I should not mind if I were to die among them. But not here, not here in the snow of the mountains ! " Very dolefully he raised the wail of distress that speaks in every language.

Yet in another month — a month of such hardship as the old man had predicted — they were safe in Captain Sutter's hospitable fort, and Chinook was having his first sight of the Californians, Spanish and Indian. It was strange indeed to observe the many Indians who worked all day at farm and forge and mill, making the big fort a beehive of industry.

Then, after rest and reprovisioning, they travelled south down the river valleys to leave California by the easier Old Spanish Trail. Down they went through the land of the Mission Indians and of the disbanded neophytes who had become the "Horse-Thief" groups; then across the low southern pass into desert country again.

All the way across the Great Basin their path was dogged by hostile Ute; Carson and Godey made their gallant foray to aid two Mexicans who were the survivors of a slaughtered party; one of the Frémont men, seeking a stolen horse, was ambushed and slain. Chinook felt that there were other dangers than ice and snow before he should attain his desire.

In the mountains they found the Ute at war with the Arapaho. Cautiously they made their way past the very scene of a hostile encounter in which hundreds of naked braves were engaged. Through the unfriendly Arapaho they made their way to Bent's Fort on the Arkansas, the first structure of the white man's building to greet their eyes since they left California.

There was still a long journey across the plains before the settlements were reached. The Cheyenne, just returned from a sortie to the east in which they had dispatched a goodly party of Delaware, were anxious to entrust to the white men a message which might forestall the vengeance the Delaware would be seeking. They let the government party pass in peace; but the Pawnee whom they met farther to the east were insolent and menacing. Chinook was as glad as his white companions when they were clear of that unpleasant village.

And now they were getting nearer and nearer to the

villages of the white man. It was late summer when they reached St. Louis. It was marvellous enough; but still greater wonders awaited the young Indian. Chinook went east with Lieutenant Frémont to Washington; then to Pennsylvania where a hospitable home was opened to him. He spent the winter studying much and seeing much.

The next summer Chinook rejoined Frémont in Washington. He had achieved his desire to see the whites and was now ready to start back to his own people.

"Chinook been Quaker all winter," he said, as he proudly exhibited the parting gifts of his host. Among the treasures he was carrying back was a large Bible with attractive illustrations. He opened it to show the blank pages between the Testaments.

"Here," he laughed, "Chinook put name all wife and all horse !"

So back he went to his people on the Columbia to give them his impressions of the marvels he had seen in the white man's country.

VI

CHINOOK's winter among the people of peace may have helped to keep his tribe friendly in the outbreak that came a year or two after his return. So many warring influences were at work that there was need of any gleam of kindliness that might be found.

The Nez Percé, remoter and already traditionally friendly to the whites, did not participate in the uprising. Eliza Spalding's quiet and arduous ministrations had raised up for her a body of Indian friends who were her protection.

But the Cayuse, in and around Fort Walla Walla, grew more and more angered as they saw white men and their families pouring in over the Oregon Trail. Wild rumors flew about that these men would claim the whole land for themselves. They would drive the Indians away from their homes, from their fishing and hunting grounds. The Whitman mission at Waiilatpu sheltered too many of these intruders.

When Dr. Whitman was away in the East an angry band of Cayuse had burned down the mill at the mission. His return with a party large enough to change the balance of the white population from English to American did not make them less hostile.

An epidemic of measles in 1847 proved to be cause or pretext for an outbreak. The Cayuse professed to believe that the doctor was planning to poison them wholesale and had spread among them the seeds of this plague. Forty years before, it was said, a trader had threatened to let the smallpox out of a bottle among the Indians. The ill-timed jest had borne much evil fruit since that day.

The year before this, the long standing boundary question had been settled, and a provisional government was in operation. But the country was still outside the pale of American law. When Marcus and Narcissa Whitman and a dozen others were murdered, and forty-eight women and children carried off to satisfy the vengeance and lust of the Cayuse braves, there was no American Army to call upon, no American court to invoke. It was Peter Skene Ogden, who had succeeded Dr. McLoughlin as Chief Factor of the Hudson's Bay Company, who succeeded in buying from the Indians the freedom of these pitiful captives.

The Cayuse war followed with many tribes in open battle against such troops as the new land could muster. At the behest of the government all Protestant missions were withdrawn from this section for a generation.

The faithful Nez Percé, weeping to lose their friend, brought Mrs. Spalding and her children out to safety. They were not to see her again; already she had fallen a victim to tuberculosis. But the memory of her teachings stayed with many of them through the long years and the " first church of Oregon," started by the Whitmans and Spaldings, is represented by a group of churches today. Near one of these the body of Eliza Spalding, brought back in 1913 to the Clearwater country, rests beneath a monument which tells something of her work and the devotion the Nez Percé gave her. They are still proud to do her honor.

In that first church of ninety years ago there was one non-missionary member, Charley Compo the interpreter. He had a little son a year and a half old, who was the first child baptized after the organization of the church.

A nonagenarian still lives out on the reservation on the Clearwater. His name is Billy Compo. Name and manner alike show the French intermixture. Billy apologizes for his poor English which makes it difficult for him to tell the many things he recollects of his ninety years of living.

He explains the reason for his halting tongue. His mother, he says, was a Cayuse. When he was a small lad he could speak English better, but his mother took him for many years out among the wild Indians and he lost all knowledge of the tongue.

Billy is not a member of any one of the six Presbyterian churches which the devout Nez Percé maintain at various points on their reservation and from which they frequently send out missionaries to the other tribes. But it looks as if he might have been one of them ninety years ago.

CHAPTER XII
The Old Southwest

I

I N THIS prairie country beyond the Missouri to which the Delaware had come after generations of westward travel, they were well content. For near neighbors they had the Shawnee, whose old people, like their own, looked back to the days on the Ohio. These elders would tell of the time when their grandfathers fought together against Fort Pitt and gave up their white prisoners to Colonel Bouquet. But with the white man today their relations were as a rule friendly.

East of them it was not a long journey to the big bend of the Missouri River where a few small villages marked for many years the last advance of white settlement. Twenty miles beyond that border was the soldier town, Fort Leavenworth, established in 1827.

And westward, across the plains, all, north or south, was Indian country. Two famous trails forked apart just after leaving the white settlements. The one to the north, first the way of the trader and the trapper, was later marked by the rolling Conestoga wagons of the homeseeker bound for the Oregon country. The southern route, traversed first by mules and later by oxen, saw each summer the great caravans of merchants going along the dry plains to Santa Fé, in the Spanish speaking world.

While they kept on the north bank of the Arkansas River they were in the Indian country set aside for the

tribes by the United States. Below that stream was
Spanish territory — Mexican, rather, since the revolution of 1822. But the roving Kiowa and Comanche, and
the Apache of the plains, cared nothing for international
boundaries. Up and down this country they rode and
hunted and fought, and if they hesitated to come north
of the Arkansas it was not the white man but the red
that deterred them. For this central country, west of
the definite location of the Delaware and the Shawnee,
was becoming more and more the hunting ground of the
northern tribes — Cheyenne, Arapaho, Crow, Pawnee.
Even the Sioux, above these and helping to push them
southward, now and then found their way down for war
or adventure or trading. The buffalo hunt brought even
the Ute from the Rockies, and the Osage, Wichita, and
many others from the eastern plains. To all of these
tribal rights and prerogatives meant a great deal more
than national boundaries. Many were the wars whose
only historians were the wrinkled old men and women
who crouched about the campfires at night and recounted the exploits of their youth.

All through the days of the Santa Fé Trail the Kiowa
and Comanche, from the south, were at war with the
Cheyenne and the Arapaho from the north of the Arkansas. None of them settled upon that river. Its valley
was the theater of their warfare as well as the scene of
many a buffalo hunt and of attack upon a trader's caravan when one chanced to come along and offer opportunity. But these merchants were well armed and kept
strict guard night and day. Only occasionally was there
a chance to stampede their stock and capture booty.
Smaller parties were legitimate prey; these too kept
closely with the great caravans whenever they could.

With the bodies of merchants or travellers would be

Delaware warriors journeying as hunters and guides. They loved the life; the guard and the reading of Indian sign, the heat of conflict and the glow of victory. Let the women and the old men stay at home and raise corn as the white agent advised. That was fitting work for squaws. For braves there was better employment.

This permanent frontier, it will be seen, looked toward civilization on one side; but it had a more interested eye out toward the wild life of the tribes of the plains.

II

YELLOW WOLF of the Cheyenne was returning from a horse-hunting raid south of the Arkansas. He had had good fortune and a string of Comanche horses were proof of his prowess. Crossing the river near the mouth of the Purgatoire he came upon a camp of white men. They were not Mexicans but the less usual kind that came from the East. They seemed friendly enough. Yellow Wolf stopped to pass the time of day with them.

The Cheyenne liked these white men from the first. They were looking over the country and planning to build a trading post. Where could they find a place that would be most suitable for the Cheyenne ? Yellow Wolf considered gravely. Near the mountains ? No, that was too far from the buffalo range. The tribes of the plains would not come so far to it. It must be above the Arkansas, if he wished the Cheyenne to be his patrons. Somewhere in this region near the mouth of the Purgatoire would be a very good neighborhood. The Bent brothers and their partner, Ceran St.Vrain, agreed with the Cheyenne chief.

"When you have built your walls," said Yellow Wolf, "I shall bring my Cheyenne people to you with furs, to buy your flour and gunpowder. And because we shall always be friends, we Cheyenne people will always call you, Charles Bent, by our own name of White Hat. You, Ceran St. Vrain, shall be known to us as Black Beard. And to you, William, brother of Charles, because you are still a stripling, shall we give the name of Little White Man. But later when you are a full warrior you shall have another name among us."

Yellow Wolf had watched the trading post grow during four years in the spot he had helped to choose. It took a long time to make and put in place so many blocks of adobe. The Cheyenne marvelled often at the work and at the men who helped to build it. But it was with friendly eyes that they looked on.

Other eyes were not always so friendly. Yellow Wolf heard from Black Whiteman and from Little Turtle the story of a raid the Crow made, one winter night, on a camp where a few of the workmen were gathered. He was a scamp, that Black Whiteman, to run away with another man's wife; but so good-looking a young brave that no one could blame Otter Woman for preferring him to the husband who had duly bargained with her father and paid ponies for her.

According to Cheyenne custom her elopement with Black Whiteman would be ratified if they could get safely away. So with his friend Little Turtle to help him, the young brave took his woman and started out toward the place where the new fort was rising.

The three spent the night at the camp where a dozen workers were under the leadership of the trapper whom they called " Kit " — a small man and not old in years but both brave and cautious. Yet he seemed neither this night; for in the morning they found that all the horses and mules of the white men had been carried away. A raiding party of sixty Crow had passed by in the night. Those Sparrow Hawk people clearly earned their reputation for being the cleverest at acquiring horses of all the tribes of the region.

Black Whiteman and Little Turtle's horses had not been with the rest and so were spared; so they offered to go with the eleven white men who were starting off afoot to recover their animals. Otter Woman stayed in camp with the Mexican herder and cook.

It was a great tale Black Whiteman brought back to her — how they had travelled many miles through the snow and the brush; how at last they had found the Crow camp in the evening, all a scene of feasting and dancing and merriment over their capture of the white man's horses; and how the eleven white men had caught them unawares and routed the whole sixty Crow braves. The two Cheyenne warriors, meanwhile, had been helping by stampeding the horses. They counted coup, none the less, on the two dead Crow left by their fleeing comrades. Many a time in after years the story was told at the Cheyenne camps.

Yellow Wolf heard it and added another white man to his list of friends. When at Bent's Fort, not long after, he met Kit Carson, he gave him, too, a new name. Thereafter the Cheyenne called Kit Vih-hiu-nis — Little Chief.

The friendship grew greater when the younger Bent took to wife a Cheyenne girl, Owl Woman. Her father was Grey Thunder, keeper of the sacred medicine arrows which the Cheyenne people had guarded with mysterious rites ever since the world began. Other ceremonies and dances they had learned from various tribes of the plains, but this was their own, their holy of holies. No white man could even see the ceremonies. The keeper of the arrows was revered by them all. That he should give his daughter to a white man was a mark of highest confidence.

During this time while the Southern Cheyenne traded at Bent's Fort on the Arkansas, Black Beard and his brother Marcelline had a smaller fort on the South Platte, which was the special haunt of the Pawnee. Marcelline's wife was a Pawnee, a thin beanpole of a woman, whom the Cheyenne called Tall Pawnee Woman. They liked her and they liked especially the fine garden she raised around the trading post, with pumpkins, melons, and beans as the season went on. It was good to visit Fort St. Vrain.

Down below the Arkansas, to the fort called Adobe Walls, Yellow Wolf did not often lead his people. They were still at war with the Comanche and the Kiowa — a war that had gone on for years untold and promised to go on forever.

But a different idea now began to prevail. The white men suggested it. The older men among the Indians took it up.

"Why do we not make peace with the tribes below? We are at peace with the Arapaho and allied with them. They have made an agreement and no longer war among themselves. It would be good if we could meet and agree."

Slowly the idea prevailed; it was in 1840 that the old time enemies met in council on the banks of the Arkansas not far below Bent's Fort. It was a great gathering, remembered always.

North of the river were the great villages where lay encamped the Cheyenne and the Arapaho. South of the stream stretched the tepees of the Comanche, the Prairie Apache, and the Kiowa. Instead of attack and raid, there were dancing and drumming. After days of council and feasting they were agreed.

"Come over to see us," said the tribes of the south; "but bring no horses with you. We have so many already. Come afoot, and we shall send you back riding and driving horses before you."

Dohausen of the Kiowa, Yellow Wolf of the Cheyenne, and many another chief and warrior finished the council of peace and moved up the river to pay their respects to the fort which had held their friendship always. They nearly exhausted its stores in making presents to ratify the new pact.

So the tribes of the southern plains smoked the calumet. Thereafter they raided and fought together, against the white man crossing the plains or against their standing enemies of New Mexico and Texas.

III

In 1845 the fierce Arapaho saw for the first time the bluecoats of United States cavalrymen. The dragoons made a great march that summer, out from Fort Leavenworth to the trading post Fort Laramie in the Wyoming hills, south to Bent's Fort on the Arkansas, and back across the prairie to their starting place.

It was heralded far and wide among the whites as a great achievement. The Indians too were obviously impressed. It was thought they had received an object lesson on the power of the United States which would be lasting.

While some of his men travelled as far as the Sweetwater, the Horse-Chief of the Long Knives (Colonel Stephen Watts Kearny) sat at Fort Laramie and sent out word to all the neighboring tribes to send their chiefs in for council. Many came, Arapaho warriors among the rest. They were amazed indeed at the numbers of the white men, their equipment, their shining weapons, their precise drill.

The Arapaho were taken to task for their recent behavior. They had been doing quite a little to thin the white population of the region.

" Do you see these great lines of men ? " This was the burden of the talk. " Do you see these great guns, going off twice at one shot ? If you kill any more white men, these lines of soldiers will march against your nation and wipe out every one of your villages."

When this impressive threat was followed by rockets shooting fire into the sky and the discharge of the marvellous howitzer the fear and surprise of the Arapaho were unbounded. Some fell flat on their faces. Others shrieked and ran as fast as they could from the spot. This was big magic indeed.

They remembered this threat. Indeed they remembered it for several months. Then one of them was unduly tempted and made way with two trappers whom he was able to surprise in the mountains.

Bitterly the tribe reproached him saying that the horse soldiers now would come according to the promise. They sent a delegation in to Fort Laramie with a gift of horses to pay for the crime. To their surprise there were no dragoons there; and the trader would take neither the horses nor the guilty man whom they offered to give up.

So the threat of vengeance had been hollow and the whites were poor weak creatures who did not try to avenge their dead. The Arapaho would place no more reliance upon the Long Knives and their rows of soldiers. Let them come on; they would find resistance quickly enough. The bluecoats were nothing but old women, fine for talk but hiding when there was danger. Such a spirit as this brooded on the plains in the summer of 1846.

And before that summer had faded, there came the day when the Army of the West came marching out from Fort Leavenworth across the plains on its way to the little New Mexican capital of Santa Fé.

IV

THE TOWN of Santa Fé which General Kearny entered as peaceably as if it had been a Missouri village was in the midst of a score of Indian villages that spread along the Rio Grande and its tributaries. These were not the tepee villages of the roving buffalo hunters but closely packed rows and terraces of stone and adobe houses. They had been standing for many a generation sheltering these agricultural Indians from the constant forays of the wilder tribes about them.

To the north the line of villages, each with its near-by Mexican town, stretched out for eighty miles — Tesuque, Nambe, San Ildefonso, Santa Clara, San Juan, Picuris. Finally, and strongest, Taos, the outpost to the north. Taos was most warlike, its people most accustomed to the outer world of Ute and Apache and Mexican and mountain man. The high-terraced Indian village and the famous center for the mountain men almost chummed together in this little-tenanted country. They were but two or three miles apart.

Southward were still more villages — Jemez, Sia, and Santa Ana on a tributary stream; Cochiti, Domingo, San Felipe, and Sandia on the main waterway as one went from Santa Fé down to Albuquerque. Then turn-

ing westward, following another stream, one found
Isleta, no longer an island; Laguna, its lake long since
vanished; Acoma, set high on her rocky pinnacle in the
land of the Mesa Encantada. Still farther, beyond the
reach of the Rio Grande, were the clustered houses of
the Zuñi. So far beyond as to seem almost legendary
the Hopi held their inaccessible mesas. Since 1680 they
had defied the sway of the Spaniard or the Mexican.

And all about and around was the land of the Navaho
and the Apache. Defence against the red marauders
colored the life of the Indian villages, set their homes on
high waterless summits, their tiny gardens in rude
crannies of the rocks. The Pueblo Indians, as the Spanish had named them, could not be non-combatants if
they wished to retain their lives and homes.

To them all — village folk or nomad, Queresan or
Tewan, Navaho or Ute — had come a change of allegiance whose meaning they could not as yet even guess.
Rumors were rife in the towns and across the desert.
Red men far and wide knew that the Horse-Chief of the
Long Knives had come into the land and that the Mexican Governor Armijo had fled without giving battle. If
the American war chief were looking for battle would he
not turn next upon the red man?

A young chief from Taos with a group of his warriors
made the mountain journey down to Santa Fé to look
upon the American commander and the soldiers of
whom he had heard such tales.

"We have heard of General Kearny," he said, "and
have come to see him. Does he intend to protect the
pueblos or to murder us? We have been told that the
Americans will plunder and kill us and take our wives
and daughters away from us; that you are going to brand
us on the cheek with red-hot irons.

" General Armijo wished us to fight for him; but the old men of our pueblo, the wise and experienced ones, told him that there was no use fighting the Americans. If you kill one army another will keep coming from the east as long as the sun shines.

" So we decided to come first and have a talk with the leader of the Americans and learn whether to prepare for peace or war."

The young war chief was received kindly and returned happily to Taos laden with gifts from the American war chief.

Below Santa Fé the departed Governor Armijo was said to be having better fortune in rallying the Mexican and Indian population. The general deemed it wise to make a demonstration by marching in that direction.

They passed through the Indian town of Santo Domingo, which today bears the reputation of being less kindly disposed to outsiders than any of her sister pueblos. The chief or alcalde of the Indian village came out to meet the American Army at the head of " about seventy dashing cavaliers," bearing a white flag in token of amity.

" They made a sham charge and performed several evolutions about him, displaying consummate horsemanship and brandishing their pointed lances, as if to show what they were capable of doing had their intentions not been peaceable and friendly." The volunteer portion of the Army, two or three miles distant, at first thought they were meeting with real resistance at last; but " we were soon satisfied of the sham and concluded the general might drink his wine and puff his cigaritos without our aid, so we moved onward."

Thus peaceably had New Mexico fallen into Kearny's hands. He chose Charles Bent as governor of the territory and made ready to press on his way to California. He sent word to Doniphan's column to pause on its way to Chihuahua and make a treaty of peace with the Navaho.

Just before the general left for the West he received a visit from the head of a New Mexican band of Apache, presumably a Mescalero. These Apache of New Mexico were unruly at times but in the light of the manners of their Arizona cousins they seem mild indeed. General Kearny made the visitors a long speech through an interpreter, bidding them to till the soil, to be industrious and quiet, and to refrain from robbery and depredation. " If they would do so they should be his brothers; but if they failed he would send his soldiers and wipe them from the face of the earth."

" Father," was the old Apache's reply, " you give good advice; but I am now old and unable to work and my tribe are unaccustomed to cultivating the soil. The Apaches are poor; they have no clothes to protect them from the cold and the game is fast disappearing from their hunting grounds.

" You must, therefore, if you wish us to be peaceable, speak a good word to the Comanche, the Yutaw, the Navaho and the Arapaho, our enemies, that they will allow us to kill buffalo upon the great plains.

" You are rich; you have a great nation to feed and clothe you — I am poor, and have to crawl on my belly like a cat, to shoot deer and buffalo for my people. I will take your counsel because I am weak and you are strong."

Blankets, butcher knives, beads, and mirrors made the hearts of the band glad and they departed promising faithful allegiance to the nation.

V

WAR BETWEEN the Navaho and the Mexican was a standing engagement, a lifetime occupation. Stealing of cattle and sheep and horses and individuals had gone on for generations untold. It was a toss-up at any time whether there were more Mexican and Pueblo slaves held by the Navaho or Navaho slaves held by the people of the Mexican and Indian villages. Adoptions by each were equally plentiful. Today, retaining their Athapascan language, their pastoral life, and their primitive ceremonies and cults, the Navaho are less a tribe than a mixed people, a combination of different strains.

While the American troops were passing near the pueblo of Isleta a party of Navaho warriors descended upon the village, killed eight Mexicans and Indians, and carried off a woman, five children, " and a great number of sheep, cattle and mules." Captain Burgwin from Kearny's command, at Valverde for the protection of the traders' caravan, sent off a detachment in pursuit of the marauders. Sixty Americans and seventy natives followed the Navaho to a remote cañon where a fight resulted in the recovery of the stock.

Doniphan's command came up to find the village of Isleta in great happiness, dancing in honor of their victory. The scalps of three Navaho warriors, their long black locks streaming in the wind, were the immediate cause of rejoicing. This was perhaps a foretaste of the relations existing among the three races of the land which the colonel was expected to compose by an incidental treaty.

When, after many an adventure, a group of Navaho headmen had been gathered for council they presented no objections to signing a treaty of peace with the " new men." They had no idea that the document would apply to others than those who affixed their marks to the paper. As for letting the agreement interfere with their relations with the Mexicans and villagers, that must be a joke on the part of the American.

"This is *our* war," the Navaho said, genuinely surprised that this newcomer from beyond the plains should imagine he had any right to interfere with that ancient heritage.

Doniphan found even greater animosity when he took his three Navaho chiefs to make peace with the Zuñi villagers on the Gila. The three stayed close by the American colonel; but in spite of this protection the Zuñi were quite determined upon detaining the Navaho as prisoners of war. For a time it looked as if the new men were fomenting battle instead of peace.

One of the Navaho chiefs discussed the situation:

"The war between us has been waged for plunder. You Zuñi kill and drive off our flocks and herds. To resent this we have plundered your village. Lately you have been unsuccessful. We have outstolen you, and therefore you are mad and dissatisfied about it."

The Zuñi spokesman replied in kind threatening to hold the Navaho as hostage.

"You may be sure," retorted the Navaho, "that we did not come over here relying on *your* good faith. We rely on the Americans and their ability to protect us. We trust ourselves with a more honorable people."

After more acrimonious debate a treaty was concluded. Doniphan had now carried out his commission as a peacemaker and went on his more warlike journey to Chihuahua.

General Kearny, before he had reached California, had an offer of alliance from no less a person than Mangas

Coloradas of the western Apache. At the Gila copper mines he met the advancing Americans. He was accompanied by twenty of his warriors and some of the women of the tribe. They were Mexican in dress and arms, but their shields of rawhide and fans made of buzzards' wings were of original invention. The purpose of both was to shield their eyes from the blinding sun of their semi-tropic land.

One of the Apache chiefs suggested that they go on together to take Chihuahua and Sonora.

"You fight for glory; we fight for plunder. So we shall agree perfectly." He did not succeed in winning Kearny's consent to this proposition.

The last encounter of the desert was with a very different people — the quiet corn-growing Pima folk. The general left with them a message and goods for Lieutenant-Colonel Cooke who was coming later with his Mormon Battalion, building a road across the wastes.

Cooke found them better than their word. When they brought him the message they brought him also twenty-two mules that had been abandoned by the troops along their way. Now, refreshed by rest and pasture, they were ready to rejoin the American Army. The aims and actions of the Pima were a refreshing contrast to the designs of the Apache.

VI

KEARNY had gone on. Doniphan had traversed the country. Cooke and his Mormon Battalion had passed through. Presumably New Mexico was at peace under her new rule.

The governor of the new region, according to General Kearny's appointment, was a man who was friend to everyone — American, Mexican, Indian. For more than twenty years he had traded and lived in the province. While his brother William was living at the fort on the Arkansas he had made his home in " old Touse," and had chosen his wife from a leading family of the New Mexican town. The Taos Pueblo folk, nearby, were his friends and neighbors.

In November Governor Bent wrote to the Commissioner of Indian Affairs at Washington, for as governor he was ex-officio in charge of the Indians of the region. He gave an account of the different tribes and their manner of living. For securing future peace he thought a visit to Washington on the part of some of the chiefs would be most useful. " They have been so long in the habit of waging war and committing depredations upon the Mexicans with impunity that they still show a disposition to continue."

He did not include among these warriors his neighbors the Pueblo, though he thought a group of them might properly accompany the delegation. They were " Pueblo or civilized Indians who are by law citizens of this Territory and of the United States. They compose a very considerable portion of the population of New Mexico and if excited so to do might cause a good deal of difficulty here."

Already the difficulty was rising. Mexican and Pueblo were joining forces in a plot to murder all the new officials and indeed all the Americans within the Territory. In December the existence of the scheme was discovered and it was believed that the conspirators had been thwarted. In January Governor Bent was warned, as he started from the capital to visit his home and family at Taos, that trouble was brewing.

" I am not afraid," was his answer. " The Mexican

and Indian people have always found me their friend; they will not harm me."

But on the early morning of the nineteenth of January, 1847, a crowd of Indians and Mexicans burst into his home, shouting their threats. Their leader was Tomasito Romero, alcalde of the pueblo of Taos hard by.

They scalped Governor Bent while he was still living; they slashed him with knives and shot him; and then from the corpse they hacked the head and bore it on a pole about the streets of the town. Others, too, were slain here and elsewhere in the towns of the Territory. Only one American of Taos escaped to slip away by night and carry the news to Santa Fé.

When the news came to the fort on the Arkansas the Cheyenne Indians were eager to send a war party against the people of Taos to avenge the murder of their old friend. But William Bent wisely restrained them. It was the soldiers of Colonel Sterling Price from Santa Fé who brought the rebellion to an end.

They found the Taosan insurgents entrenched in the old church at Taos pueblo. It was besieged boldly and defended desperately. All day the soldiers charged and battered, trying to scale the adobe walls with ladders or to make a breach with their cannon. At length they succeeded and put the defenders to rout. Next morning the Pueblo came with flag and crucifix, suing for peace, ready to deliver the murderers for trial.

This was the third of four battles that were necessary to bring the short-lived rebellion to an end. After a time there was quiet again along the Rio Grande.

WALPI — THE PUEBLO ON THE TOP OF FIRST MESA, HOPILAND, ARIZ.

PUYÉ CLIFF DWELLINGS ON THE SANTA CLARA RESERVATION, N. M.

THE PUEBLO OF TAOS, NEW MEXICO

VII

OUT IN California twelve Delaware Indians were taking a part in important events. Two of them were not to see again their home in Kansas. Frémont had taken them on his third western journey. Swanok and Sagundai were their chiefs. Crane, one of their number, had won the special fondness of the young leader of the expedition. He was " unusually grave, even for an Indian; " " One of the men I always liked to have by me."

The Delaware scouts had hunted and kept guard across the land to the very coast. Sometimes it was hard to restrain them from making the journey a continual warpath. They had enjoyed a brush with the Horse-Thief Indians. They had stayed the three days with the mountain men on Gavilan Peak and had wondered at the failure of the Californians to carry out their threats to attack. Then they had all gone northward to the land of the Klamath Indians.

A group of them who were with Frémont hurried back to meet Lieutenant Gillespie coming from the south with dispatches. It was that night that an unexpected attack from the Klamath came upon them. A groan from the dying half-breed Denny and the sound of the English half-axe that buried itself in the head of the voyageur Basil Lajeunesse awoke the others of the party. In the sharp fight that followed Crane fell with five poisoned arrows in his body.

" With our knives we dug a shallow grave and wrapping their blankets around them left them among the laurels. There are men above whom the laurels bloom who did not better deserve them than my brave Delaware and Basil. I left Denny's name on the creek where he died."

The Delaware Indians went into mourning. "With blackened faces, set and angry, they sat around brooding and waiting for revenge."

When the party moved on the Delaware braves stayed in ambush waiting for the Klamath to loot the deserted camp. They flaunted two scalps when they rejoined the rest of the expedition. They were more abundantly revenged when they reached the village of the attackers and put them all to rout, killing some of the warriors and burning their deserted tepees.

"When the Klamath tell the story of that night attack when our comrades were killed there will be no boasting. They will have to tell also of the death of their chief and of our swift retaliation; and how the people at the fishery had to mourn for the loss of their men and the destruction of their village. It will be a story for them to hand down while there are any Klamath on the lake."

VIII

BESIDES these belligerent Klamath, the United States had fallen heir to many other nations in its new territory. Oregon had brought her Shoshoni, Bannock, Ute, Crow, Nez Percé, Flathead, Cayuse, Yakima, and scores of smaller tribes along the coast and sound. Texas had wished upon the nation the never-ending wars with Kiowa and Comanche and Apache of the prairie. New Mexico had added more Ute, many more Apache, a vast expanse of Navaho tribesmen, and the high villages of the pueblo dwellers. When the treaty should be complete there would be also the southern agriculturists, Pima and Papago, with the wilder Yuma.

Here in the California country there were tribes, east of the Sierras, Pai-ute, Pah-ute or Washoe, who had but recently looked first upon the faces of white men. "Diggers " was the name which indicated their laborious lives in an inhospitable land.

" In the Great Basin," Frémont wrote, " where nearly naked he travelled on foot and lived in the sagebrush, I found the Indian in the most elementary form, the men living alone, the women living alone, but all after food. Sometimes one man cooking by his solitary fire in the sagebrush which was his home, his bow and arrows and bunch of squirrels by his side; sometimes on the shore of a lake or river where food was more abundant a little band of men might be found occupied in fishing; miles away a few women might be met gathering seed and insects, or huddled up in a shelter of sagebrush to keep off the snow. . . The labor of their lives was to get something to eat."

On the other side of the Sierras the beautiful river valleys made a striking contrast. Here life was easy. Yet this was the home of innumerable unrelated smaller tribes whose story is no more heartening than the other. A long chain of missions, in Spanish days, had gathered in great numbers of these native people for their centers of industry and religion.

Already under the mission rule the numbers of the Indians diminished. With the secularization of missions the decline was accelerated. With the coming of emigration from the East the disaster was complete.

As the tide set in, there was infinite possibility of trouble with any of the tribes along the various routes or at the end of the journey. If it had been a normal flow of population the greater elements of danger might have been foreseen and in part averted. The country was vastness itself, and the Indians, save in a few sections, were never in great numbers.

But this was no normal influx. The tide of Oregon immigration was in itself an epic, but when the end of the decade brought the astonishing news of the discovery of gold in California, the rush across the plains took on the proportions of a stampede. It was as headlong, as unreasoning as the onrush of a herd of frightened cattle. It was as irresistible as fire on the autumn prairie. Many a band went down before it.

The Pilgrim Fathers, someone had said, fell first upon their knees and then upon the aborigines. It is not recorded that the gold-seekers paused for any gesture of piety.

CHAPTER XIII
The Fighting Fifties

I

IT IS said that as President-elect Zachary Taylor rode toward the Capitol to take the oath of office he confided to the retiring President Polk, who sat beside him, his plan for disposing of the new territory which had been added to the United States by the war in which he had won his glory and his election. Let new states be organized, he said, in these new western lands. Then, when they were all ready, let them go by themselves in another nation. The western boundary of the United States should remain at the line of the Rocky Mountains as it had been in the days when President Jefferson bought Louisiana.

Apparently the idea gained no more favor elsewhere than it did with Polk, whose own administration had been devoted to enlarging the boundaries of the nation. Instead of diminishing governmental powers or boundaries Taylor found himself, in his year as President, erecting a new cabinet office, a new department to deal with the many problems of the new West. In 1849 the Land Office and the Bureau of Indian Affairs were turned over to the Department of the Interior — twin activities that were to furnish not a " problem," but an unending series of problems for years to come. The controversy as to whether the Indians should remain under the new jurisdiction or be turned back to the Army and Department of War was a burning question for forty years thereafter.

With the great rush of gold-seekers and settlers to the Pacific came political organization all along the coast. Oregon had been organized as a territory in 1848. Two years later California had grown to such proportions that she attained statehood at a leap. About this time New Mexico became a territory. The Mormons, settling around their Great Salt Lake and growing rapidly in numbers and prosperity, had a commonwealth of Deseret which was ready for statehood by all criteria of size and development but which was held in territorial status by differences of belief.

And what had become of the " Indian country," of the " permanent " frontier, of that barrier which was to stand forever between the United States and the western wilderness? Changed indeed was the map of America in those fateful forties. Even greater change must come to the plans which had been based upon the older boundaries.

The unorganized Indian country had shrunk mightily. From the Missouri west to the Rockies the tribes still might roam but even here not with the freedom of a decade or two before. For while few white men lived in the land those who traversed it were many. Instead of the handful of hardy trappers and traders who had made their way into the wilderness at stated seasons, there was now a constant flood of men, women, and children, their household goods piled in great prairie schooners. In 1836 Narcissa Whitman and Eliza Spalding had been the first white women to cross the Rockies. Fifteen years later, scalps with long light hair attached were no longer a novelty to the wilder tribes.

While it would be another fifteen years before the railroad would actually cross these western plains, yet the hope of its coming was an important factor in the aban-

KLAMATH LAKE
From Frémont's Report

ATTACK BY KLAMATH INDIANS
From Frémont's Report

donment of the frontier idea which had been held for a generation. The age of rapid transportation was at hand. Actual settlement had not in recent years pushed far beyond the Missouri borders; but communication lines to link the Mississippi Valley with the western coast were increasingly important. If the red man stood in the way of these things, he must step out.

To "Fort Laramie in the Indian Territory" — now the eastern part of the State of Wyoming — there came, in the early autumn of 1851, a great gathering of Sioux, Cheyenne, Arapaho, Crow, Assiniboine, Gros Ventre, Mandan, and Aricara, to make treaty with Indian Agent Thomas Fitzpatrick whom they had known these many years past as old-time mountain man and trapper, Broken Hand.

By this treaty the Indians promised to keep the peace with one another and to recognize the right of the United States to maintain roads and military posts within their territories. The lands of each tribe were duly set forth and bounded in the agreement.

In return the United States was to pay the tribesmen an annuity of fifty thousand dollars a year for fifty years to come. When the agreement reached the Senate thrift was the order of the day. The fifty years were reduced to fifteen and the treaty returned to the tribes for their agreement. The assent of all except the Crow was procured at a subsequent council and the amended document became law.

The following year the Apache came to council. Of these red rovers Governor Bent had written:

"They know nothing of agriculture or manufactures of any kind but live almost entirely by plundering the Mexican settlements. For many years past they have been in the habit of committing constant depredations upon the lives and property of this and the adjoining territories and states, from which they have carried off an incredible amount of stock of all kinds.

"Several bands have for several years past received a bounty of so much per diem per head, from the government of the State of Chihuahua, but still without having the intended effect of preventing them from plundering the inhabitants."

To this Apache treaty of 1852 came, among others, Mangas Coloradas, who had conferred with Kearny upon the Gila. All duly promised perpetual peace with the United States. They even went further and undertook to refrain thereafter from raids and incursions into Mexico. In return they were promised "donations, presents and implements" — amount not specified — and "such other liberal and humane measures as said government may deem meet and proper." The treaty took some time in ratification and amendment; it was promulgated in the spring of 1853.

Hard on its heels came another council called by Fitzpatrick, this time with the Comanche, Kiowa, and Kiowa Apache, at Fort Atkinson. These tribes likewise promised to give up the raids into Mexico which had up to this time been their chief occupation. They also engaged to keep the peace with all travellers through their lands and to refrain from depredations upon the military posts. As a reward they were to receive, in money or goods, the sum of eighteen thousand dollars, delivered to them each July " at or in the vicinity of Beaver Creek." Dohausen of the Kiowa signed as their principal chief; Satanka as war chief. When they came the following year to receive their payments they gave their assent to the amendments that had been made by the Senate. In time this treaty, like the others, became the law of the land.

Now the plains are at peace. The way is made clear north and south. Nothing remains but to give these red children their yearly presents and enjoy their friendship.

II

BESIDES these wilder bands that had just promised to keep the peace, there was still to be considered that fringe of red tribes adjoining the frontier settlements. These were the people who had come from their eastern lands to carry out the policy of a permanent Indian border. This was the country that a few years before had been dedicated forever to the use of the Indian, as long as grass should grow and water run.

Permanency is one of the recurring delusions of mankind. Now the northern Indians could stay a little longer in their land of lakes and timber. West of the State of Arkansas, the Five Civilized Tribes were off the main line of travel and need not be disturbed for the present. But that central territory between the Arkansas and the Platte, where a score of eastern tribes had been settled — that was quickly in dispute, involved in the great and ever greater controversy between slave state and free.

About this time Commissioner of Indian Affairs, George W. Manypenny, " visited the Omaha, Oto and Missouria, Iowa, Sauk and Fox of the Missouri, Kickapoo, Delaware, Wyandot, Shawnee, Potawatomi, Sauk and Fox of the Mississippi, Chippewa of Swan Creek and Black River, Ottawa, Peoria and Kaskaskia, Wea and Piankeshaw, and Miami, all of whom, except the Omaha, and Oto and Missouria, were Indians who had been transplanted by the government in pursuance of the law of 1830. He did not find these Indians as prosperous or as far advanced in civilization as he had been led to expect from the reports made from time to time of their condition. . . The commissioner came to the conclusion that the administration of the affairs of the Indians was not wholly free from abuses, and that such of the Indians as resided near Fort Leavenworth and the Missouri line, were more demoralized than those who lived in localities more distant." So wrote Commissioner Manypenny himself, in a book published a quarter of a century later.

The Kansas-Nebraska Act threw wide open the question of slavery in the territories and sent a host of eagerly contentious settlers across the Indian frontier. All the Indian country north of Oklahoma was in effect thrown open to the white man. It was several years before the war tide of Bleeding Kansas should inundate the entire country; but in the meantime there were groups of Indians who stood in the very heat of the conflict without having much idea what it was all about.

Getting them out of the fray was the job of the Indian Bureau. Our form of government makes it always possible for an Act of Congress to supersede a prior treaty. It is just as feasible for a new treaty to supersede an Act. Obviously the situation required more use of pens and paper. No wonder Commissioner Manypenny wrote in his official report for 1856 of the three years just preceding: " In no former equal period of our history have so many treaties been made, or such vast accessions of land been obtained."

In these central treaties of 1855 we find some of the tribes going a bit farther west, deeper into the plains, as did the Omaha; but more of them giving up their lands along the frontier to take their places near the Five Civilized Tribes. To this section south of the Arkansas River and west of the state of the same name, was restricted, from this time forward, the name of "the Indian territory." Up by the Great Lakes was still "Indian country"; here tribes of red men lived and the Indian title had not yet been extinguished. But this lower country was "the Indian territory," the district unorganized to which that elusive character of permanency had now attached itself.

And thither are going the Delaware and the Shawnee, making the last of their many migrations; the Iowa and the Sauk and Fox; the Kickapoo and the Miami from Indiana; the Wyandot or Huron remnant from the northern country; and in the extreme northeastern corner of the territory was found a place for the confederated Kaskaskia and Peoria, Piankeshaw and Wea, remnants of the Illinois tribes now gathered into one. Here came the Quapaw from Arkansas. These tribes had at last found a location which has so far proved really permanent.

But not all went; nor did all who departed do so with the best of grace. We have to this day recalcitrant remnants such as the little group of Sauk and Fox who took their annuity money to purchase Iowa land and settled themselves in the rich centre of that farming country. There were Shawnee and Delaware people who remained behind and became Kansas farmers; "Citizen Potawatomi" who did the same, while others of the tribe went on to the south. There were Kickapoo who fled afar, to be known later as the "Mexican Kickapoo" because of the constant raids and forays across the border in which they indulged.

And it must always be remembered that great numbers of these tribes lost themselves in the white blood and the white civilization. No historian or scientist has yet given adequate attention to the extent to which aboriginal American blood has entered into the making of what we now call an American. That it has been a widespread admixture, especially in the region of French influence, even the casual reader of events must admit.

III

THE ADMINISTRATION under which Manypenny was Commissioner was one which looked toward the west with vaulting plans. The project of a series of surveys across the country to determine the best course for the Pacific Railroad which the future was to see, was approved by Congress. Three routes — southern, central, and northern — were chosen and three parties sent out to examine the ground. Oddly enough the first transcontinental railway to be completed did not follow any one of the three paths.

Jefferson Davis, Secretary of War, naturally hoped that the surveys would prove beyond a question the superiority of the southern route. It swept far below most of the dangers of cold winters, steep mountains, and hostile Indians.

Captain Gunnison was in charge of the party covering the central route. His wagons cut a deep swath up the narrow gorges of the Arkansas in the heart of the Rockies. But the turbulent Ute was his undoing. Disaster and death were the end of the story. The difficulties of the central passage were illustrated as completely as the Secretary could wish.

On the northern route Davis met his match. Major Isaac Stevens, veteran of the Mexican War at thirty-five, resigned his commission in the Engineer Corps to accept two assignments from Congress either of which would have been a huge undertaking. He was to make the northern survey across the Minnesota forests, the Dakota plains, and the mountain country of the always embattled Blackfoot; then he was to be Governor of the new Territory of Washington and ex-officio superintendent of the conglomerate tribes of the mountains, the Columbia, and the Sound. Stevens started off on his long journey in the summer of 1853.

From Fort Snelling the party struck out to the northwest meeting on their way to Fort Union the hunting expeditions of the Red River half-breeds. This was introduction to the Indian tribes to be met later. The Assiniboine chief said to Governor Stevens, in council:

"My father, we hear that a great road is to be made through our country. We do not know what this is for, we do not understand it, but we think it will drive away the buffalo. We like to see our white brothers; we like to give them the hand of friendship; but we know that as they come our game goes back. What are we to do?"

The Governor explained to them that implements of agriculture would be sent, that they might learn to till the soil. To them this conveyed as little enlightenment, it is to be feared, as the purpose of the road of the steel rails. It was the irreconcilable conflict of two different stages of civilization.

Four days later they were at Fort Union, where the Missouri crosses the western line between today's States of North Dakota and Montana. Assiniboine, Crow, Gros Ventre and others of the roving northern tribes came here to trade. Culbertson, the chief agent at this post of the American Fur Company, had for wife a woman of the Blackfoot tribe. From Fort Union Stevens sent out messengers telling the Blackfoot to meet him for council at Fort Benton, hundreds of miles to the west, near the Great Falls of the Missouri. To them he brought the same message as to the Gros Ventre:

" Live in peace with all the neighboring tribes, protect all the whites passing through your country, and the Great Father will be your fast friend."

He urged upon them to meet the Gros Ventre in a peace council. Later among the Flathead he broached to them the same project. They shook their heads over the idea of trusting the Blackfoot. The idea grew that when he had assumed the duties of the Governor of Washington he would return to gather into council all these tribes of the Northwest. Through this section the journals of the Jesuit Father de Smet were his guide, and in the Flathead missions he met the chief Victor, long a friend of the missionary priests.

Then on across the mountains they pressed to Colville and to Spokane where Chief Garry, educated by the Hudson's Bay Company at the Red River settlements, welcomed them to a comfortable lodge where he could dispose hospitality not unlike that of the white man.

Southwest now, in the Walla Walla country, they found a trading firm occupying the site of the mission where the Whitmans had blazed the way. Pio-pio-moxmox, the Walla Walla chief, impressed them favorably. When the Cayuse suggested that he share in the spoils of the looted mission he had refused saying he was afraid of neither whites nor Indians. " He has the air of a substantial farmer," Stevens wrote.

Down the Columbia went the indefatigable Stevens to the coast and spent the rainy winter months in touring the sound in an open boat, making acquaintance with the tribes along the shores. An old chief of the

Lummi still remembers that canoe that brought him his first sight of the white man.

The survey was over. Now for a trip back to Washington and an unexpectedly glowing report of the northern railroad route. Then in the fall of 1854 Governor Stevens came again to his wide western domain, this time in full panoply as a commissioner to make treaties with tribes unnumbered.

IV

ALL ALONG the coast there were treaties and still more treaties. In California a group was made in 1851 and 1852. They are still unratified, and claims against the United States are still pending. A friendly suit is now planned to bring about adjudication in the courts, and an official is enrolling Indians of the Sierras to determine their relationship to the early treaty-makers. The upshot may some day be an award to the grandchildren of the natives who saw with amazed eyes the great rush of white men to find the yellow metal in the hills and streams.

In both California and Oregon the rush of settlement had preceded any arrangements with the Indians as to land. The long ill feeling between American and British trappers had left abiding dislike and distrust in the Indian mind. The Cayuse outbreak was the beginning of a long series of conflicts. Some of these preceded the making of treaties, some followed them. The Indian was unaware of any connection between the two.

The series of Oregon treaties began with the Rogue River tribe in September 1853. There were the usual cessions, promises of peace, establishment of annuities, and gifts at parting. Then the Rogue River Indians went on the warpath for the summer and returned in November 1854 for more treaty-making and more gifts. This time bands of Chasta, Umpqua, and Scoton Indians came along and entered into like agreements. Other bands of Umpqua and Kalapuya made their promises about ten days later.

It was the council season. Indian tribes were always ready to make promises and receive gifts in the winter when food was hard to get and fighting rather too arduous. Spring weather would often revive their spirits and set them out again upon the warpath. The white man's annuity payments helped to bridge over the time when they were accustomed to refrain from fighting in any case.

Now Governor Stevens in December 1854 sallied forth for his round of councils. First he met a group of the little "fish-eating" tribes around the waters of the sound. The old Lummi chief, his head flattened after the ancient fashion of his people, remembers when as a lad he went with his father to this treaty-making. Nine little tribes participated — of whose names the Nisqually and the Puyallup come nearest to being pronounceable by non-Indian vocal cords. They accepted a defined reserve on which to live and ceded their rights in the rest of the land to the government for payment in annuities and goods. Lesh-high, one of the earliest signers of the treaty, was chief and instigator of the Indian war which broke out the following year.

In January it was Oregon's turn and Superintendent Palmer made agreement with eleven bands of Kalapuya, with Molalla, Tumwater, and Clookamu. Superintendent Stevens was not behind him; on the same day, January 22, he was meeting the head chiefs and delegates of twenty bands to make the treaty of Point Elliott.

The old chief Seattle said: "I look upon you as my father. All the Indians have the same good feeling toward you, and will send it on paper to the Great Father."

Four days later Stevens went on to Point No Point, Suquamish Head, to confer with the chiefs and head men of the S'Klallam, Sko-ko-mish, To-an-hooch, and Chemakum tribes. The Sko-ko-mish were at first reluctant to enter into the treaty but after much discussion with the other Indians and with the whites they yielded their consent.

The last days of the month were spent at Neah Bay, to this day scarcely to be reached save by water. Here the head men of the Makah met to discuss their boundaries. This was Governor Stevens' ultimate west unless he were to press onward to the Sandwich Islands.

"I bring you this white flag," said one old chief. "See if there are any spots on it. There are none on our hearts."

The council of the next month was less successful. The Chinook, Chehalis, and Coast Indians were summoned to meet on the Chehalis River above Gray's Harbor. About three hundred and fifty Indians met the fourteen whites. For several days of feasting and talking good feeling seemed to prevail. But Tleyuk, the young chief of the Chehalis, resented the fact that the proposed reservation was not on his land that he might be head chief over all the five tribes represented. His father, Carcowan, the old chief of the tribe, fomented his discontent with whiskey smuggled into the camp against the rules of the white men.

Next day Tleyuk in council voiced his belief that the

Americans designed putting all the Indians on steamers and sending them out of the country. He gave the names of several white men who had told him this. He aroused his following to disorder and was insolent to the Governor who destroyed the paper he had given the young man as token of his chieftainship and dismissed the conference. It was nearly a year later that these tribes at last signed the agreement.

In both territories during this spring of 1855 active little wars were springing up here and there. Nevertheless, as May came on, both Superintendent Palmer and Governor Stevens travelled over the mountains to the Walla Walla Valley to confer with the Walla Walla, the Cayuse, the Umatilla, and the Nez Percé. Between five and six thousand Indians assembled there, and of them all only the Nez Percé were in friendly mood. The white men all told numbered fewer than a hundred.

The unwillingness of the tribes to enter upon a reservation soon became apparent. Pio-pio-mox-mox voiced their feeling: " In one day the Americans become as numerous as the grass. This I learned in California. I know it is not right; you have spoken in a roundabout way. Speak straight. Goods and the earth are not equal. Goods are for using on the earth. I do not know where they have given land for goods."

Late that evening Lawyer, head chief of the Nez Percé, came to Governor Stevens. The Cayuse and other tribes had been holding nightly councils to which the friendly Nez Percé were not bidden. Lawyer had discovered their plan which was for a sudden uprising and the murder of all the whites upon the council ground.

Not without reason had the Hudson's Bay Company given Lawyer his name. He had a plan ready to avert disaster.

" I will come with my family," he said, " and pitch my lodge in the midst of your camp that those Cayuse may see you and your party are under the protection of the Nez Percé." And though it was now midnight his lodge soon stood beside the tent of the commissioners. Next morning the conspirators knew, with no word said in explanation, that the whites would not be undefended.

The council went on for days thereafter. The proposed treaty was modified to give the unfriendly tribes a location that pleased them better. Finally they agreed to sign. The many crosses on the bits of paper represented the Walla Walla, Cayuse, and Umatilla in one treaty, the Yakima and the thirteen smaller bands in another.

The third treaty was that of the Nez Percé. Looking-Glass, their old war chief, had come in with the scalps of victory during the negotiations. He resented bitterly the fact that Lawyer was recognized as head chief; but the Nez Percé people in council had so declared it. Lawyer was the first signer of the Nez Percé treaty. Looking-Glass followed him. Third was Joseph, father of that Chief Joseph who was to lead a masterly retreat more than twenty years after. The following day the Nez Percé celebrated the conclusion of the treaty by dancing about the scalps Looking-Glass had brought them.

Later in this month Palmer met and councilled with the tribes of Middle Oregon — seven of them. The first of July Stevens exchanged promises with the Quinaielt and Quilleute tribes.

Stevens was now warming up for a big journey. In mid-July he was far in the interior, in the Bitter Root Valley, covenanting with the Flathead, Kootenai, and

Pend d'Oreilles; and by autumn he had penetrated to the upper Missouri, near the mouth of that Judith River named by Captain William Clark some forty years before. Here he councilled with more Flathead, more Nez Percé, and with the Blackfoot tribes — Piegan, Blood, Blackfoot, and Gros Ventre. Not land was the purpose, but the establishment of peaceful relations among the Indians themselves.

Palmer was long outdistanced. A mere Indian superintendent could not fare so far as a governor and commissioner. The Oregon man made the last score of the year, however, in his treaty with the Molalla on December 21.

While Governor Stevens was in the mountains the Yakima arose and killed their Agent Bolon. There was a general outbreak both east and west of the Cascades, in both Oregon and Washington. Hundreds of red warriors were in control of a large part of the land. An expedition that autumn, of regular soldiers supplemented by local militia, was a failure.

Pio-pio-mox-mox, who had plundered the old fort at Walla Walla, freed a half-Indian captive that the boy might carry a message to Governor Stevens. It was to the effect that the Indian chief intended to take the Governor's scalp. Many thought Stevens would never get back to his home in the territory; but he found the Spokane not unfriendly and the Nez Percé loyal as ever. He made the journey in safety.

He found the country prostrate. It was not until the following spring that a measure of security was restored. Actual peace was much later than that.

But it had been a fine year for treaty-making.

V

On the plains all had been far from peaceful, in spite of the treaty at Fort Laramie. The Brulé and Oglala Sioux held a little reunion and celebrated the occasion by butchering some "white buffalo" left by an emigrant party along the trail. Great consequences were to follow this appropriation of a poor old cow turned out to die.

Spotted Tail was not chief of the Brulé at this time but he was already winning renown among them by his daring. He had won the love of Appearing Day but not the consent of her father. Running Bear, having more horses, was the favored suitor. The two lovers fought a bloody duel with their long knives. Their people found them locked in an embrace, Running Bear dead and Spotted Tail very nearly so. After that the survivor had no opposition in his suit and so devoted to Appearing Day was he that it was not until after her death that he followed the tribal custom and welcomed a plurality of wives to his lodge.

This deadly encounter won him more than a wife for it so impressed his fellows that they passed over hereditary aspirants to the chieftainship and in time chose him as leader. Before this election, however, he had triumphed in other encounters.

Following a feast of the Brulé on emigrant cattle Lieutenant Grattan and a detachment of thirty soldiers visited the Indians and remonstrated with them. The upshot was the death of the Lieutenant and all save one of his command. Little Thunder was the leader of the Brulé at this time, but Spotted Tail bore a distinguished part in the slaughter.

Next the triumphant Indians attacked and vanquished a mail party. They now found themselves in all but undisputed possession of a large part of the country along the upper Platte and during the winter of 1854 they rested upon their laurels. According to custom many of them came in to the Indian agent to be fed during the cold winter.

The War Department had a different plan of treatment. General Harney was recalled from a leave of absence in Paris and in the spring of 1855 set out upon an expedition designed to restore peace in summer as well as winter. The Brulé were now upon the warpath again and Little Thunder sent word to Harney that he was ready either to fight or to shake hands.

The trader who brought this message carried back Harney's ultimatum. The young men to whom Little Thunder attributed all the ill doings of the past year must be surrendered for punishment. Instead of doing so the chief preferred to meet the paleface in combat; and near Ash Hollow on the Little Blue Water Creek in western Nebraska he met a decisive defeat.

This was in early September. For the remainder of the open season the Indians kept out of the way of Harney's scouting parties and before the winter was over they were glad to meet him and arrange an armistice.

While the General was at Fort Laramie Spotted Tail and two others of the young warriors who had been foremost in the destruction of the Grattan party dressed themselves in full panoply of war. So attired and chanting their death songs they came in to give themselves up to the surprised garrison at the fort. This was their atonement for the ill deeds of the tribe. They fully expected the death which Indian custom would have meted out to them.

The white man's way was not that of the red man.

The warriors were held prisoner for due inquiry into the crime and as hostage for the good behavior of their people. After many months of imprisonment Spotted Tail escaped and returned to his band. They welcomed him now as doubly the hero and his road to the chieftainship was assured.

VI

By the Treaty of Guadalupe Hidalgo the United States acquired from Mexico a great expanse of territory and a crop of Indian wars. The pueblo of Taos had inaugurated the difficulties of the Southwest by joining in the murder of Governor Bent. The Navaho, making peace with Doniphan, took the treaty as an impetus to warfare which was practically continuous for fifteen years. The Ute began to emerge to public notice with a series of depredations and the murder of Gunnison. More than all, the Apache began the primary instruction in what was to prove a thorough course of education for the Army.

The first lesson came with the murder of the men of a small party of citizens returning to Santa Fé from St. Louis. James M. White was among those killed, and his wife and ten-year-old daughter were carried off by the victorious Apache raiders. News of the affray came to Taos, and Major Grier led a party of dragoons in search of the captives. Kit Carson joined the party.

For several days they followed the trail of the fleeing Indians. At many of the old camps were found bits of the dress of Mrs. White or articles known to have belonged to her. Probably the wretched woman hoped in this way to aid in her rescue.

The Apache camp sighted, Carson judged that the attack should be made immediately. The less experi-

enced army officer halted for a parley. This gave the
Apache just the moment's delay that they wanted.

They were actively on their way when the white men
reached the abandoned camp site. Beside it lay the body
of Mrs. White, still warm. She had been shot down as
she started in the direction of the rescuers. The body of
the little girl was never recovered, though Congress —
some months later — appropriated a goodly sum to
procure her release.

Raids upon the settlements from various bands of
Apache and Ute continued. The Navaho, to the west,
were less troublesome because in their land settlement
was more scanty. Four campaigns were made against
them in a dozen years; but they remained defiantly
unconquered. Forts began to dot the desert — from
Union and Marcy in eastern New Mexico, to Yuma on
the California side of the Colorado River.

The Navaho received no annuities because they could
not stay at peace long enough to have a treaty ratified.
Ute and Apache would come in peaceably to receive
their presents and immediately start out afresh upon the
warpath. Their annuities of goods and supplies were
obviously bribes; and quite as obviously bribes that
failed of their purpose. Whenever the red men came in
for presents the Army rejoiced in a peace and the Indian
Department was assured of future tranquillity. But
soon it was all to be done over again.

They might have been doing it yet had it not been for
local volunteers — Mexican, Pueblo, mountain men of
Carson's breed, all of whom knew the Apache and his
way, all of whom had vivid recollection of long years
of foray. Not without reason had Mexican and Indian
village huddled together these centuries past. The
menace of the *Indios salvajos* had been with the land
years without number.

VII

SUCH was the "comparative tranquillity" of the fifties. In California the inrushing prospectors were completing the extermination Spaniard and Mexican had prosecuted so successfully. In Texas raids of Kiowa and Comanche went on as ever. The attempt to concentrate these fierce rovers ended in the determination to expel them forever from the borders of the state.

In the sadly shrunken Indian territory where the Five Civilized Tribes were colonized there were intertribal dissensions almost without end. The Cherokee clung to their factions. Group warfare and private sniping were the order of the time. The Seminole protested vigorously at being quartered with the Creek. The Chickasaw were no less indignant at being forced to share the Choctaw country. In the end these smaller tribes were assigned individual lands where they might maintain their civilization uncontaminated. Harney was sent to Florida and spent three years there gathering up a few more Seminole for the West.

As the decade wore on the northern Sioux were again in commotion, Cheyenne and Arapaho devastated the plains, and in the far Northwest were new outbreaks and new campaigns. These were certainly not times of piping peace.

And yet in view of the decade that was to follow this may indeed have been a time of "comparative tranquillity."

CHAPTER XIV
The Civil War in the West

I

IT IS not surprising that the four years of deadly conflict between the North and the South were also years of acute troubles among the Indian tribes. During this period, whenever any Indians became restive, it was the custom to suggest Confederate influences as the reason for their disaffection. But there was usually little warrant for such a view. Obviously, the Confederacy had more important and nearer affairs to adjust; whereas the warlike disposition of the Indians of the plains had been manifested many years before this and would still be in evidence when the fires of the Civil War had burned low and been extinguished. In one section only was there actual Confederate approach to the tribes. This was, of course, in the Indian territory west of Arkansas. Both by location and by their quasi-independent position these " civilized tribes " invited diplomatic relations. They were originally from southern states and the most prosperous of them had long been slaveholders. Indeed, the Cherokee remnant left behind in the Carolina mountains were loyally following their colonel into the ranks of the Confederate Army, not primarily as Indians but as Southern citizens. That the Five Tribes in the West should follow their example was only to be expected.

They were not unanimous in this, however. So far they had never achieved unanimity on any subject.

In March 1861 they met in "international council" at the Creek agency. The Choctaw were urgent that an immediate treaty of mutual aid be made with the Confederate government. Captain Albert Pike, Commissioner of Indian Affairs for the Confederate States, stood ready to promise them all the protection and comfort they had received from the United States.

The Chickasaw, at whose instance the council had been called, were divided in their views. The Creek, with old Opothleyaholo at their head, inclined to a negative vote. The Seminole for once agreed with them. There was much division among the Cherokee. John Ross, now past seventy years of age but still their head chief, urged a neutral policy with the ill luck which usually comes to neutrals.

The deciding argument was that the Confederacy was there, while the Union forces had hastily departed leaving their forts to the first comer. Texas troops were quick to enter and make this land a base for their operations on the plains of Kansas. The gifts the Indians regularly expected from the United States could not come to them across the lines of battle.

So it came about that Elias Rector, Superintendent of Indian Affairs for the Southern superintendency, who in 1860 made report to the United States Commissioner of Indian Affairs, was outlining the condition of the same tribes, a year later, in his official report to the Commissioner of the Confederate States. Rector had changed his allegiance but not his title. Three thousand Indians of his superintendency were enrolled under the Southern banner. Again their star of destiny had shed a false light upon them. Once more they had chosen the losing side.

For the first year it looked as if they might have picked the winner. Stand Watie with his Cherokee troops, McIntosh with his Creek companies, did valiant service to the Southern cause. The opposition within the nations, though strong, was far from organized.

By the second year of the war members of the tribes began making their way up into Kansas to take refuge with the Federal Army. In the dead of winter old Opothleyaholo, holding his leadership among the Creek factions to the last, brought a great body of his people north to safety. The Commissioner of Indian Affairs hastened to Kansas to see what might be done for the refugees.

" Collected for the journey, with scarcely a moment for preparation, amid the confusion and dismay of an overshadowing defeat; in the dead of winter, the ground covered with ice and snow, and the weather most intensely cold, without shelter, without adequate clothing, and almost destitute of food, a famishing, freezing multitude of fugitives, they arrived in Kansas unexpectedly, where not the slightest preparation had been made to relieve their sufferings or provide for their wants."

In some manner these six to eight thousand Creek refugees were at length cared for. As the war went on other tribesmen came until at the close of the conflict between fifteen and twenty thousand Indians were being rationed by the Government. It was not until the war was well over that they could go back to their own land.

Some of the men enlisted in the First and Second Indian Regiments that were now being formed. The Kansas Indians had proved loyal in the main though most of them suspected the Osage of playing a double game and getting remuneration from both sides. The Delaware had volunteered almost to a man. In fact they liked nothing half so well as fighting.

The Indian regiments presented an odd combination of savage and soldier when they started out from camp. The uniforms furnished by the United States Army were little calculated to fit the Indian figure and they either hung too amply or stretched too tight. The high-crowned issue hat, of stiff wool, oddly surmounted the long black braids that hung down over each shoulder. These tall men with their long squirrel rifles appeared to dwarf the small Indian ponies they bestrode. When the whole array of Indian soldiers, full panoplied, started up the long shrilling war-whoop that ran again and again from the front of the line to the rear, it was a sound to cause a shiver of anticipation.

They did not retake the territory, however, not even when the third year of the war added a third regiment, mainly of Cherokee who had finally decided to espouse the Union cause. John Ross, caught between two fires and called upon for troops by both Federal and Confederate forces, came out with the last retreat of the Northern army and went to Washington to try what diplomacy might do.

Opothleyaholo, old as he was, told the Commissioner of Indian Affairs that if furnished arms and supplies he and his men would fight their way back to the strongholds of the Creek nation. The Commissioner urged upon him the necessity of making peace with his brethren when the conflict should end. He commended mercy to all, especially to the women and children who should always be spared.

The old warrior did not agree with this. It offended his primitive logic. " When a man has a bad breed of dogs," he assured Commissioner Dole, " the best way to get rid of them is to kill the bitch."

Opothleyaholo did not live to wreak vengeance or to offer mercy. He died in his Kansas exile while the war was still raging.

II

MINNESOTA seemed far enough from the path of conflict to enjoy quiet. Yet here in the summer of 1862 occurred one of the most harrowing events of the western warfare.

The Sioux of the Mississippi, as these northern bands were designated, had been restive ever since the treaty of 1851. By this agreement they had given up all their lands except a narrow strip along the Minnesota River. The northern part of the territory was left to their ancient enemies the Chippewa, while in the south white settlements began to come nearer and nearer.

Missionaries had been among them since the thirties. In those days the white man still believed in the gospel of work, practised it, and preached it. Accepting the white man's religion was construed to mean accepting industry, cleanliness, monogamy, and Sabbath-keeping. Many of the red men listened and started upon " the white man's road."

Two factions thus grew up among the Minnesota Sioux. There were the " farmer " Indians who were willing to learn to till the soil, to give up to a considerable extent their roving habits, to try new ways of living. The " scalp-lock and blanket " party, adjuring " cut hair and breeches," wished still to live by the chase and the warpath like their western roving brethren the Sioux of the Missouri.

Little Crow, hereditary chief of the Mdewakanton Sioux, was now a man of sixty years. He seemed to have the diplomatic situation well in hand and was in good favor with both parties. Fifteen years before he had asked that a missionary be sent to his village. Since that time he had given the mission his countenance by attendance and approval.

Little Crow could have provided a fair-sized congregation for the mission from his thriving family of six wives and twenty-two children. He did not carry his religious fervor to the point of embracing monogamy. Liberal in political as well as religious matters he had signed the treaty of 1851 and was recognized as the leader of the opposition which had been maintained to that document ever since its signing.

Opposition was growing stronger in these war days. It was not that vague rumor of malevolent agents of the Confederacy lurking about which led up to the outbreak of the summer of 1862. Much more obvious was the incentive offered by the fact that a large proportion of the able-bodied whites had marched away to don suits of soldier blue. And a much harassed Congress delayed in making the appropriations which would send the annual boxes of gold to keep the Sioux in kindlier humor. Times were hard and the traders were not so free with goods and credit as they had been. There was grumbling everywhere.

Little Crow had plans laid for a rather general uprising. He was expecting allies from the hordes of Sioux to the west. Meanwhile he consulted with the Indian agent about a new brick house which the government was to build for him. It would need to be rather large for all that family of his.

On Sunday, August 17, he attended church as was his wont at the Episcopal mission. But four of his young men had grown impatient. Heavy potations of fire-water incited them to start out on a murdering and pillaging expedition of their own. As a result five persons were murdered that afternoon.

" This, probably," said the Lieutenant Governor of the State in his official report to Governor Ramsay, " was one of those accidental outrages at any time to be anticipated on the remote frontier." One of the amenities of Minnesota life, as it were.

" It fell, however," the Lieutenant Governor conceded, " like a spark of fire upon a mass of discontent, long accumulated and ready for it."

Little Crow learned of the accidental outrage and decided he could do no other than follow it up. " It must come," he said. " Now is as good a time as any. I am with you. Let us kill the traders and divide their goods."

By daybreak on Monday morning the work of destruction and death had begun. Little Crow and a large band of warriors swept through the pleasant countryside while the thrifty German settlers were beginning the day's work in the harvest fields. They spread desolation in their wake. By nine the fleeing settlers had reached Fort Ridgely with the news of the outbreak.

Captain Marsh and fifty men started out to the rescue. The fifteen survivors of his party crept back to the fort at dusk. All the rest had met death at the hands of the Sioux warriors.

Strangely enough, at noon of that very day the delayed payment money came to the fort. But the embattled Sioux were collecting from the towns and farms they were ravaging, far more than the government had to give them.

For days the fleeing settlers poured into the little fort. Poorly located on a bluff surrounded by ravines ideal for Indian approach, without a fireproof building in its little collection of log and stone huts, Fort Ridgely was ill adapted to stand a siege. By great good fortune a hundred men arrived to reinforce it on Tuesday of the first week of warfare.

On that day the Indians were attacking in force the town of New Ulm. Houses were fired and their fleeing inhabitants shot down all through a bloody afternoon. In the evening a company of cavalry from the fort reached the town and drove the Indians off. About half the village had been burned.

The next three days were spent in besieging the fort, but it was able to hold out against attack. Discouraged, Little Crow and his men returned to the raiding of New Ulm. A new week began with the evacuation of the entire town. A strange procession went, guarded by soldiers, along the road to Mankato — men, women, and children fleeing from their homes and farms; the wounded racked by the shaking of the rough wagons as they toiled over the road. The prosperous countryside of ten days before had become a deserted land.

The end of harvest month came. Little Crow had won no decided victory but he had suffered no decided reverse. He and his men had terrorized the state and had withdrawn northward, driving before them great herds of cattle, laden with rich spoil of money, food, and tons of ammunition. Nearly a thousand whites had been dispatched by the braves; not more than a tenth of the number men in arms, the others citizens in the pursuit of their daily labors. If Little Crow were not followed he would eventually make his way westward to the Sioux of the Missouri, to inflame them with his story of successful warfare.

Little Crow had suffered a slight wound in the attack on Fort Ridgely; but his vigor was not lessened. His

Indians crossed the Minnesota border and attacked Fort Abercrombie in Dakota. At Wood Lake, late in September, General Sibley won the victory which brought peace to the distracted region.

Little Crow and a few of his warriors fled westward to the Yankton Sioux. Three hundred captive warriors were tried by court-martial and sentenced to hanging. Appeals for clemency were made. Dole, Commissioner of Indian Affairs, maintained that "in spite of most horrible and atrocious crimes, which shock every feeling of humanity," such "indiscriminate punishment" was "contrary to the spirit of the age and our character as a great, magnanimous and Christian people." Accordingly, President Lincoln pardoned all but thirty-eight who were positively identified as having been seen in the commission of the murders. These met death on one scaffold on February 26, 1863. It was about six months after their start upon the warpath.

Little Crow himself had but a few months longer to live. That summer, returning to Minnesota on a little private raid, he was stopped in his career by the bullet of a settler whose instinct for self-preservation outweighed for the time being his magnanimity and Christianity.

With the settlers of the entire region fear was the dominating motive for the present. It brought the reiterated demand for the removal of the Sioux outside the boundaries of the state.

Other Indians were strongly suspect. The Chippewa had in the main been quiet, but Hole-in-the-Day, second of the name, had followed a devious course of resentment and insult to the Commissioner and his messengers. Public sentiment would be satisfied with their retreat a little farther into the northern woods.

The Winnebago, a small and harmless band in the lower country, had sent only a few disaffected young braves to the support of Little Crow. In the main they had been friendly. But their presence among the settlers was no longer tolerable. They too must go.

In the summer of 1863 the remove was made. A new agency was created at Crow Creek, near Yankton Agency in Dakota. Here were taken such of the Minnesota Sioux as were not in jail or out upon the warpath.

Here too went the Winnebago, protesting that they had lived so long among the whites they were now as much afraid of the wild Indians as any paleface might be. But they realized life was no longer tenable in Minnesota. The residents in the southern part of that state would tolerate no Indians among them after the uprising of '62.

The Winnebago took things into their own hands, made canoes, and slipped on down the Missouri from their new reservation to the home of the Omaha, a people to whom they felt more nearly related. The farmer party among the Sioux quieted down in their new abode; the scalp-lock and blanket contingent made common cause with the western plainsmen.

The seven bands of the Sioux of the Missouri made general war upon the whites in the summer of 1863.

III

THESE were lively days for the warriors of the plains. Where the Sioux left off raiding the Cheyenne and Arapaho braves began. Below them thousands of Kiowa and Comanche kept the trails well watched. Travel beyond the Kansas frontier was always dangerous and often impossible. The Territory of New Mexico and her newly formed sister territory, Colorado, found themselves often without means of communication with the East, without needed supplies, without protection.

Actual invasion by troops of the Confederacy had been turned back after a battle or two. But this portent of the hostile braves was no question of pitched battle and single sharp engagements. It was a daily menace to travel and communication. It threatened something like siege to the remote villages of mountain or desert whose dependence was all upon food and munitions brought by pack trains across the prairies.

Bent's Fort had disappeared these ten years past. Colonel William Bent, finding the United States Government unwilling to buy it at a satisfactory price, blew it up one fine day and abandoned the site. Somewhat farther down the Arkansas the military had set up Fort Wise. Here had been made a treaty with the Cheyenne and Arapaho Indians, nominally confining them to a three-sided reservation angling out toward the plains. With the coming of the Civil War Wise joined the Confederacy, and the fort which had borne his name was rechristened Fort Lyon.

Discovery of gold in the Rockies had brought a rush of miners in '59, resulting in the creation of the Territory of Colorado in the following year. These were the days of overland freighting and the pony express, with both of which institutions Indian fighting played frequent havoc.

Opinions are sharply divided on the events which led up to the so-called " Chivington massacre." One may read unsparing condemnation for the soldiers who came down from Denver to their bloody work. On the other hand, there are still to be found in Colorado old residents who maintain stoutly that the Indians didn't get half they deserved on that November morning in 1864.

In the spring Governor Evans of the territory had issued a proclamation urging friendly Indians to go to the protection of the soldiery and the Indian agent at Fort Lyon, and there to refrain from wandering and murdering upon the plains. During the summer season his proclamation won no notice. Depredations, captures, and murders went on.

There was a premeditated attack all along the stage line from the Missouri. Nearly every one of the relay stations suffered attack. Buildings were burned and stock driven away. Colorado Territory was cut off from communication with the states to the east.

In the mile-high table-land that fringes the Rockies, late September holds more than a hint of approaching winter. The lengthening frosty nights warned Black Kettle, leader of the Cheyenne, that it was time to gather into winter quarters at the agency, to receive annuities and presents, to get fresh store of ammunition in readiness for another summer. Accordingly groups of his followers began to appear at Fort Lyon, professing friendliness and the desire to smoke the pipe of peace with the white man.

Already the military authorities had awakened to the need for action and a campaign was being prepared against the hostilities. The Indian agent, bringing a party of red men up to Governor Evans at Denver, was told that the power to make peace had now passed from the Governor's hands. On their part the Indians admitted depredations in conjunction with Apache, Comanche, and Kiowa, and with thirteen different bands of Sioux who had crossed the Platte and made common cause with the other warriors of the plains. Black Kettle and White Antelope, Cheyenne chiefs, and the representatives of the Arapaho Left Hand, were now willing, they said, to take the white man by the hand. They found the white man not so willing. Governor Evans said: "The war is begun, and the power to make a treaty has passed from me to the great war chief."

It was November when Colonel Chivington, the "fighting parson" whose Colorado troops had turned back the Confederate invasion, was ready to charge upon the Indians. He made his way, not to the plains where in spite of the advanced season he might still have found some marauding parties, but to the camp on Sandy Creek where the Cheyenne and Arapaho were gathered.

The attack was unexpected; the Indians were badly outnumbered. The result was an indiscriminate slaughter of men, women, and children, despite, so some said, the raising by the Indian leader of the flag of the United States as a protection. There were scalpings and mutilations such as Indians themselves might have perpetrated. To the soldiers this seemed only a fair return for the summer of horror. To the onlooker, especially at a distance, it was a fiendish attack upon confiding innocents. A Congressional investigation, the following year, brought out many statements, from which the only sure conclusion to be drawn was that settlers and roving savages could not peaceably occupy the same territory.

Colonel William Bent, whom the Indians now called Grey-Beard, testified at this hearing. So did his oldest half-Cheyenne son Robert, who had been interpreter to Chivington's command. Bent's two younger sons, George and Charles, were in the Sand Creek camp when it was attacked. They escaped to become leaders of fierce marauding bands in the years of plains-fighting that followed.

Colonel Chivington thought he had killed Black Kettle and won for himself a general's star. He was mistaken in both assumptions. Black Kettle lived to fight the whites through other summer campaigns and died in another winter raid made by General Custer upon the Washita, four years later.

IV

THE SOUTHWEST had been at war since the dawn of history. It was now more thoroughly so than ever.

"Even before the acquisition of New Mexico," Kit Carson had testified before the Congressional committee, "there had existed a hereditary warfare between the Navaho and Mexicans; forays were made into each other's country, and stock, women, and children stolen. Since the acquisition, the same state has existed; we could hardly get back from fighting and making peace with them before they would be at war again."

In the winter of 1860–61 General E. S. Canby had engaged in another one of the series of Navaho campaigns which had been a steady need ever since American occupation. Besides his regular troops he had Mexican volunteers and a goodly number of Ute and Pueblo Indians as scouts and soldiers. As Navaho campaigns went this was rather more than usually successful. When the Indians thought it a good time for a truce, they declared themselves ready to receive congratulations and presents according to the usual formula. This time, twenty-two chiefs signed the articles of capitulation. But Canby's back was no sooner turned than the Navaho were at it again.

Followed the fighting of white against white, and when the regulars, the Colorado and New Mexico volunteers and the friendly Indians combined had sent the raiding Texans back to their own country, it became evident that this conflict had left in its wake a war with the Mescalero Apache in southeastern New Mexico.

Perhaps the Texans, now withdrawn, had been the cause of the Mescalero troubles. But all outsiders looked alike to the embattled red man and revenge was to be taken on the New Mexicans near at hand. General Canby had now been sent north and his place taken by General James H. Carleton, with Kit Carson as his right hand man.

"During the raid from Texas," reported General Carleton, "the Indians, aware that the attention of our troops could not, for the time, be turned against them, commenced robbing the inhabitants of their stock, and killed, in various places, a great number of people; the Navaho on the western side and the Mescalero Apache on the eastern side of the settlements, both committing these outrages at the same time."

Starting out after the Mescalero, Captain Thomas Graydon made short work of a party led by old Manuelito, head chief of that band. It was said that they were headed toward the white man seeking peace, not war. Certainly, after the death of Manuelito and his fellow leader, José Largo, the Mescalero were all eager for submission. They hurried to Fort Stanton to Kit Carson, known to the Indians far and wide as "Father Kit" and their good friend.

Carson sent them under escort to General Carleton at Santa Fé. That soldier, profiting by the failures of his predecessors, decided that something more than a mere treaty was needed to reduce the wandering tribes to a real peace. He established a reservation on the Rio Pecos and sent the Mescalero thither. There they were to remain until all the tribe should be gathered and ready as a whole to acknowledge the rule of the white man.

Like many another man, Carleton thought he had hit upon a solution of " the Indian problem." He thought that if these wild Indians of the desert should be collected on a reservation, fed, clothed, and taught the arts of farming and industry, they would soon " become what in this country is called a pueblo." In other words, he was going to do with the nomads what centuries before the Spanish *padres* had done — not without blood and tears — for the tribes already inclined toward agriculture and village life.

But the Navaho and Apache tribes were of Athapascan stock, rovers who, judged by linguistic standards, must have made their way to this land from the far, all but arctic, Northwest. The Pueblo Indians, on the contrary, had come up from the Central American tribes, far more advanced culturally and industrially than any of the more northern peoples. Many centuries of development lay between them. Even at that, the development of the peaceful pueblos had been no matter of a year or two, but a change that came with centuries of intermingling and intermarriage.

Through their constant taking of captives from other tribes and from the Mexicans, these desert people had become as well mixed in blood as might be expected. But they clung tenaciously to the fierce roving ways they had brought with them from the Northwest. Settling down is even yet far from their desire.

To the Bosque Redondo, however, on the Rio Pecos, went the Mescalero. Fort Sumner was established as the means of keeping them there. Early in 1863 most of the Apache of this group had come in or had been brought in to the reservation. A few marauding bands were still at large while some had fled westward to the Apache of the Gila river. These farther Apache bands were to vex the newly formed Territory of Arizona through two decades of its existence.

Now it was time to give some real attention to the Navaho. General Carleton looked over a file of reports and treaties, from Doniphan to Canby, and decided that something more drastic would be required. He did not want another peaceable parley followed by renewed outbreaks. The Navaho too must come in to the Bosque Redondo and learn to till the soil.

" The purpose now," reported Carleton, " is never to relax the application of force with a people that can no more be trusted than you can trust the wolves that run through their mountains; to gather them together, little by little, on their reservation, and then to be kind to them; there teach their children how to read and write; teach them the arts of peace; teach them the truth of Christianity. . . Thus little by little, they will become a happy and contented people, and Navaho wars will be remembered only as something that belongs entirely to the past."

This does not sound like a bloodthirsty proposal. The carrying out of the plan furnished no sensational encounters. In June 1863 a proclamation was issued calling on the Navaho to surrender and go to the Rio Pecos. A refusal to do so would be construed as a declaration of war. Some obeyed the proclamation; more stayed behind.

Colonel Kit Carson established himself and his force of several hundred men at Fort Canby, west of Fort Defiance, in Arizona Territory. Carson had with him regular soldiers, Mexican volunteer companies, and a considerable detachment of Ute and Pueblo scouts and warriors. Ute and Pueblo were nothing loath to take the field against their ancient enemies.

Scouting parties went out with a bonus in prospect for all the horses, mules, and sheep they might bring in. Then as now the Navaho were shepherds. The destruction of their herds would bring about the surrender of many of them without battle.

Through the remainder of the year this method was pursued. There were frequent casualties on both sides but no pitched engagement. By September the Navaho were asking for peace. They were told that the terms were unconditional surrender. One group after another, they began to come in to the various forts to be sent under escort to the Bosque Redondo.

Following the Navaho into the rocky wastes of his country was a hard task at best. One or two places were considered quite impregnable — chief among them being the famous Cañon de Chelly, thirty miles in length, with high rocky walls that had housed cliff-dwelling people untold ages before. In this cañon were sheltered nooks and angles where corn could be raised and where peach orchards had been planted. In the stone walls the Indians had natural forts from which they could repel invasion.

A dozen years before Colonel Sumner had entered the cañon, but wisely retreated at nightfall. General Canby too had made his visit a very brief one.

The Navaho Indians still tell a story of having cornered Kit and some of his men on a high rock, holding them there for three days. This does not appear in the official reports. They give us instead a vivid story of the one picturesque and decisive event of the campaign — the traversing of the famed cañon by Colonel Pfeiffer and his troops, from east to west, without losing a man, and bringing in nearly a hundred Navaho prisoners.

This raid through their great stronghold convinced the Indians there was no wisdom in further resistance. Intelligence is the Navaho's strong point. The rivulet of Indians coming in to surrender grew to a wide and hurrying stream.

By March of 1864 practically the entire tribe was on its way to Fort Sumner. "You have doubtless seen the last of the Navaho war," reported Carleton to Washington.

He was right; even though his scheme of a reservation on the Bosque Redondo proved a failure. Fighting between Navaho and Apache, worst of enemies because of the same stock originally, successive crop failures, and, most disadvantageous of all, poor water and little of it, made it apparent before long that the Indians could not settle down here as farmers. The Mescalero were accommodated with another reservation. The Navaho, after four years of exile, were allowed to retraverse the distance across New Mexico to the desert land they loved best. Here sheep were issued to them and they started again upon their pastoral life.

They are still shepherds; but they go on forays for Mexican captives no longer. They had a severe lesson and they learned it well. By their scattered fires at evening the old Indians still tell the story of their exile at the Bosque Redondo.

v

CAMPAIGNING against the western Apache brought little result. So to the eastward, although Carson led a force against the Kiowa and Comanche at the long abandoned trading post, Adobe Walls, in the Staked Plains country, it was demonstrated that a greater force than the department could muster must be exercised if there was to be peace on the prairies.

From the Missouri to the Rockies, from the headwaters of the Mississippi to the lower Arkansas, there had been Indian fighting in plenty during these days of civil warfare. Nor did the fall of Richmond mean peace for the western plains. Sharper conflicts were to come.

The war had interrupted western settlement. It had clouded for the time that dream of the far-seeing, a transcontinental railroad. Now men's thoughts turned again to the westward course of empire. As settlers, as workers upon the advancing line of rails, as soldiers in the little forts along the way, a horde of men released from combat in the East sought adventure or fortune in the West.

An iron ring seemed to draw closer and closer about the Indians of the plains. Shorter and shorter grew the path of the buffalo. Fewer and fewer still were the other wild creatures on which the red hunters could feed. A portent of coming doom lay on the skin lodges and blackened the smoke of the council fires.

CHAPTER XV
Warfare on the Plains

I

THE YEARS immediately following the Civil War present curious contrasts for the student of Indian history. Viewed from the standpoint of diplomacy it was an era of conferences, councils, and treaties. The only thing that marred the pleasure of these resounding agreements of peace and amity was the necessity of doing it all over again the next year.

In 1865 Congress appointed a Committee on the Condition of the Indian Tribes. They made extended report two years later. They had decided that the numbers of the Indians were rapidly decreasing, that Indian wars were usually to be traced to " the aggressions of lawless white men," and that the appointment of five boards of inspection would be the best way of meeting the situation.

A Peace Commission was appointed, composed of both soldiers and civilians. Two years later was created the Board of Indian Commissioners, ten men chosen " from among men eminent for intelligence and philanthropy, who shall serve without pecuniary compensation." They were to clean up the abuses in the Indian Service and advise the executive on Indian policies.

One good result at least came out of all this — the final recommendation that the fiction of independent nationality be abandoned and the Indians treated as the

288

wards they had long since become. So, in the seventies, the farce of treaty-making lapsed in favor of agreements and laws.

But in spite of peace commissions and peace policies, and even the turning over of the Indian agencies to the guidance of missionaries and religious bodies, warfare did not appreciably slacken. The Army, Congress, the Interior Department, the churches, and the public were all considerably busied with Indian matters in these days. Each one of the participants had a different approach to the subject and a different solution of all the difficulties involved. When there was a lull in fighting the Indians, they speedily fell to fighting one another, vocally if not with fist, tooth, and nail.

The Army had long since evolved the maxim that " it is easier to feed the Indian than to fight him." The Army theory was to whip the Indian into submission, gather the survivors upon reservations, issue them rations, police them, and set them to tilling the soil.

Two factors militated against the success of this policy. Public opinion never let the soldiery finish any fight to the point of submission. When the tide turned against the Indian there was always a call for a council and another treaty. The Indian naturally construed this as a cowardly surrender.

The second weak point in the Army policy was overlooking the fact that free food does not lead men to industry. Necessity is a greater spur to action than repletion. The Indian brave despised labor and the man who engaged in it. He was accustomed to receiving presents from the white man. He would not scratch the ground with the hoe, like a squaw, when he could stride up to a complaisant agent and demand cattle and flour.

The Army pointed with justice to the corruption and

disorganization of the Indian Service in those days. Indian agents were political appointees with meager salaries and ample opportunities for " money on the side." The wonder is not that some were corrupt but that many were still honest. Corrupt or honest, they were usually quite helpless in the grip of domineering braves who saw government presents for what they were — cajolery and bribery offered by the weaker party to the stronger.

The honest Indian agent was usually quite as much at odds with the Army policy as was his corrupt brother. He furnished the Indians — ostensibly for hunting — with the latest variety of arms and ammunition; and was duly surprised when they were used in fighting soldiers and citizens. When his charges grew too violent he called on the nearest Army post for help; but he was extremely resentful of the presence of the bluecoats in times of peace. The War Department called loud and long for the turning over of Indian matters to its jurisdiction. The Department of the Interior responded that the purpose of dealing with the Indians was peace, not war.

The Congressional Committee had a criticism for both: " While it is true that many agents, teachers, and employees of the government are inefficient, faithless, and even guilty of peculations and fraudulent practices upon the government and even upon the Indians, it is equally true that military posts among the Indians have frequently become centers of demoralization and destruction to the Indian tribes, while the blunders and want of discretion of inexperienced officers in command have brought on long and expensive wars. . . Since we acquired New Mexico, the military expenditures connected with Indian affairs have probably exceeded four million dollars annually in that territory alone. When

General Sumner was in command of that department he recommended the purchase of all the private property of citizens, and the surrender of that whole territory to the Indians, and upon the score of economy it would doubtless have been a great saving to the government."

Meanwhile public opinion went all the way from that of the western settler whose wife and daughters were tortured and abused until death released them from a misery words could not describe and who felt that no punishment could be severe enough for the offenders, to that of the most remote enthusiast who saw everything Indian in a haze of romance and beauty and who felt that the crimes of America were blacker than any the red man could commit.

And while all these factions argued and contended, a tragic drama was moving relentlessly onward. For a decade after the Civil War the Plains Indians were still masters of their prairies. For all the Army and all the fighting, for all the treaties and all the councils, they were for a good share of the time in control of the situation.

But it was the last frontier and their last stand. The westward march of empire was as inescapable as the process of the suns. In their savage hearts they knew their doom was upon them.

II

GENERALS SANBORN AND HARNEY, in October 1865, made treaty with Cheyenne and Arapaho, with Apache, Comanche and Kiowa, that peace would hereafter be maintained. Especially the tribes promised they would never again interfere with the routes of travel across the plains.

In the same month at Fort Sully the various bands of Sioux were making the same promise.

Nevertheless, when the braves had received their presents and had gone forth again upon the warpath it became necessary to call another conference the following summer. The government wanted to establish and maintain a road from Nebraska northward through Wyoming and Montana, the Bozeman Trail to the northwest. Word came out that presents and feasting awaited the Indians at Fort Laramie, that they might permit the United States to carry out the plan to which they had given their consent in due form the year before.

Cheyenne, Arapaho, and Sioux of many different bands assembled. Spotted Tail of the Brulé had decided by this time to become an agency Indian. His long detention at Fort Laramie after the Grattan affair, ten years before, had taught him something of the power of the white man. Rumor told another story too of his change of heart — how his daughter loved a white lieutenant and, dying of tuberculosis, made her father promise to raise his hand no more against the bluecoats.

Whether for this or shrewder reasons, Spotted Tail stayed quietly on his reservation. Though the hotter heads among the Brulé went to war as before he no longer led them but was chief of the friendlies, enjoying occasional visits to the Great White Father in Washington at the head of a delegation of braves.

Red Cloud of the Oglala band was the striking figure of this Fort Laramie assemblage in the spring of 1866. With a party of his own tribesmen and Cheyenne warriors he had held up for a fortnight the troops and construction workers sent to begin the Powder River Road. He had flung defiance to the white men. On this matter of a road he would not treat. Now in council, tall, eloquent, determined, he repeated his refusal to let the intruder make a way across his hunting grounds.

As the council talk went on a cloud of dust rose across the plains. General Carrington was approaching with his troops. They were assuming that the Sioux would consent and that they might go on to open the way and to establish the forts for the protection of the road.

Red Cloud's anger flamed into instant action. At his word his followers flung themselves upon their ponies and dashed away from the fort. Red Cloud's shout of angry defiance rang in the ears of the councillors. The war-whoop arose as the band galloped off.

III

CARRINGTON and his soldiers went on up the trail and in August began the building of Fort Phil Kearny. For the two years of its existence this little outpost was not to know a day of peace. Every group of workmen who went to cut wood for building or for fuel had to be thoroughly guarded. Every day the lookout on the hills signalled the approach of hostile Indians and more soldiers had to be sent out to repel attack. Not a message went down the trail to Laramie, not a mail or supply train came up from Nebraska, without meeting the deadly opposition of Red Cloud and his fierce warriors. Not even the cold of the northern winter could relax his determination.

On Christmas Day the eastern public was secure in the consciousness of a land at peace. In his message at the opening of Congress the President had commented on the completion of satisfactory agreements at Fort Laramie and the assured tranquillity of the Northwest.

Rudely upon this contentment broke the news of the

annihilation, four days before, of a command of eighty-one men under Captain Fetterman. Sent out from the fort to repel an attack upon the wood train, they had too boldly rushed over Lodge Trail Ridge and into an ambush of Red Cloud's waiting warriors.

The Oglala chief, however, was not to be satisfied with anything less than the destruction of the forts and the road. In the following spring, while the daily attacks continued, he was massing his followers for an assault which should annihilate the whole garrison. When he had taken this fort he felt sure that the other two along the way would fall and the Indian would be master of the land.

Red Cloud's star was in the ascendant among his red brethren. The Fetterman victory had given him prestige such as few chiefs can claim. All the daring young men among the Sioux and the Northern Cheyenne, and not a few of the more turbulent spirits among the tribes that were in general friendly and at peace, sought him and were proud to campaign with him.

Midsummer of 1867 found hundreds, even thousands, of them gathered in the vicinity of Fort Phil Kearny. On Piney Island, seven miles away, contractors, guarded by a little company of soldiers, were cutting the winter's supply of wood for the fort. The logs were hauled on the wagon trucks, and the wagon boxes, removed from the wheels, had been arranged on the island in an oval which formed a sort of corral within which the camp supplies were stacked for protection.

Red Cloud planned to attack the woodcutters and their guard and, after overwhelming them with his vastly superior numbers, to go on to the destruction of the fort itself. Perhaps he could repeat the plan which had worked so well the winter before. By an attack and

RED CLOUD

By Courtesy of the Smithsonian Institute

GALL

By Courtesy of the Smithsonian Institute

feigned flight they might lure a party farther and farther from its base as Fetterman had been drawn to his death.

On the morning of the second of August the red warriors began operations by an effort to stampede the herd of the Piney Island camp. The woodcutters made good their retreat to the fort though with the loss of four of their number. The herdsmen were intercepted in their attempt to join the woodsmen and were engaged in defence when the little company of thirty-two soldiers, with Captain Powell in command, diverted the attack. Turning, the horde of Indians drove the soldiers into the wagon-box corral while the herdsmen were thus enabled to retreat with their fellows.

Captain Powell and his men were outnumbered a hundred to one. The shelter of the wagon boxes and the fact that they had breech-loading rifles of a new type proved their salvation. At the first furious charge of the Indians Lieutenant Jenness, second in command, was killed, and one of the privates was mortally wounded. There were twenty-eight men to resist the continued attacks of the besiegers.

There were said to have been as many as three thousand Indian braves in this fight, as great a number as were ever brought together for war. They represented many different tribes. They were determined, dauntless. So many were they that it was said a bullet from a defender of the wagon boxes would often pass through the body of one warrior and pierce another who stood behind him.

Again and again the red men charged. The soldiers would withhold their fire until the attackers were within close range. Then they would send forth a continuous volley that did deadly work. The Indians could not understand so incessant and devastating a fire. The

fight has come down in their campfire annals as "the
bad medicine fight with the white men."

Mid-afternoon found the little band of soldiers almost
at the end of its resources of strength. Another attack,
they felt, would be the end. But Red Cloud had lost all
too heavily. His dead were massed up about the little
corral of boxes. He was skirmishing, not for another
attack, but to recover as many bodies as possible, when
reinforcements came upon the scene from the fort. Red
Cloud was glad to retire.

Red Cloud's nephew, young, ambitious, daring, had
fallen in one of the charges. The dead were an incredible number. The soldiers' estimate of several hundred
seemed extravagant enough, but a year later the story
of the Indians more than confirmed it. Eleven hundred
red men had fallen in the desperate attempt to overcome
those thirty-two entrenched behind a screen of wagon
boxes.

It was a repulse that shattered Red Cloud's high hope
of razing Fort Phil Kearny. For the time being, his
hosts were shrunken and his medicine discredited.
Nearly half of his magnificent force of warriors had
made their last assault.

"I lost them," he said when, as an old man and at
peace, he talked of the days of war. "They never fought
again."

IV

BELOW on the plains there were plenty of warriors this
summer of 1867 for all Red Cloud's great assemblage to
the north. For Indian agent or Army officer, for railroad
worker or traveller across the prairies, there were no dull
moments. Where the Sioux left off the Comanche and
Kiowa began. The fighting Cheyenne and their allies

the Arapaho lent a hand to marauders of both north and south and kept the central country as active as a nest of wasps.

Something approaching a war, meanwhile, went on between Indian agents and Army folk. The conflict was not the less vigorous because it stopped short of physical encounter. The air was filled with charges instead of gunsmoke, and invectives were no less keen than the scalping knife.

While white man fought white man, Indian fought Indian. Crow and Pawnee, ever friendly to the whites because ever ready to attack their ancient enemies the Sioux, aided the Army as scouts and guides. Four Pawnee companies under the command of Major North, a white man who had long lived with the tribe, did valiant service in Nebraska and Kansas beating off the almost constant attacks of the hostile bands upon the railway workers. In spite of attacks the lines continued to stretch their way along.

The Cheyenne achieved a railroad wreck this summer about the time Red Cloud was massing his men to attack Fort Phil Kearny. Generals Hancock and Custer had been campaigning on the prairies all the season but with no great result. Still the iron rails kept advancing. Red Wolf and Porcupine, Cheyenne braves, tied a log to the track and derailed a handcar; then pursued and killed the two men who were overturned by the obstruction.

This encouraged the Indians to further experiment and they tore up a section of the rail and twisted it to one side. The oncoming freight was derailed and piled up in a confused mass. But one of the crew was left alive. He came along with a lantern and was speedily dispatched by the wreckers. Next morning they plun-

dered the train and gathered much booty; then set fire
to the cars.

Returning another day for more spoils, they found the
Pawnee on the scene. The fight that followed convinced
the Cheyenne braves of the advisability of returning to
their camp on Plum Creek until the trouble should blow
over.

And now the peace commissioners came and made
preparations for gathering together all the Indians.
There should be a great council of the plains and still
another series of treaties. First came preliminary conferences and in October the southern tribes were gathered together at Medicine Lodge Creek to receive presents from the Great White Father. At the same time the
Sioux and the tribes of the north were expected to assemble at Fort Laramie.

Kiowa and Comanche, Apache of the plains, Arapaho
and Cheyenne agreed after much powwowing that they
would settle south of the Arkansas and west of the Five
Civilized Tribes. There they would maintain the peace,
learn habits of industry, send their children to school,
and give up their roving ways. The United States
promised to provide agents and teachers, farmers and
blacksmiths, to give the red men food and implements
and seeds, to supply needs of all sorts.

As earnest of the bargain, three great piles of presents
were spread out for the assembled Indians. Distribution was made to every family among them. So much
was given that the Indians could by no means carry it
all away, but left piles of clothing and blankets and provisions on the ground to rot. The braves were put to the
indignity of walking away from the place of council, for
all their many horses were laden with gifts. So heavily
laden were they that they, too, had to walk slowly.

This was in October of the year 1867. " From this time forward all war between the parties to this agreement shall forever cease." So began the long treaties one and all.

v

THE WINTER was comparatively quiet, as winters are apt to be. As summer came the Cheyenne began to grumble that there was not another round of presents. Especially they desired arms and ammunition. When these arrived the Indian agent, with sublime confidence, issued them to the waiting tribesmen. Presto — they were at once off on the warpath.

Roman Nose, better known to his followers as The Bat, was hero and victim of the Beecher Island fight, which signalized the waning of this battle summer of 1868. On the Arickaree Fork of the Republican, just within the eastern border of Colorado, fifty-one scouts under Major Forsyth were besieged on an open sandy island. For nine days they held out until the Indians tired of the attack and starvation was the greater danger. Their horses were all killed and the able men would not leave the wounded behind.

The attackers were Cheyenne, Brulé, and Oglala Sioux, and a scattering of Arapaho warriors. There were hundreds of them to charge again and again across the shallow stream. Roman Nose was not a chief, but as a valiant fighter they looked to him for leadership in time of battle. This first morning of the attack he stayed out of the fight until the other warriors wondered. They came to taunt him with his delay.

Evil had befallen him. His medicine war bonnet, whose function was to protect as well as to ornament him in battle, had been given him with the advice that its medicine would avail him only so long as he ate no food that had been handled with metal. And this morning, unwittingly, he had partaken of meat in the Sioux camp, which a Sioux woman had taken from the stewpot with an iron spoon.

By a long ceremony he might purify himself and restore the efficacy of his bonnet. But by that time the fight would be done. Roman Nose knew that if he ignored the warning the fight would be his last. He put on his war bonnet, sang his death chant, and threw himself into the fray.

He was right. The taboo he had violated was fatal. His was one of the bodies the Indians bore away from the field.

In pitched battle the Indians did not always score a victory. It was in the smaller raids on settlers or travellers that the most deadly work was done. General Sheridan, in command of the department, decided on a winter campaign. November was nearly at an end and a blizzard raging, when Custer and his men rode out to attack the Cheyenne camp upon the Washita.

The Cheyenne historians still maintain that Black Kettle was not really a hostile. The soldiers and dwellers on the plains took a very different view of the matter. This raid of Black Kettle's village, however, ended both the life of the old chief and some of the hostility of his people. Before long the southern tribes began to gather in the western part of the Indian territory. It was a belated fulfilment of the treaty made at Medicine Lodge Creek.

The peace commissioners had planned a treaty with the Sioux to follow the one in the South; but Red Cloud was still defiant. When runners came to him he sent back word that he refused to parley with the white man until all the forts were removed from the Montana country.

As it was impracticable to remove forts at the beginning of the winter, the commissioners meekly asked Red Cloud for a truce until spring. When spring came the forts were abandoned. The rejoicing Indians flocked in and burned the deserted buildings.

Red Cloud then signified that he was willing to receive presents. He came in for his treaty at the end of April 1868, when Sioux of many bands gathered for treaty-making and gifts. The commissioners promised that white men should be kept out of the Sioux country. Food and clothing, ploughs and cattle, schools and teachers should thenceforward be furnished the tribesmen.

Red Cloud as an individual kept his agreement. He and Spotted Tail thereafter vied for honors as agency Indians. But a great band of Brulé, Minneconjou, Sans Arc, and Oglala braves, biding their time, remained hostile.

"From this day forward all war among the parties to this agreement shall forever cease."

VI

THE DECADE that had begun with so much warfare went out with something approximating peace. The Commissioner of Indian Affairs, reporting for 1870, congratulated the Secretary of the Interior on the fact that relations with the tribes had been " as favorable as could be expected," that the year preceding had seen " no serious outbreak or demonstrations of hostility."

There had been a few exceptions, however. He noted them briefly.

The Piegan Indians, a band of the Blackfoot, had committed murders among the Montana settlers, and a command of cavalry had been called out to subdue them.

While Red Cloud had happily been pacified by a triumphant visit to Washington and other eastern cities, about a third of the Sioux remained disaffected. But in spite of the organization of a group of people in Wyoming to explore the Big Horn country, there were to be charged against the Sioux "a few murders and depredations only." These difficulties were " caused by roving and irresponsible bands, and were not the result of any general organization of the Indians for purposes of mischief or outrage."

The Ute too were giving some trouble. They also had made treaty in 1868 promising to remove to a certain definite territory. To date they had refused to carry out their promise insisting on receiving their presents at their old locations. The Commissioner recommended that they have their desire in the matter.

The Cheyenne and Arapaho had called a council with the Kiowa and Comanche designing that they might all go on the warpath together. So far the final arrangement had not been effected. These Indians too were demanding a different location for their agency.

Kiowa and Comanche had been guilty of various murders and outrages during the year. They had kept the warpath busy with raids against the Texans, " killing citizens, capturing women and children, and stealing stock; and have set at defiance the military — audaciously inviting them out to battle. The Indian Bureau is wholly powerless to prevent these raids," the Commissioner explains. The Indians protest that the Texans are enemies and point out the fact that the soldiers too were fighting them only a few years ago. " But in my judgment," says the Commissioner, " they know better."

The Apache of New Mexico had caused but few complaints; those of Arizona were as wild and warlike as ever. " Their thirst for rapine and blood seems unquenchable and unconquerable." There was further trouble in Arizona with the Pima and Maricopa tribes. " During the present year the conduct of these Indians has been more insolent and arrogant than ever."

Intertribal wars had gone on about as usual. The Sioux were " gratifying their thirst for blood by raiding upon weak neighboring tribes, and no argument can induce them to abandon the practice. They will reply, ' It is no business of the white man what the Indians do among themselves.' "

Aside from these difficulties everything was peaceful.

Lest the Commissioner who made this report be suspected of an anti-Indian bias, it is well to note that he was himself of Indian blood, General Ely S. Parker, an aide of Grant during the Civil War.

Let it be noted, too, that this was the time of the new " Peace Policy "; that Congress had passed a law forbidding Army officers to be assigned as Indian agents; that the various religious denominations, and notably the ultra-peaceful Friends or Quakers, had been asked to take charge of the different Indian reservations and assign agents to each; that the fiction of Indian tribes as separate nations was being abandoned and the theory of wardship adopted as a guide to action.

It was felt that a new day had dawned. The sun was arising in full splendor.

Here and there, however, a cloud still drifted across the sky. . .

CHAPTER XVI
Last Stands

I

THE BELLIGERENT Sioux and Cheyenne had amply shown the white man that a peace policy is one thing and actual peace another. Nevertheless, as the seventies wore on, the peace policy began more and more to prevail and became something like actuality.

It was not alone that public sentiment became increasingly enlisted in favor of the red man and in sympathy with his reluctance to give up the life of the plains. It was not alone the greater interest in Indian training and education, as shown by largely increased appropriations and more liberal laws, as well as by popular movements in missionary and educational work. Feeling in the eastern part of the country rose to tidal proportions during this decade; yet the tide might have ebbed again fruitless had not the undercurrents of destiny worked in the same direction.

Railroad building went on; and when the railroads had spanned the plains the rule of the red man was definitely challenged. Construction gangs on the Union Pacific and the Kansas Pacific had fought their way west. Many a day they threw down pick and hammer to snatch a gun from the pile stacked up for instant use. Hard-bitten " tarriers " themselves, they welcomed a fight as part of the day's work or the evening's carouse. The ties were laid and the rails pounded into place to the sound of the war-whoop.

For many a year before this the range of the buffalo had been shrinking. The first guns that sent the Sioux down on the plains started the decline. Long since the shaggy herds had retreated from the valleys of the Ohio to come no more. Generations had passed since the far western tribes, Nez Percé and Bannock and Blackfoot, had noted that longer and longer journeys to the east were necessary for their annual hunt. The Indians of the central plains still thought the buffalo inexhaustible; but their brethren of the remoter lands could have told them otherwise.

The decade of the seventies saw these limitless hordes reduced to a mere handful. The coming of railroads and white settlement meant eventual extinction. The sudden awakening of the white hunters to the profits to be gained brought about in a few years what might have taken much longer.

With the departure of the buffalo forever, there was nothing for the red rover to do but to settle down, reluctantly though it might be. So fire wagons and fire-arms worked for the success of the peace policy and the fires of battle died down.

But north and south, in the mountains and on the plains, there was many a fitful flare of rebellion before the inevitable change.

II

The Modoc were too small a tribe — only a few hundred at best — to attract much notice. But for a few months in 1872 and 1873 the country waited breathless for the news of their warfare among the lava beds.

Twenty years before, in the days of the earliest emigrants, there had been enmity and conflict, in which white man and Indian were about equally guilty. These Modoc, in a loosely united band, roamed and hunted a bit over the Tule Lake country where Oregon and California meet. South of the lake was a pedregal, or lava-covered waste, some miles in extent; a country all but impossible of passage, traversed by jagged rock gullies and sown with blackened stones whose edges cut the feet of man or horse all but unbearably.

Not far from here were the mettlesome Klamath, ancient enemies of the Modoc, and thorny people in their kindest aspects. The reservation idea being strong, the government assigned to the homeless Modoc a place on the Klamath reserve. There was room enough so far as land was concerned; but there is never room for enemies to live together. The Klamath were the stronger and the little Modoc band was harried from one point of the reserve to another. Finally they decamped and returned to their old roaming grounds on Lost River.

These Modoc folk had become used enough to the ways of the white man so that they all spoke English after a fashion. They dressed in habiliments not unlike those of the poorer white prospectors or settlers. Captain Jack, one of their leaders, gained his name by his fondness for some discarded bits of uniform that were part of his usual attire.

To some of their Indian customs they still clung; and when one of his family was ill Captain Jack had recourse to the incantations of the Indian medicine man. The practitioner of his band being away on a marauding expedition, he was forced to ask the services of the Klamath healer.

The work of the medicine man was unsuccessful. According to Indian custom, Captain Jack then killed the medicine man. The Klamath, however, demanded that the white man's law be invoked to punish the Modoc leader.

For a year or two after this episode Captain Jack's band roamed about the northern California country. They indulged in no very serious depredations but they objected strongly whenever a proposition was broached of a return to the Klamath land. They asked instead that they be given a place to stay on Lost River.

But Captain Jack with his handful of ragged followers was no Red Cloud backed by the guns of thousands of braves. The Indian Office refused his request, asking that troops be sent to round up the band and return it to the reservation. The Modoc resisted arrest and retreated to their ghastly stronghold — the lava beds.

Here, in the hideous rocks they knew well, they were able to remain perfectly concealed and to pick off the white soldiers who tried to approach. At first the white men laughed at the boast of Captain Jack that he could stand off a thousand soldiers. But after a few days of fighting in the "land of burnt-out fires," of receiving the bullets of an unseen enemy as they struggled over the jagged rocks, there was no more laughter. Captain Jack had not boasted; he had spoken simple truth.

Parleying followed, for the peace party was strong and General E. S. Canby, in charge of the department, was an earnest advocate of peace and a good friend of the Indian, as well as a soldier of experience and reputation. All through the winter and into the spring messages came and went between Captain Jack and his band in the lava beds, and the Peace Commission headed by the General. But Captain Jack refused to give up those of his band who had been guilty of murder and outrage; refused to consider a return to the Klamath reserve; demanded, instead, a reservation on Lost River and immunity for past deeds. Spring came and an agreement seemed as far off as ever.

A conference had been postponed because the signal man on the lookout over the lava beds announced that in addition to the six Modoc councillors in open view, twenty armed warriors were secreted in strategic spots nearby. Nevertheless when a second conference was proposed by the Indians, the commission accepted, though the indications were plain that treachery was intended.

Toby Riddle, a Modoc woman whose white husband was interpreter for the commission, knew that there was danger. She and her husband urged the commissioners not to go. Three of the five knew the situation well enough to agree with her that it meant going to their death. They had given the Indians their promise to come unarmed. General Canby and Dr. Eleazar Thomas, the remaining two commissioners, declared that their honor was pledged to carry out the council as agreed upon. Both were well known to be the Indian's sincerest friends.

When they met it was obvious that the councilling Indians were armed. There was a brief and excited parley; Captain Jack's demands were heated and wild. Suddenly other Indians appeared laden with rifles.

" At-tux ! " (All ready !) shouted Jack, and shot General Canby full in the face. Boston Charley dispatched Dr. Thomas as promptly.

" Maybe you believe next time what squaw tells you," he said as he emptied the barrels of his revolver.

Riddle and two of the commissioners were able to escape. Toby herself escaped death only through the intercession of Scar-faced Charley, the Modoc. As she raised herself from the ground she saw one of the mur-

WI-NE-MA.
(The Woman of the Brave Heart.)

A Modoc woman, and a full cousin to Captain Jack. Her fidelity and her heroism in the Lava Beds, in 1873, won for her a place in history which can never be disputed. After warning the Commission of the impending danger, unavailingly, she went to the ill-fated Council as interpreter; and when the attack was made, she sprang to her feet, and by almost superhuman efforts saved my life.

A. B. MEACHAM,
Chairman of the late Peace Commission to the Modoc Indians.

TOBY RIDDLE

By Courtesy of the Smithsonian Institute

derers preparing to scalp the apparently lifeless body of
Meacham, the fifth commissioner.

" Soldiers are coming ! " she cried; and the scalping
was forsaken. The Modoc band fled back to the shelter
of their caves in the lava beds.

Meacham, whom the Indians had thought dead,
eventually recovered. Later, Toby was voted a pension
by Congress for her rescue of the commissioner.

Even after the Modoc band had thus destroyed the
leaders of the peace party and their own best friends, it
was a matter of weeks of desperate fighting before they
were captured. In the end it was their own disunion that
brought them out of the pedregal and into the hands of
the soldiery. The worst of them saved their lives by
turning state's evidence. Captain Jack and three others
met death on the scaffold about a year after the beginning of their outbreak.

The offenders who survived were sent *en masse* to
Baxter Springs, Kansas. Before long they were quietly
located at Quapaw agency in the northeastern corner of
the Indian territory. They were farming and working
after the manner of the white man. Only six years after
the affair of the lava beds, Steamboat Frank, one of the
group known as " the murderers " because of their attacks upon white settlers, was ordained in the Christian
ministry and was given charge of a church among his
people. It was a speedy transition.

III

APACHE wars were perennial. In the sixties it was Mangas Coloradas; in the seventies it was Cochise; in the
eighties it was Vittorio and Geronimo. Nor were these
the only trouble-makers.

There were many bands of these fierce warriors, roaming through northern Mexico and the southwestern territories of the United States. Linguistically they are related to the Navaho, and like them, call themselves *Dinné* — " the people." But in ferocity and endurance they put even the Navaho to the blush.

They could traverse a country and gather sustenance where the white man would perish. They could find shelter in a land so bare that a cactus plant is a tree and a depression in the sand a river bed. They fought the Mexican for centuries; and when settlers from the States came into Arizona, the newcomers were quickly adopted into the list of enemies. When the territory was formed and for thirty years thereafter, its white inhabitants were firmly of the opinion that the Apache was as deadly a creature as the rattlesnake and deserved the same summary treatment. They would have been quite as willing to adopt a peace policy with wildcats or grizzlies as with Mangas Coloradas or Cochise.

The Mimbreno chief, Mangas Coloradas, had been one of those who promised peace when Kearny went through in 1846. His promise had been about as good as any of the others. An alliance with Cochise of the Chiricahua aided in the terrorizing of the white settlements. Mangas Coloradas had been captured and killed in 1863. Years later Cochise was still keeping up their old activities. Troubles were rife in the territory when President Grant asked General O. O. Howard to leave for a time his Freedmen's University and try his hand at pacifying the Apache.

The measure of his undertaking may be gauged from one of his initial difficulties, which was persuading the citizens of Arizona to return to the Indians a group of captured children they were holding as servants or hos-

tages. General Howard naturally inclined to the feeling
that the children should go back to their relatives the
Arivipa Apache, but the Governor and Attorney-General of the territory protested strongly, threatening appeal to the Attorney-General of the United States.
Against their protest, the soldier-commissioner decided
to put the young captives in escrow with a kindly sergeant's wife, pending the decision of the President. The
decision was a disappointment to the territorial forces
but a great satisfaction to the Indians.

The main object of General Howard's mission was to
pacify if possible Cochise and the Chiricahua. A former
Commissioner had made the effort but had been unable
to get within a hundred miles of the stronghold where the
wily chieftain kept his camp. After much search the
General found a frontiersman by the name of Tom Jeffords, reputed to be a friend of the Chiricahua. On several occasions of attack the Apache band had spared
him. Jeffords was willing to take General Howard to
Cochise if he would go without any escort of soldiers.
It was so agreed.

There were five in the party that after days of hard
journeying reached the wary Apache chief in his rocky
cañon — the General, Jeffords, Captain Sladen, and
two friendly Apache scouts, Chie and Ponce. These two
Indians told Cochise who General Howard was and what
he had come for.

"Nobody wants peace more than I do," said Cochise.
"I have killed ten white men for every Indian I have
lost, but still the white men are no less; and my tribe
keeps growing smaller and smaller. It will disappear
from the face of the earth if we do not have a good peace
soon."

Cochise was an old chief by this time. He was tired

of constant foray and flight, and was ready to take his beef and flour and settle down. But he had sent his twelve sub-chiefs out to plunder, and the decision must await their return. The General must stay with them ten days or more.

Like General Canby, Howard was a lover of peace and of the Indian. He had no fear of treachery. He settled down to make friends with them all, children as well as elders, sharing his meals with them and teaching a younger son of Cochise to sign his name "Natchez."

It was a name that was later to stand beside that of Geronimo as a symbol of outlawry. But for the present General Howard's peace efforts were successful. The various captains came in; great council was held. The bands agreed to settle upon a Chiricahua reserve in southeastern Arizona with their friend Jeffords as their agent.

Cochise kept his promise of peace for the remainder of his life. Dying, he passed on the obligation to his eldest son, who was likewise faithful. But in 1876 both had made their last ride. Continued forays across the Mexican borders, not construed by the Chiricahua as a violation of their promise, led the government to abolish the reservation. The order went out to remove the band to the San Carlos reservation to the north.

The Indian Office was now endeavoring to carry out a "policy of concentration." New policies bloomed at least every fourth year, and sometimes much more frequently.

This new policy sent a few Indians to the new reservation. It sent a greater number over the border into Mexico. Again the Indian Bureau had to ask the War Department to step in.

IV

SETANGYA, known to the whites as Satank, was long a chief of the Kiowa. He was one of the young warriors when the Kiowa and Comanche made peace with Cheyenne and Arapaho on the banks of the Arkansas in 1840, following the advice of William Bent. Even then he was a recognized leader and a maker of potent medicine.

Six years later he was head of a delegation taken to visit President Polk in Washington. "A fine looking man of good size and middle age, and evidently a man of talents," the President found him. Satank decided as a result of this visit to the United States that the white men were more numerous than the stars and he gave up trying to count them.

Satank's name is first on the list of Kiowa chiefs signing the treaty of Medicine Lodge Creek in 1867, twenty years later. Next in order is that of Satanta, his second in command, a warrior twenty years Satank's junior.

Signing the big treaty and retiring to the general vicinity of the Canadian River did not, in the opinion of the Kiowa and Comanche, obligate them to keep peace with the Texans. The new reservation was most invitingly close to the Texas border. The horses and cattle so abundant on the Texas plains afforded an excellent substitute for buffalo hunting. If human beings were killed, too, that was but an incident in the life business of raiding and hunting.

"Without any provocation from officers, soldiers, or citizens," writes the good Quaker agent at Fort Sill on Ninth month 1, 1871, "the Indians of this agency have been carrying on a continuous war in Indian style in Texas, with very short intervals, and occasionally saying that they intended to continue it until the soldiers followed them to their camps, as they wished to prove that they could whip all the soldiers that could be brought against them."

Satank had boasted to Agent Tatum of the exploits of a party of a hundred he had lately led to the Texas plains. They had attacked a pack train, killed seven men and captured all the mules. The people of Texas were asking that the murderers be arrested. Satank, Satanta, and Big Tree were taken by the soldiers.

But Satank, now the old warrior, was not to go to Texas for trial. When about a mile away from Fort Sill he sang his death chant and tore the fetters from his wrists. He sprang upon his guard with a knife which he had hidden beneath his shirt. A shot ended his rebellion and his life.

Satanta and Big Tree were turned over to the Texas authorities and stood trial. The verdict was murder; the sentence, death by hanging. Milder counsels prevailed and the sentence was commuted to life imprisonment.

Two years they spent in the Texas State penitentiary. In their absence, Lone Wolf was chief and spokesman for the hostile Kiowa. He refused to promise good behavior or to relinquish white captives until Satanta and Big Tree were released. A council called by the quieter Indians of the Five Civilized Tribes had no effect upon the determination of the Kiowa. They would not listen to their red fellows who had found the ways of peace more satisfactory than the warpath.

The United States Government appealed to the Governor of Texas to exercise clemency. The two chiefs were released on parole. They were to be free so long as their people would refrain from war. It was not long.

The Southern Cheyenne, at the agency to the northward, grew more and more restive as they saw the white man making short work of the buffalo on the plains. In 1874 their discontent culminated in open warfare. With them they carried a good portion of the Kiowa and Comanche malcontents.

Across to the west in the Texas panhandle stood the old adobe walls that had long been a landmark for Indians and whites, the remains of the southern fort of the Bent brothers, long abandoned and left to the slow erosion of sun and wind. Here, ten years before, Kit Carson had fought his last and fiercest battle. And here, as headquarters and rendezvous, were gathered the buffalo hunters. The Indians decided upon this as their first point of attack.

Isatai, Comanche medicine man, had promised them that he would protect them against all harm. His incantations and charms would assure their complete victory.

As the event proved, a recollection of the white man's religious teachings might have stood them in better stead. They made the attack on Sunday morning, when the frontiersmen, if not keeping the Sabbath holy, were at least abstaining from the hunt and remaining in force at their camp. A week day would have been a far wiser choice.

Isatai, however, said that their fatal mistake was the killing of a skunk as they started out on their expedition. That had destroyed the value of his charms. But the disgruntled Indians, fighting most of the long summer day with little effect upon their enemies and considerable loss to themselves, would not accept Isatai's explanation.

One Cheyenne, in his rage, even raised his horsewhip against the medicine man, but the others dissuaded him from this retaliation. Isatai slunk off unharmed, but his medicine was no longer in demand among the tribes.

Smarting from their defeat, the war-party started for the plains. Meeting a family of travellers, they killed the elders and took four daughters captive. In due time the soldiers came into action — by autumn, that is. They came from four different directions and four different commands, with the usual crop of confusing technicalities.

After months they brought something like peace to the southern plains. One by one, during the winter and spring, the chiefs with their villages came in to surrender and were held as prisoners of war by the soldiery. On March 6 the main body surrendered to Miles.

Satanta and Big Tree had been taken under guard before this. Satanta was sent back to Texas, where a few years later he committed suicide by throwing himself from the window of the prison hospital. Big Tree was held at Fort Sill during the troubles; when released, he proved that he had learned his lesson by settling down and adopting the ways of the white man.

It was decided to send the ringleaders in this little war away as prisoners. Thirty-three who were identified as the perpetrators of specific crimes, were selected for exile. On an appointed day the Indians were lined up, but when afternoon was come only fifteen had been marked out for removal. The officer in charge selected eighteen more at random, as a sort of hostage, intending on the next day to exchange these for some of the identified criminals.

Tomorrow was too late. As they were fixing handcuffs upon one of the young braves, he was stung to rebellion by the taunts of a squaw nearby. He knocked over the guard who was beside him. Instantly all was turmoil. The prisoner was shot and one of the guards was wounded. The Indians had by no means surrendered all their arms when giving themselves up to the soldiers.

The braves fled to a nearby sandhill where for hours they stood off three companies of cavalry. Then night came, and the Indians made their escape. Three or four hundred of them took their way northward to join the northern Cheyenne and the hostile Sioux. The most warlike of the bands had already gone in that direction.

The thirty-three who had been set aside for deportation were sent to Fort Marion, Florida, the old Spanish fort near Saint Augustine, the scene of Osceola's capture a generation before. Lone Wolf, chief of the Kiowa, was one of their number. He served his three years on the sandy Atlantic shore.

Oddly enough, from this group of prisoners came the nucleus, a few years later, of an important new movement in Indian education. Lieutenant R. H. Pratt, detailed to take charge of them, busied himself in teaching, with a success that led him, when the three-years' imprisonment was over, to suggest the sending of the younger ones to school at Hampton, Virginia. Their progress here pointed to the possibility of an eastern industrial school. So Carlisle was founded and from some of the most warlike of Indians arose the most peaceful of institutions.

But peace was not yet with the plains tribes. The land below the Arkansas was somewhat quieter after the rebellious Cheyenne had fled to the north. They had transferred the scene of their activities, changing their scene but not their spirit, as the old Roman put it.

v

THERE was welcome for warlike spirits in the North. Red Cloud had made his peace with the white man, but Crazy Horse the Oglala, Gall and Sitting Bull of the Uncpapa, Two Moons the Northern Cheyenne, and other chiefs were patently hostile. The treaty of 1868 had submitted to Red Cloud's condition that the forts along the Bozeman Trail be abandoned and the road leading to them closed.

The noted generals who framed that treaty perhaps thought that although they could not control the Indian, they might be able to control the white man. Six years later it was obvious they could do neither. The march of white settlement was going up the Bozeman Trail just as surely as it had gone down the Ohio and up the Missouri.

The Army itself could not be kept in line with the treaty its leaders had made; for in 1874 General Custer led an exploring expedition to the Black Hills. Soon the word was bruited about that there was gold on their slopes. If it had been difficult before to keep the white man away, it was impossible now.

The Indian Bureau had no realization of the number of hostile Sioux still at large. The Pawnee knew more about the matter for when the hostile bands had fewer white men to disturb them they were able to pay more attention to their Indian foes. The Pawnee agent reported it as a good year that had seen only a half-dozen Sioux raids, and not more than a score or two of his people fallen victim to their ancient enemies.

After a particularly savage and fatal encounter at the buffalo grounds one summer, the Pawnee decided they would not wait for a promised or expected removal to

SITTING BULL

By Courtesy of the Smithsonian Institute

the Indian territory. They began to wander down in that direction by themselves, in small bands. The United States then was awakened to their need and arranged for them the purchase of a reserve west of the Five Tribes. Here the Pawnee were eventually settled. They had been able to help the white man in protecting the advance of the railroad, but for themselves they could find protection only in flight.

Nevertheless, in his report for 1875 the Commissioner of Indian Affairs said quite confidently that the hostile Sioux " could not muster more than three hundred warriors." A year later he had a very different opinion.

The order was issued that these recalcitrant red men, known as Sitting Bull's Band on the Yellowstone, must come in to the agency and be enrolled with the friendly Indians who were receiving their supplies from the government. Forty thousand of the Sioux were being rationed at this time, a pound of beef and a pound of flour daily for each of them. No wonder there was scrambling for these fat contracts.

The beginning of the year 1876 was set as the deadline. The year began, and the hostile Sioux did not come in to enroll. In February the Army took the matter in hand. Sitting Bull, meanwhile, had issued his call. Emissaries went to all the twelve Sioux agencies and to tribes far and near, eastward even to the Chippewa, westward far beyond the Rockies. While most of the tribes as a whole resisted his invitations and his threats, considerable numbers of the Sioux of all the bands and of the more reckless youths of other tribes, found their way to his camp while the blue-coated soldiers were making ready for the campaign.

The Indians called Sitting Bull " the man with the big head and the little heart." Certainly his heart was never bold enough to lead him into battle. But his head was useful enough to ensure a success which broke up all the white man's anticipation of an easy victory. In spite of the Fetterman disaster, in spite of Red Cloud's signal triumph in the removal of the forts, there were still men to echo Fetterman's boast that he " could take eighty men and ride through the whole Sioux Nation." He had ridden to them — but not through. Another band of cavalrymen was to meet a similar fate.

Three lines of soldiers were advancing to round up the warring red men. General Gibbon was marching from the western part of Montana; Crook was coming up from the south; and Custer with his Seventh Cavalry started out to the westward from Fort Abraham Lincoln on the Missouri River. Each commander hoped he might be the one to meet the enemy and win a decisive victory.

Crook's engagement on the Rosebud River with the warriors of Crazy Horse on June 17 was far from a victory. True, he forced the Indians to retreat somewhat from their position and by a hair's breadth he saved his men from falling into an ambuscade that would have meant complete annihilation.

Crook's Crow and Shoshoni helpers, three hundred or more, did valiant service against the hated Sioux. Old Chief Washakie led his Shoshoni ably. But when the Sioux withdrew at the end of two hours' severe fighting, Crook realized that he could not pursue. He must return for supplies and to care for his wounded.

Putting the best face he could upon the matter, it was a drawn engagement. The Sioux and Cheyenne had overcome the usual Indian reluctance for a pitched battle and they had given the white troops a decided check.

General Custer did not know of this engagement when he rode out from the camp on the Powder River a few days later. His orders were to meet General Gibbon on June 26 near the Little Big Horn. He was there a day earlier and met, instead, the great encampment of hostile Indians.

Custer's scouts were Crow and Ree, and his guide was one Mitch Buoyer, half French and half Sioux, who had lived long among the Crow and married among them. The scouts, who were enlisted for spying out the land and not for actual warfare, managed to save themselves when they saw that a battle was impending. Buoyer warned Custer that the hostile village they were approaching was of immense proportions. Custer in reply intimated that Buoyer might, if he wished, retire with the scouts, since he might not want to fight against his own Sioux people. Perhaps Custer counted on rousing the Indian's quick pride. Buoyer stayed and met his fate with the others.

Opinions differ as to the number of hostile Indians engaged in this battle of the Little Big Horn. It was a great village stretching down the valley almost as far as eye could reach. Many years after an Indian investigator said there could have been no more than twelve hundred warriors with their women and children in Sitting Bull's camp. Contemporary and later estimates of white men and of Indian scouts ranged from two to six thousand warriors. Three thousand might be a fair estimate; but even the smallest number was far in excess of those opposed to them.

Custer's force of six hundred or so was divided into three detachments, each isolated from the others during the engagement. Reno and his men, attacking one end of the great Sioux camp, were repulsed and virtually held prisoners on a hill. They knew nothing of what was going on elsewhere. Benteen with the pack trains came up too late to take any part or be of any assistance. Custer, with a few more than two hundred men, rode along the ridge above the river to the attack. A cloud of dusky warriors rose up all about him. Their numbers must have seemed an incredible host to the little band. In half an hour, the tale goes, not one of the soldiers was left alive.

When Gibbon and Terry came up according to the plan they found a deserted camp and a battle-field strewn with mutilated corpses. After a night of rejoicing and dancing the Indians had moved on to the north.

Gall of the Uncpapa Sioux had been the head chief in this battle; Two Moons of the Cheyenne an able lieutenant. Sitting Bull, he of the big head and the little heart, had not been on the battle-field at all. He had been up in the hills making medicine. Yet so shrewd was he that he convinced the Indians it was his medicine making which had won the victory. So his prestige was greatly augmented although his contribution to the battle had given him no moment of danger.

From that time, however, there was a rift between the two Sioux leaders, and though they fled together into Canada when the campaigning of next year proved too hot for them, they were no longer friendly.

Generals Crook and Miles had many a hard march and hard fight in the year that followed the disaster upon the Little Big Horn. The defeat of Crazy Horse in December was the turning point. By the spring of 1877 more than two thousand of the hostile Sioux had come to the Army to be fed. They were willing to promise to settle down at their agencies and fight no longer.

Just above the Canadian border the hostiles still had

their camp. Canada gave them none too warm a welcome and no food at all. They missed the regular issues of beef and flour. These were lean seasons.

One band after another came back to the country of the Long Knives. It was five years before Sitting Bull returned to promise peace.

" Tell them," he said, " that I am the last to give up my rifle."

CHAPTER XVII
The Fires Die Down

I

THE TWO great events of the Nez Percé history
were the coming of Lewis and Clark and the journey of the four messengers to St. Louis to learn of the
white man's Book. But to most people the tribe is
memorable chiefly for the fight and masterly retreat of
Chief Joseph, the year following the battle of the Little
Big Horn. The Nez Percé themselves do not feel that
way about the matter. The greater number of them had
always been proud of their friendly relations with the
white man.

All the headmen of the tribe were signers of the
Stevens Treaty of 1855. The reservation which it gave
them had been made far larger than their needs, with the
design of incorporating upon it the Walla Walla, Cayuse,
and Umatilla. Pio-pio-mox-mox had frustrated this
plan. The Nez Percé were left a great territory along the
tributaries of the Snake River.

But in a few years gold was discovered, with the usual
unhappy results. For a time miners overran the country. Lewiston was settled within the borders of the
reservation. It became necessary to make a new treaty.

In 1863 the agreement was reached which secured to
them a diminished but still rich and ample country, with
a quarter of a million dollars in payment for the land
relinquished. Lawyer, the head chief, signed and many
other leaders with him; but a few held out against it.

Old Joseph had signed in 1855; but he was now gone. His half-Cayuse son Young Joseph was foremost in his opposition to the new boundaries. Henceforth the division of the Nez Percé was between the treaty and the non-treaty party. The latter numbered at most no more than a third of the tribe. They were the group that had always been the "pagans," the "wild Indians," the recalcitrant remnant generally.

The great contention of the non-treaty Nez Percé was with regard to the Wallowa Valley to which they claimed right as a hunting and fishing preserve. They did not wish to live here permanently; the winter season would always see them back on the Clearwater. They did not wish to cultivate the land for they were "Dreamers." Their belief was that it was wrong to insult their mother, the earth, with planting and reaping.

In pursuance of Grant's Peace Policy this claim was favorably considered. An Executive Order in 1873 gave Joseph and his non-treaty Indians the right to live in Wallowa Valley. If the land was to be wholly in the possession of the red men there were a few white settlers who would have to be bought out. Congress failed to make any appropriation for this purpose.

When two years had passed it was apparent that Joseph and his band would not accept the valley as a residence. Permanency of abode was contrary to the tenets of the Dreamers. So the Executive Order was revoked and the word was sent forth that the non-treaty Nez Percé must return to the main reservation.

This they failed to do. As they continued to roam in the Imnaha and Wallowa Valleys relations between them and the white settlers grew more and more strained. A Commission appointed by the President met the bands in council at Lapwai but no satisfactory settlement was reached. The Commission recommended the return of the recalcitrants to the reservation but did not indicate how this might peaceably be brought about.

General Howard, a member of the Commission, was in charge of the Military Department of the Columbia. He was now given the problem of Joseph to solve. Perhaps he thought of his sojourn in the power of the Apache Cochise, when a season's effort resulted in a peace lasting three or four years. Perhaps he thought of General Canby, treacherously shot in the country of the lava beds. Most probably he prayed more fervently than usual and went ahead doing his duty, however hard it might be; for that is the kind of a man he was.

So in April and May he met the non-treaty Nez Percé and the Dreamer band, who were seceded Indians from various northwestern reservations. He counselled with them and told them of the order that had been sent out for him to execute. He rode with Joseph and the other chiefs, Looking-Glass and White Bird, over the long miles from Lapwai to the Kamiah Valley, up hill and down dale, that each might choose a desirable place for himself and his followers.

On May 14 they parted with the promise of the red chiefs that in thirty days they would come in voluntarily to the reservation and accept the locations assigned to them. General Howard's return to Portland, his headquarters, closed a four-hundred-mile journey.

Howard had trusted the Apache, Cochise, and had not been disappointed. Surely, he thought, he could put faith in the promise of a Nez Percé leader. But Joseph was half Cayuse and all Dreamer. The day of the promised removal, June 14, was the day of the beginning of warfare. The intervening month had been spent in drill, in securing ammunition, and in making ready for a departure northward, not to the reservation.

Down on White Bird Creek, sixty miles or more south of the agency, twenty-one settlers, men and women, were attacked and killed, professedly in retaliation for the death of an Indian of Joseph's band at the hands of a settler more than two years before. The few troops that could be mustered at Fort Lapwai were hastily sent to the spot. They met the Indians in White Bird Cañon and were speedily defeated with great loss. The next month, against a larger force on the Clearwater, Joseph was again the victor.

But victory could not bring him peace. The greater number of the Nez Percé had promptly ranged themselves on the side of the whites. At Kamiah, with warfare raging twenty-five miles or so away, Lawyer had formed his people into a company to protect the school and government property there and had brought the employees in safely over the hills to the fort. The reservation had no welcome for Joseph and his allies. They could see no welcome nearer than British Columbia where hostile bands were gathered. This was a thousand miles away, across rugged steeps. They must begin by the passage of the dreaded Lo-lo Trail.

Joseph did not welcome the idea of retreat. He appealed to his people in council.

"What are we fighting for ? Is it for our lives ? No. It is for this land where the bones of our fathers are buried. I do not want to die in a strange land. Stay with me here now and we shall have plenty of fighting. Let us die on our own land."

But the voice of the band was for the northward journey.

Chief Joseph and his followers knew this country well.

The white soldiers were in a strange and difficult land. The Indians had an abundance of ponies and could have fresh mounts at will. The soldiers, having no others to draw on, must take every care of their mounts. General Howard's main body was ere long outdistanced.

A body of hastily assembled settlers was induced by the clever chief to give his people safe passage. Along the Bitter Root Valley the citizens aided the Indians on their way, not so much through sympathy as with a desire to hurry possible trouble along to some more distant location.

General Gibbon's troops, warned of the need, met the Indians in an all day fight. It resulted badly for the white man. After this the retreating hostiles killed the settlers they met. General Sturgis with some exhausted troops met them. They fought him and hastened on their way.

Up in the Bear Paw Mountains Joseph thought he had eluded all pursuit. Another day or two would bring him to the Canadian refuge of Sitting Bull. Joseph had not counted on the telegraph which had brought Miles with fresh soldiers to the attack.

This last blow was the telling one. Joseph surrendered. He promised the surrender of all his followers, but White Bird and his band took advantage of the darkness to escape over the border.

In the Army, the usual wrangle ensued as to the proper distribution of credit for the capture. There was always plenty of fighting, but there never seemed to be glory enough to go round.

Joseph had surrendered with the promise that he would be permitted to return to his own country. Orders from Washington overruled this and sent the band down to the Indian territory. Here for years they suffered from malaria and homesickness and made desperate appeals to be permitted to return to their own country.

In the very month of the outbreak four young men of the Nez Percé proper had gone to Portland and received ordination into the Christian ministry. During these years of exile the tribe sent missionaries and helpers to their brethren in the South. When, in 1885, they were permitted to return, all who had shown themselves no longer hostile came to the Nez Percé reservation. Those who still defied all efforts at civilization, with Chief Joseph at their head, were sent to the Colville reservation in Washington.

Joseph lived for nearly thirty years after his famous war, visiting often the Nez Percé reservation. He became the warm friend of his captor, General Miles. On his trips east he was lionized to his heart's content. He died in 1904.

A year or two ago an attorney for the Nez Percé tribe was discussing in council the various items to be brought up when the tribe should institute suit in the Court of Claims. Royalty on the gold mined by prospectors and miners, mainly Chinese, who swarmed in on the reservation during the sixties, was one of the possibilities. A claim for the relinquishment of the hunting and fishing rights in the Wallowa Valley was mentioned. Even Joseph himself had claimed no title to the land.

When the subject was broached, a descendant of Chief Lawyer rose in protest.

" For the Nez Percé as a whole," he said, " I wish to disclaim any right to the Wallowa Valley. This was a claim of Joseph and his followers, but it was never the claim of my people the Nez Percé. If any money is to be obtained from such a source, we do not wish to share it."

He sat down. There was no word of dissent. The Nez Percé people, proud of their long friendship with the white man and their long adaptation to his ways, had spoken.

II

THE victory over Custer in 1876, the all but triumphant march of Joseph in the following year — little wonder that the Indians of the Northwest were excited. The Bannocks conceived the idea of rousing the tribes of the region to concerted hostility.

The Crow scouts in the service of the United States had temporarily forgotten their enrollment when the Nez Percé went by. It was not Joseph so much as Chief Looking-Glass who enlisted their sympathy. A few years before he had given them notable aid in their perennial warfare with the Sioux. This was a time to return the favor. The Crow remained conveniently blind and deaf to the progress of Looking-Glass and his band.

This, however, was just such surreptitious disobedience as any schoolboy practises. Rebellion was something quite different. Although Buffalo Horn, the Bannock, had been with the Crow at times in their scouting from Fort Custer, he did not win them to his side when he started out on his own little uprising in 1878.

Buffalo Horn had accompanied General Howard in the pursuit of Joseph, and in various subtle ways had been able to hinder the progress of the soldiers. He took umbrage at being refused permission to kill three friendly Nez Percé who had come along as herders. Again he was disgruntled when urged to bring back the horses his fellow Bannock scouts had stolen.

The Bannock returned to their reservation at Fort Hall with the determination to make a campaign that would be even more memorable than that of Joseph. Discontent with the policy of concentration, the irritation of constant minor conflicts between white settlers and little roving bands of Indians, and the racial tradition of warfare, were all factors aiding this resolve.

On their reservation at Fort Hall the Bannock had their own complaint. They shared this great reserve with the Shoshoni, and so long as the proud and warlike Bannock were in the majority they did not object. They roamed as they pleased over the wide country, returning to the agency only for the regular issue of food and clothing and ammunition. But as the concentration policy progressed the quieter Shoshoni came in more and more. Soon they, remaining on the reservation and falling in to a greater extent with the industrial plans of the government, were receiving the larger share of the white man's gifts. The Bannock had to content themselves with stealing from the more favored Shoshoni. They were not content.

They did not count on the Shoshoni as helpers in the war for which they now made preparations. Instead, they sent their messengers far to the west to the Piute and to the roving tribes up toward the Columbia.

The term Piute has always been an indefinite one, applied loosely to many different bands of Indians in and around the Great Basin. They were a very scattered people, often but not invariably Shoshonean in language. As a rule they were not inclined to war.

As emigration came on they gathered on reservations — some at Pyramid Lake or Walker River reservations in Nevada, others at the Malheur reserve in eastern Oregon. One of these little groups produced a remarkable Indian woman who was a leading figure in the Bannock campaign — Sarah Winnemucca.

Sarah Winnemucca's book, " Life Among the Piute," published in 1883, was said by its editor to be " the first outbreak of the American Indian in human literature." Even under the handicap of written instead of spoken language, it breathes that fully Indian, impassioned eloquence which is unfailing in its appeal. Sarah's stories of her people and their needs and wrongs, as she visioned them, were tremendously effective when, after her period as a campaigner, she blossomed out as a lecturer. It was in the capacity of interpreter — for she had been educated by white friends and spoke English fluently — that she joined General Howard's forces against the embattled Bannock and Piute.

Throughout the winter and spring the trouble had been brewing. In June two hundred Bannock braves started out across the Camas Prairie that lay between their reserve and the city of Boise, killing and plundering the settlers as they went. About the same time the Piute on the Malheur reservation took French leave and vanished from the ken of their agent, making their way southeastward. The rendezvous was to be the Juniper or Stein's mountains in southeastern Oregon.

Winnemucca's band, the group of Piute who gave their allegiance to Sarah's father, had gone with the rest. Sarah herself had not been at the agency when they left. She came to General Howard and told him she believed she could make her way to the hostile camp and bring out the Piute. She felt that many of them had gone under duress.

The General promised her a reward if she should carry out her plan. With two friendly Piute men she started over the mountains to the hostile camp.

Buffalo Horn, the Bannock, did not live to reach the rendezvous. At South Mountain, in Idaho, he and his

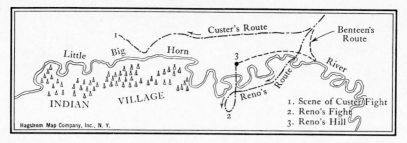

IX. SCENE OF CUSTER'S ENGAGEMENT, JUNE 25, 1876

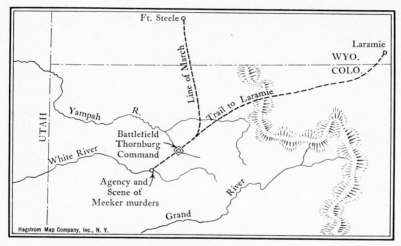

X. SCENE OF UTE OUTBREAK, 1879

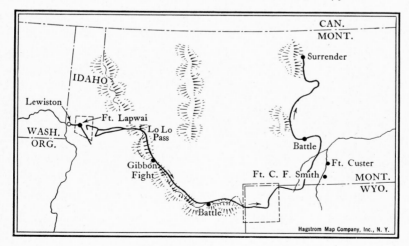

XI. RETREAT OF CHIEF JOSEPH

band met a party of volunteer citizens. Napoleon's definition of a battle as two bodies of men trying to frighten each other seems to apply admirably to this engagement. A scout, Piute Joe, claimed the credit for the death of Buffalo Horn. The Bannock braves hurried on to the mountains and the volunteers fell over one another getting back to their homes.

To the camp of Bannock and Piute in the rugged mountains came Sarah Winnemucca, disguising herself in blanket and warpaint and mingling with the hostile Indians. She made her way to her father's camp and they laid a plan for the escape of his band. Seventy-five of them secretly left the hostile headquarters and fled for protection to the Army.

" I went for the government," says Sarah in her book, "when the officers could not get an Indian man or a white man to go for love or money. I, only an Indian woman, went and saved my father and his people." It was boastfully said; but it was none the less true.

Egan of the Piute was now chief of the hostiles, with Oytes the Dreamer as his chief coadjutor. Egan had before this fought against General Crook. His great resource was not open battle, but sudden foray and quick retreat. The difficulty would be not to conquer him but to overtake him.

Egan made for the Umatilla reservation for reinforcements. Many of the Umatilla and other tribes of this reserve had listened to the promises and prophecies of the Dreamers. Egan himself had not been entirely convinced but he had seen the wisdom of fighting.

The Army fed its captured people without labor, while the Indian Bureau was trying to make the Indians do some cultivation of the soil in return for their rations. Before leaving Malheur reservation Egan had said that he did not expect to conquer the whites but he would fight as long as he could. Then he thought the Great Father in Washington would give him more supplies and would no longer try to make his people work.

Egan was not to benefit by this foresight. The soldiers overtook and repulsed his men at Umatilla. Seeing which way the wind was blowing, the hostile people of that jurisdiction, Umatilla, Cayuse, and Columbia tribesmen, decided to make their peace with the military. They even showed their friendliness by making war on Egan's people.

" In fact," their agent reports, " they showed their animosity to the hostiles by doing more damage to them while in the vicinity of the reservation than was done by all the troops that fought them during the campaign."

Their chief, Umpaine, now offered to go out after his erstwhile friend Egan. He returned with the bloody head and his people had a dance of rejoicing about the pole on which they impaled it.

The remainder of the campaign was a series of pursuits of scattered small bands until they were willing to surrender. As General Howard said, his purpose was not to kill them but to hive them, as in his boyhood he had seen his father gather in a swarm of bees. One by one the bands came in and went to their destined places.

The trouble with the Sheep-Eaters, the following year, was the last of it. These were a mixed band of Bannock, Cayuse, Umatilla, and Piute Indians, hiding in the mountains and depending upon the mountain sheep for food and clothing. When they had surrendered the Department of the Columbia was fairly well pacified.

Under orders from headquarters Army officers took the Piute to join the Indians on the Yakima reservation in the State of Washington. The Piute had objected to

Malheur agency; but they liked the new location even less.

Sarah Winnemucca became the spokesman for her tribe. First in California, then in the East, she lectured to audiences who were thrilled by her pathetic appeals.

Sarah praised the Army, but attacked the Indian agents with eloquent fervor. She won great popular approval, riding on the crest of the tidal wave. The Secretary of the Interior wrote her a grudging and somewhat evasive permission for her people to return to Malheur, but as no means of transportation was offered the journey proved impracticable. It was discouraged by those on the spot, who knew that a departure without funds or supplies would bring about further depredations and renewed warfare. Eventually, however, they slipped off and made their way to their own country, band by band.

III

THE UTE had always been a restless and warlike people, but settlement had not come very close to their mountain country until the days of the Pike's Peak rush for gold. There were several divisions of these people, some much more amenable to ideas of advancement than others. The southern group, along the western part of the border between New Mexico and Colorado, had profited much by their contact with New Mexican settlement. They had opposed the idea of leaving when a treaty fixed the great body of the Ute reservation farther to the north.

The White River Ute, whose reservation this Colorado land was supposed to be, did not wish to stay upon the great tract reserved for them, though it was rich in soil and in forest and game. It would serve them as a place to receive their liberal annuities and as a point of departure for trips. So they continued to roam, hunting or visiting with the tribes to the north and west.

So little did they stay at their agency on the White River that no trading post had been established there. They went off their reservation to traders' stores in western Colorado and in Utah where they could exchange the annuity goods furnished by the Great White Father for firearms and whiskey. They were thoroughly unconvinced of the power of the white man and considered these annual gifts as a tribute exacted by their own superior prowess. In this they were not far from right.

There had been various treaties with the different Ute bands. From among their leaders Ouray, one of the southern group, had been designated as head chief of the tribe. Ouray had been a friend of Kit Carson. He was on good terms with the Mexican people and had aided the whites in many ways. So far as the untamed Ute recognized a head, he was the head man, a natural leader. His own advancement in the ways of the white man was considerable, and the Indians most in contact with him were far more receptive to new ways than their tribesmen to the north.

In the latter seventies there came as agent to these turbulent people on the White River one N. C. Meeker, a man in his sixties, a veteran journalist who had been the mainspring of Greeley's famous dictum " Go west, young man ! " He had been a leading spirit in the founding of the Greeley colony in Colorado, and was an enthusiast about the country and its agricultural possibilities. He set devotedly to work at his task of introducing the White River Ute to tillage.

The White River Ute required no lessons along this

line. They had never cultivated the soil and had no intention of learning to do so. While game roamed in the mountains and generous gifts came at regular intervals from the government, there would be no need to spur their intentions. Furthermore, they would not submit to having the ground plowed by anyone else.

In the late summer of 1879 the agency farmer started on some fall plowing. He was threatened by two Indians with guns. When he returned to his field the next day a shot from a nearby cluster of sage-brush barely missed him.

Shortly after Agent Meeker himself was assaulted and injured by one of the chiefs of the band. There were two of these head men, Douglas and Johnson. They were constantly in dispute with each other, but were as one in their opposition to the plans of the government.

In this remote country the only approach by road was from the north, the nearest fort being over the Wyoming border. Here, at Fort Steele, Major Thornburgh was in charge. All during this year, from time to time, word had come to him of depredations committed by Ute parties here and there; but he could not take action until his orders came from Washington.

This was frontier country indeed; the last stand of the lawless element that is always to be found on the borderland of civilization. Consequently there were greedy traders who were glad to profit by Ute trade and indifferent to the ill results that might flow from the unhampered use of rum and revolvers. There were border roughs of various types, cattle rustlers, outlaws, and renegades, who found the Ute both an aid and a cover in their own illicit farings. The situation was not a simple one. Situations seldom are.

But when Chief Johnson assaulted him and drove him

from his home, Agent Meeker knew that more was needed than his unarmed authority. He sent messengers out to the railroad with a telegram which, dated September 10, reached Washington late on Saturday the thirteenth. It was a striking illustration of the difficulties under which he and many another Indian agent had to labor, meeting urgent necessities by long distance appeals rather than action.

On Monday morning the War Department telegraphed Major Thornburgh to proceed to White River. On the twenty-fifth of September he sent a messenger ahead to the agency to ascertain the situation and to advise of his arrival in four days more.

Ute chiefs met the command on Bear River and advised Thornburgh that he should not take in his troops. They insisted that he encamp, and himself go on to the agency with a guide and no more than five of his soldiers. To this he agreed but maintained that his instructions did not leave him liberty to halt his troops at so great a distance. Accordingly, he would march within twenty-five miles of the agency and there leave his force.

Their way led through a narrow cañon which they entered on the morning of the twenty-ninth. Not fewer than a hundred armed Indians sprang from concealment and fell upon them. Major Thornburgh and several others were killed in the retreat to the baggage train. Hastily using the wagons for breastworks, the remainder defended themselves as best they could against a continuous fire rained upon them by assailants from the bluffs all about them. Here they were held until the second of October, when a company of colored troops relieved them.

A swift runner from the Indians brought the news of this morning encounter to the waiting Ute warriors

around the agency by afternoon. This was their signal
for attack upon the defenceless agency employees.
Every man was killed and all the buildings burned to the
ground. Agent Meeker's wife and daughter, and the
wife and children of one of the employees, were carried
off into a captivity that was a long, hideous agony.

When, by the fifth of October, an adequate force of
troops had reached the scene, they found only dead
bodies and the ashes of the agency buildings. The Ute
band had helped itself to all the agency goods in the
warehouse and had fled the spot.

It was Chief Ouray who came to the rescue. He and
his people were about to start on a long hunt when he
heard of the disaster. He changed his plans and issued
an order commanding the peaceable to stay at home and
the White River band to cease from their hostilities.

His order was obeyed. Ouray sent an escort to attend
a special agent, General Charles Adams, who went to
demand the return of the captive women and children
and the surrender of the perpetrators of the agency outbreak. Adams brought back the pitiful captives, but no
culprits were given up. After months of parleying,
Douglas, the chief who had headed the attackers on the
agency, was surrendered. He suffered a year's imprisonment at Fort Leavenworth.

The remainder of the band was given a reservation in
Utah, where the Uintah and Uncompahgre Ute were
already domiciled. The relinquishment of their Colorado lands put a large sum of money into the tribal
treasury so that their annual payments were larger than
ever. Liberal provision was made for improvements and
benefits at their new home in Utah. In general their
misbehavior had been a source of much profit and
emolument.

After such a lesson it is not surprising that a generation later found the White River Ute still rebellious, still ready to threaten the warpath though not actually entering upon it. Nor is it surprising that today they are notably the least advanced of all their people, clinging to the smoky wickiup while the Uintah and Uncompahgre dwell in neat homes.

Ouray died the following year. But the impetus he had given his people was by no means lost. Today the southern Ute, in the southwestern corner of Colorado, afford, on their irrigated farms, a striking contrast to the hunters and warriors of fifty years ago.

IV

IT WILL be recalled that after the death of Cochise and his eldest son the policy of concentration had untoward results down on the Chiricahua reservation. Geronimo and Natchez had taken southward flight. From a more northern Apache reservation, the Ojo Caliente, a band under Vittorio, had similarly decamped. Now in Mexico and now in the United States, the Apache under these leaders made life sufficiently miserable for both nations. They knew every nook and corner in their rugged country. They had little difficulty in living by a series of raids upon villages and wagon trains, eluding every attempt at capture.

Now and then, however, it was good policy to surrender and be entertained for a time at one of the reservations. Geronimo was particularly adept at this form of diplomacy. After his first flight into Mexico he and his band returned to Ojo Caliente and, being apprehended, settled down peaceably for a time on the San Carlos

OURAY

By Courtesy of the Smithsonian Institute

GERONIMO

By Courtesy of the Smithsonian Institute

reservation. In 1882 he led a raid into Mexico, until captured by General Crook, when he came back again to San Carlos.

Two years later he was off again for more extensive raids and depredations. His base of operations was in the Sierra Madre mountains below the Mexican border. His attentions to both nations in the matters of forays was quite impartial. Mexico and the United States had an agreement to co-operate in capturing the Apache raiders — or rather in trying to do so.

Vittorio had been killed by Mexican troops before this time, and Nana, his successor, was an old man. Geronimo, however, was in the prime of life; and Natchez, younger son of Cochise, was an unusually vigorous and stalwart young raider and warrior.

General Crook enlisted supposedly friendly Apache companies to aid in the pursuit of the hostile ones. Divided so as to follow the scattered bands, they made brave marches and advances. Here they gathered a few prisoners, there they scattered and dispersed a marauding band. But it was a weary task.

The story of the march of Captain Crawford's company of Apache scouts into Mexico was a tragedy of errors. Two lieutenants, a quartermaster, an assistant surgeon, and the hundred Indian scouts made up the battalion which left Fort Apache in November 1885.

The first conflict was between the scouts and the peace officers of a Mexican village. One death resulted and a fine was paid by the captain to get his Apache scout out of jail. The next trouble was a visit from the United States Marshal. Dutchy, one of the scouts, was wanted for a peculiarly cold-blooded murder of a white man up in Arizona. Neither the Captain nor the Marshal was in a position to quell the rebellion that Dutchy's arrest would occasion. So they wisely decided to defer action until they had come back to the vicinity of white settlements.

They now struck the trail of the hostiles and laboriously followed it up the difficult mountain passes. When they reached the camp, however, it was deserted. They found there only an old woman who indicated that Geronimo and Natchez were willing to enter into a parley.

Next morning they were attacked, not by Indians, but by a company of Mexicans who mistook the scouts for hostile Apache. Lieutenant Maus, who spoke Spanish, was able to bring about a cessation of hostilities. He was making explanation when another body of Mexicans came up.

Directions not to fire were shouted out, in both Spanish and English. But a shot was fired, none the less, and in a moment there was a general volley from both sides. There were two hours of fighting before further explanations could be made.

All the Mexican officers were dead and Captain Crawford was mortally wounded. The Mexicans were still distinctly resentful, even after explanations, and the next day tried to resume the fight. The Apache scouts were more than willing to do so and it was with difficulty that the Lieutenant managed to restrain them.

The next day, according to request, the Lieutenant went unarmed to meet Geronimo, Natchez, Nana, and Chihuahua, Apache chiefs, who came to the meeting with fourteen of their men, all fully armed and with their belts full of ammunition. The hostile Apache proposed to surrender as they had done on previous occasions, keeping all their plunder. The Lieutenant was scarcely in a position to make more favorable terms.

They begged of him and got some sugar and flour.

But from the Apache scouts the hostiles bought a good supply of ammunition at a dollar a pound.

The way back was beset with many difficulties. At the Mexican town of Bavispe, Maus found it hard to avoid encounter between the local troops and his scouts, who were excited by large draughts of the native *mescal*. The next battle was among the scouts themselves, part of whom were White Mountain Apache and part Chiricahua. The Mexican drink revived their ancient antagonisms.

Geronimo and his hostiles had been coming along at the rear of the Army party in order to have a parley with General Crook. The next fight was to their credit, *mescal* again furnishing the match for the explosion. There was firing in their camp all night and Natchez shot his wife.

Geronimo told General Crook, when they met, that he would come in on condition that the band go east for not more than two years. He was in a position to dictate the terms of the agreement. They were fifteen miles below the border, well armed, well supplied with ammunition, in a camp on a rocky hill that was a natural fortress. Only a few Apache came in sight at any time, but others were on hand and watchful. They had come thus far voluntarily and were as free as ever. They would come farther on their own terms or not at all.

General Crook told them to come in and telegraphed his decision to Washington. Three days later he received an answer saying that only unconditional surrender would be acceptable to the President. Meanwhile Geronimo and Natchez had tired of waiting and had decamped with thirty-five of their followers.

Crook was tired, too, when he received the telegram

from headquarters. He asked to be relieved from command of the department.

General Miles, who came to succeed him, adopted the plan of spreading his men in small detachments all over the Territories of Arizona and New Mexico. When Geronimo and his men came in on a raid they would be pursued by one group. Having safely eluded that one they found to their surprise that their trail was taken up by another.

General Miles in his story of the summer's campaign credits most of its success to the use of the heliostat, a device for signalling from station to station by means of sunlight flashed upon mirrors. Thousands of messages were sent from one to another of the twenty-seven stations he set up.

The General also became convinced that the assemblage of Indians at Fort Apache was a menace to the country. They were denominated prisoners of war, but were neither dismounted nor disarmed. They could transform themselves into warriors at any moment. Good judgment dictated that their capacity for trouble-making be reduced. After endless negotiations, dispatches, delegations, and discussions, the General was authorized to send them east for a term of years. They were entrained for Fort Marion in Florida.

When, next autumn, Geronimo came in for his regular gesture of surrender, he was amazed to learn that there were no more of his people at Fort Apache. An exhibition of the powers of the heliostat added to his astonishment. He sent out a runner to Natchez at once.

"There is something here I cannot understand; come in, and come quickly."

Natchez and his group soon came; and before long the last of the hostiles was on his way to Florida. Later, these Apache were removed to Fort Sill, Oklahoma, the country of the Kiowa and Comanche. Here they or their descendants live today, still officially designated as prisoners of war.

v

TECUMSEH had his Prophet; Chief Joseph his Dreamer; and from time to time there would arise in this tribe or that a new seer, with another vision of the triumph of the red man over all his adversaries. The Messiah craze which swept the country in 1889 and 1890 was not unlike others that had gone before. Under normal conditions it might have subsided harmlessly or calmed down into a religious manifestation of a fairly conventional sort, like the "Shaker" churches that are to be found today among some of the tribes in Washington and Oregon.

The craze, unfortunately, coincided with a period of unrest among the Sioux; and the combination of dissatisfaction and prophetic frenzy wrought both red man and white to a pitch of excitement where anything might happen, and far too much did.

Over the Rockies came the story that a Piute medicine man had seen great visions. Wovoka or Jack Wilson, a young and personable fellow whose boyhood had been spent much in the company of the family of a white rancher, was much affected by an eclipse of the sun coinciding in time with a serious illness. In his delirium he visited the spirit world, bringing back with him the message of a coming day when the glory of the red man should revive. The old mighty leaders would come back, bringing with them the vanished hordes of buffalo and troops of wild horses only waiting for the lariat.

To bring this about it was necessary for all to join

with fervor in dancing, six days at each time of the new moon, making invocation for the return of the spirits. In due time the reward would come.

The Piute danced; and the neighboring tribes caught the infection. Away off in Oklahoma Cheyenne and Arapaho heard the news and sent a delegation of inquiry to the Shoshoni. They returned convinced of the imminence of the Messiah. Eastward the word spread. In due time it reached the Sioux agency at Standing Rock and the camp on Grand River where Sitting Bull sat in sullen gloom, regretting his diminished state and power.

This looked to him like an opportunity. Sitting Bull's people began to dance.

There were seven of these Sioux reserves, immense in size still, though diminished by a recent treaty. Three stretched along the South Dakota-Nebraska border line, west to east — Pine Ridge, Rosebud, and Yankton east of the Missouri. Up the Missouri, where it turns sharply west, was the Crow Creek agency. Above that, but still on the river, were the huge twin jurisdictions, Cheyenne River and Standing Rock. Apart from the others and farther east was the home of the Sisseton Sioux. All these great reserves were in South Dakota, but Standing Rock, the northernmost, straddled the dividing line and spread its bulk in North Dakota too. It was just at the time of the division of Dakota Territory into two states.

On Standing Rock agency the ghost dancing was confined to Sitting Bull and his band. The greater number of the Sioux were slow to be infected. The farmer party by now was in the ascendancy and the missionaries had many sincere followers. Nevertheless, the new idea made a strong appeal to the deepest instincts of the Indian heart. The white man watched the manifestation with growing apprehension

The craze was at its height at Pine Ridge. The Indian agent became alarmed. The Army was asked to take charge. Newspapers all over the country began to fan the fires with highly colored accounts of the frenzied dancers, the wild excitement, the burning prophecies. At this distance it seems that the white man was quite as susceptible to fantastic rumor as the red man. All through the autumn of 1890 the situation grew more and more tense.

Various causes had made a large party among the Sioux more discontented than usual. Crops had been poor; rations had been somewhat scanted this year from the million dollars' worth that had been previously distributed; the Indians resented a census which had disclosed their real numbers and consequently reduced the issues to some bands whose accounts had been padded successfully before that time. The opponents of the recent treaty, although a minority, were a substantial and vocal minority. The summer had brought grasshoppers and the winter was bringing an epidemic of that new and fatal ailment which men called *la grippe*.

Altogether, it was time to dance in the millenium. Groups of Sioux from other reservations began to slip away to Pine Ridge and to the Bad Lands. It was rumored that a general uprising was at hand. The newspapers quaked with terror.

Late in the fall the Army sent Colonel Cody — Buffalo Bill — to arrest Sitting Bull. The old chief had travelled America and Europe with Buffalo Bill's Wild West Show and had a friendly feeling for its proprietor. Major McLaughlin, the Standing Rock Indian agent, begged for delay. He felt that arrest would be the precipitation of trouble; he hoped that the advent of a bitter Dakota winter would discourage dancing about a pole in the open. But December came and the recalcitrants on Grand River were still dancing and seeing visions.

His faithful Indian police, many of whom had also been in the tours of the Wild West show, brought Agent McLaughlin the word that Sitting Bull and his people were preparing to slip away to the Bad Lands. Thirty-nine of these loyal Sioux went out to Grand River to arrest and bring in the old medicine man. White soldiers were to attend at a distance.

On a grey, cold morning, the fifteenth of December, they reached the house of the old leader. He did not protest but delayed long while his two wives assembled his best clothing. When he emerged from his doorway, a hundred and fifty of his followers, well armed, were crowded around.

Sitting Bull was still " the man with the big head and the little heart." He did not resist; but his son Crow Foot was a youth of more fire than wisdom. He shouted a taunt to his father. It was a call to battle. Guns flashed almost simultaneously. Sitting Bull fell and so did two of the Indian police, Lieutenant Bull Head and Sergeant Shave Head.

In the *mêlée* which followed the loyal Indian police stood their ground bravely, repelling attack though six of their number fell as the morning wore on. When the white soldiers finally came, they were masters of the situation. The unwounded drew themselves up for formal salute, proud to have done their duty.

Two weeks later the bands in the Bad Lands surrendered at Wounded Knee Creek. Told to give up their arms they offered a few guns. A crazy boy, so the

Indians maintained, fired the first shot. No one stopped to investigate; the shooting became general in a moment. When the fighting was over there were a hundred and fifty dead Indians strewn along the way of their flight. The troopers had twenty-five dead and thirty-five wounded.

It was a strange chance by which Custer's old command, the Seventh Cavalry, was thus the instrument for a bloody revenge for the defeat of fourteen years before. It was a last chance as well. Never again have the Sioux gone upon the warpath. A summer or two ago they all furbished up their automobiles and drove over the Custer National Highway to the Black Hills to welcome the President of the United States as an adopted member of their tribe.

CHAPTER XVIII
The Red Man at School

I

A CENTURY of Indian warfare died down with the passing of the Messiah craze. After the fight at Wounded Knee Creek General Miles pressed the often repeated recommendation that the Indians, and especially the Sioux, should be turned over entirely to the jurisdiction of the War Department.

The time had gone by for a decision in his favor. Too many non-warlike activities were already being prosecuted by the Indian Bureau. Too strong and too vocal had public opinion become as to the need for pacifying and civilizing the Indian. There had once been a body of two-fisted citizens who insisted that the only way to solve the Indian problem was to exterminate the Indian. They had had their day and it was over. The tidal wave of sympathy for the red man was at its height.

All during the century of conflict there had been a less noticed current of honest endeavor toward the education of the Indian and his adaptation to the changes he would inevitably meet. Even while the Revolution was in progress Congress remembered Dartmouth College, which had been started in pursuance of the colonial plan for Indian education, and voted money for the training of Indian boys there.

But during the first three quarters of the nineteenth century such government appropriations as had been made for Indian education had been passed over for use to one or another of the many missionary bodies. These had worked diligently in many different tribes and with varying results.

Joseph Brant, in the days before the Revolution, had gone to a mission school kept by the Reverend Eleazar Wheelock. Sequoyah of the Cherokee had gained his impetus toward learning from long association with a devoted missionary to his people. Faithful converts among the Minnesota Sioux had carried their mission friends to safety when the storm of massacre broke in 1862; just as earlier, in the far Northwest, friendly Nez Percé had protected Mrs. Spalding and her little ones when the Cayuse rose to slaughter the mission group at Waiilatpu. It is even said that the scanty English Chief Joseph knew was learned from Mrs. Spalding in his almost baby days, before his Cayuse kinsmen carried him off to the wild life.

All across the continent there was a trail of sincere endeavor and worthy accomplishment as well as a pathway of blood and struggle. But the Indians who welcomed instruction rather than battle were the happy people who had no history. Few troubled to tell the outside world of the combats with the three R's and the victories of soap and scrubbing brush.

In 1819, when Congress began the appropriation of a definite sum yearly for Indian education, the President directed that the plan of education, in addition to the usual subjects, should include " the practical knowledge of the mode of agriculture and such of the mechanic arts as are suited to the condition of the Indian." He also contemplated that the girls should be instructed in " spinning, weaving, and sewing." For many years after this time, however, the money was not expended directly by the government, but was distributed among various mission schools for their support.

With the new policy of 1870 came an increasing interest in education and greatly augmented appropriations for the purpose. By this time the government had started boarding-schools on Indian reservations here and there. A system that was no system at all was growing up. In some places the missions owned the schools and the Indian Bureau paid the teachers. Sometimes the government supplied the plant and the church boards the service. Sometimes the government paid tuition for Indian pupils at a mission school.

There was no supervision over either processes or results. The frequent good results were due to devoted and fine individuals rather than to the encouragement they received from outside, either moral or financial.

As government appropriations grew — and they did grow steadily during the last quarter of the century — the conviction gained power that the schools supported by public moneys should be wholly governmental institutions; while the mission schools should be completely supported and managed by their churches. The American theory of the division between church and state was to have a new field of application.

The change dragged out over decades, but in time it was accomplished. Some of the churches united in a self-denying ordinance and refused longer to accept government funds for their schools. Others were inclined to hold on to the bitter end. They even went to the length of court action when Congress finally passed a law that no more funds should be supplied to denominational schools.

Indian affairs have always been complicated with fine-drawn interpretations and decisions. The Supreme

Court of the United States finally decided that Congress could rightfully refuse to bestow gratuity appropriations upon religious bodies. Yet the Indian tribes, if they possessed funds held in trust for them by the government, might request that such funds be appropriated for use in mission schools. Accordingly there are to be found today, scattered variously over the country, a score or more denominational institutions where Indian tribal funds are received each year for the support and education of the pupils. With these exceptions, however, the mission schools are supported by their various denominations, while the government schools are maintained apart from any religious organization.

Among most of the tribes, particularly among the plains Indians, boarding-schools were at first the only feasible method of training. An Indian village was too movable an institution. Its youthful inhabitants might come to school today and tomorrow be in a distant county. Even during a period of semi-permanency it was apparent to the teachers of an earlier day that a few hours of instruction were insufficient to cope with the influence of tepee life, the dirt, the idleness, the incitements to savage ways. Twenty-four hours were few enough to eradicate the backward pull of such conditions. Day schools must await the period when life among the elders had attained a greater degree of stability.

They were a motley lot in those early Indian boarding-schools on the reservations. They were young and old, grown men almost at the warrior stage perhaps stumbling with their first unaccustomed English words. The missionaries often taught " in the vernacular," but after long and tense discussion this was abandoned in favor of instruction in English. The Indian resisted this change as he did all others.   Primitive and conservative are all but synonymous.

II

THE HEAVY walls of the old Spanish fort at Saint Augustine do not hint at educational enterprise.   Yet it was here that a plan was evolved which had vast effects upon Indian youth.

Lieutenant R. H. Pratt was in charge of the prisoners sent from the reservation of Cheyenne, Arapaho, and Kiowa in the Indian territory, to this far-off post, in the seventies.   He and Mrs. Pratt busied themselves in giving instruction to those of the prisoners who were capable and willing.   When the three year sentence was at an end a number of the younger men were willing to stay in the East for further training.

Philanthropic friends were interested with the result that these young students were entered at Hampton, Virginia, where had been established an admirable industrial school for freedmen.   Here the Indians were successful enough to suggest and justify a widening of opportunity.   With the permission of the authorities Pratt visited the Sioux reservations and enrolled a number of students, both boys and girls, for instruction at Hampton.

At Carlisle in Pennsylvania was an old Army barracks.   The western settlements of Pennsylvania no longer listened apprehensively for the sound of the war-whoop.   For a long lifetime the Iroquois had ceased from troubling, and Shawnee and Delaware were far to the westward.   The idle plant suggested something to the eager mind of Lieutenant Pratt.   He borrowed the place and opened an Indian boarding-school.   More

CHIRICHUA APACHE
as they arrived from Fort Marion, Florida, November 4, 1885

THE SAME CHILDREN
Four months after arriving at Carlisle

than two hundred children were the pupils in that first year of 1879–80. They represented many different tribes but were chiefly from the Dakotas and from the western tribes of the Indian territory.

Indian boarding-schools were not new. Industrial training was not new. The real innovation at Carlisle was in the fact that it was the first Indian school established away from any Indian tribe or reservation. The great educating force was to be the contact with a new environment.

"To civilize the Indian," was the slogan, "put him in the midst of civilization. To keep him civilized, keep him there." General Pratt — as he later became — was to repeat that slogan many times, in the course of a long life.

Even more than the school itself, the "outing system" aided in introducing the pupils to the ways of the white man. Those who were apt and trustworthy were employed in the homes of the surrounding country, learning at first hand American farm and domestic methods. These were lessons that left a lasting effect.

Twenty years ago, at the remote Hopi village known as Oraibi, there was a small but vigorous little rebellion against the inauguration of a day school for the children of the village. Some of the offenders were removed. Instead of suffering imprisonment they were shipped to Pennsylvania, where under the supervision of Carlisle school they were put out to work in neighboring communities. Their two or three years of eastern farming sent them back to their sunbaked mesa with an entirely new outlook on life whose results may be seen even yet.

But Carlisle was no institution of punishment though

its routine was military and its rule strict. Nor, on the other hand, was it the college many people imagined because its pupils played football with Varsity teams. During the thirty-eight years of the school's existence Carlisle offered school work of no higher grade than a junior high school.

But Carlisle gave its pupils far more than formal education — training in industry, habituation to the ways that made for useful and worthy living. Today one may trace in the adult Indians of many scattered tribes the good results of the impetus General Pratt's ideas gave to Indian education.

But good things pass as well as ill. For a time the example of Carlisle set legislators and administrators to establishing non-reservation schools here and there throughout the country, and the idea flourished apace. After a time the impulse died down, to be succeeded by the theory that education must go to the Indian in his home. The red man must be trained with the idea of remaining always in the environment of his birth. A new commissioner arose, who knew not Carlisle, and his enthusiasm was all for attaching the Indian to his soil.

When America went to war, a dozen years ago, it proved convenient to return to the War Department the plant which it had lent to the Indian Service a generation before. So vanished Carlisle school, which in its day had been the embodiment of a new hope for Indian advancement.

General Pratt, then retired, saw the change with regret. He felt, as did many others, that a valuable link between the white man and the red had been broken when this outpost in the East went back to martial uses. In the half-dozen years which remained of his life he

was wont to dwell more and more upon the work which
had absorbed so long a period of his active days.

A librarian in an Indian school in Oklahoma had a
letter from a friend in Washington.

" Perhaps," she read, " you may know of an old gentleman who has an apartment in the same building in
which I live. He is always talking about Indians. His
name is Pratt."

In fancy one sees the white hair, the spare figure, the
keen eyes, the hand raised for emphasis. One hears
the voice:

" To civilize the Indian, put him in the midst of civilization. To keep him civilized, keep him there."

III

IN 1890 Commissioner of Indian Affairs T. J. Morgan
broached the project of permitting Indian children to
attend the public schools in the communities in which
they lived. His belief was that in this way, by association with white children, they would much more rapidly
acquire the ways and the language of the white race.
In order to meet the objection that Indians, as non-
taxpayers, did nothing toward the support of the public
schools, he proposed a tuition fee to be paid by the government for each Indian boy or girl attending.

In most of the states there was a satisfactorily enthusiastic response to the suggestion. The State Superintendent of Oregon, in his reply, told of cases under his
observation in which Indian children had been educated
in public schools and had taken their place in the life
of the state as creditably as any members of the white
race.

California, Washington, North and South Dakota,

and Minnesota added their commendation and promised their support. Only from Arizona came a dissenting voice. It was but four years since the last surrender of Geronimo, and small roving Apache bands were still a menace to the unwary traveller or the remote settler. The Superintendent of Public Instruction for the Territory sent announcement of Commissioner Morgan's letter to all his school districts, " assuming," as he said, " that the proposition was made in all seriousness." The response was a various one.

Many of the districts contented themselves with pointing out that there were no Indian families within their limits. A district in Cochise County added to this information " and hope never to come in contact with them or their parents." Remembering Cochise, Geronimo, Natchez, Vittorio, this was a not unnatural desire. Another district in the same county made the rather cryptic promise: " Should any come into our district we will endeavor to take care of them."

Tuba City reported itself as "willing to make arrangements," but added: " The main difficulty seems to be that the parents of the white children cannot afford to let their children go with the Indians, unless the Indian children are cleaned up. They are very low in their habits; they wear little or no clothing at all, except a gee string, and all are very filthy and lousy. They would have to be provided a change of clothing and their dinners when they come to school."

The Superintendent himself echoed the sentiments of Maricopa County: " We have more respect for our children than to think of educating them in such a mixed school." He told Commissioner Morgan that it was time to dispel the " mists of hysteria and maudlin sentimentalism " with which the Indian question was surrounded, and that justice to the white settler was the first necessity. He quoted with burning indignation an article by the Commissioner which said that " The Indians will not go to war except for just reasons. . . An Indian war is very often the expression of the highest manhood."

" Can it be possible," the Superintendent exclaims with biting sarcasm, " that you would permit the budding infant minds of these poor victims of the white man's avarice and barbarity to mingle with the cubs of their oppressors ? Would there not be danger of our instilling into them some of our own fiendish proclivities ? We might teach them how to steal, lie, debauch, and murder, or even to like fire-water and the noxious weed, accomplishments that, according to the same article, are now confined to the villainous white pioneer."

These fulminations serve to show what development fewer than forty years have brought about among both whites and Indians. The peace of Arizona has been long unbroken. The shadow of Geronimo and his band no longer broods on the trails. Indian children attend the public schools there as elsewhere.

Today more than half of the seventy thousand children of Indian blood who are receiving school training are side by side with white children in the public schools. In some sections, where Indian non-taxable lands make up a great deal of the school district, tuition fees are paid by the government. In others the Indians are by agreement or by virtue of their status as taxpayers, as welcome in the public schools as children of any other race. One may visit the rude frame building that houses a little country school in " the sticks " in Oklahoma, and see little dark heads bending over the primer; or drop in at the high school at Cass Lake, Minnesota, and see the bright-faced Chippewa girl who is president of the graduating class and a leader both in scholarship and in athletics.

In the past ten years the tendency has been all toward the public schools. The great advance of prices at the time of the war in Europe emphasized the fact that the smaller schools operated under a great disadvantage, financially speaking. The rule was adopted that boarding-schools having an average attendance of fewer than fifty pupils should be discontinued.

Under this ruling there have been many abandoned boarding-schools, from Green Bay, Wisconsin, to Greenville, California, and from Leech Lake, Minnesota, to Shawnee, Oklahoma. Some of these have been converted into hospitals as the growing concern for the health of the Indian has suggested such use.

At the same time the capacity of the larger schools has been increased. Today several of the non-reservation boarding-schools have a greater enrollment than was ever found at Carlisle, which throughout its long day was the largest of the Indian schools. In these big boarding-schools the work has been extended to include a complete high school course, so that today the Indian child who desires an education may receive tuition, food, lodging, and clothing without charge, from his kindergarten days until he is grown.

IV

PRESENT-DAY knowledge of the Indian seems to consist of a number of time-worn adages. Most of them are mistaken. One often heard is the dictum that "the educated Indian always goes back to the blanket."

Clothing is not, of course, the only index of the approach toward civilization. President Lincoln wore a shawl about his shoulders; yet we scarcely think of him as tending toward savagery.

That not every trained young man or woman of the Indian race lives up in the fullest measure to the opportunities that have been presented, may be freely granted. This fact is as true of any other race. Few of us in mature years would like suddenly to be called upon to read a page of Homer or demonstrate the binomial theorem. Few of us, indeed, can feel that we have quite measured up to the ideals of our school days in conduct or achievement.

Among a primitive people the task is far harder and the pull of conservatism far greater. The young Ute mother binds her baby in a stiff " baby-carrier " not because she herself feels it necessary, but because her grandmother and great aunts and cousins of remote degree in the elder generations join in threatening the displeasure of all the unseen forces of nature as well as the tribal authorities if she refuses. The Pueblo boy who knows how to do a thousand mechanical things knows also that if he stays with his people he must be reasonably obedient to the cacique or medicine man and acquiesce in practices which no longer carry any meaning to his mind. These young people submit, but in their turn they are much less inclined to force acquiescence upon their children. The growth may seem slow; but it is growth none the less.

At the time of the Minnesota uprising a Sioux family fled to Canada with other members of the tribe and did not return to the United States for a dozen years or more. The father, who had been one of the warriors apprehended and held prisoner, heard the appeals of the missionary while he was in custody. He joined with others who responded to the same appeal and a colony of the Santee Sioux was formed. It proved a credit to their profession of faith in the religion and civilization of the white man.

When the father visited Canada and reclaimed his family, a lad of fifteen years proved especially promising. After a period of training in the mission school he was sent East, where he graduated in medicine. As Dr. C. A. Eastman he was a medical officer of the government on a Sioux reservation at the very time when the least progressive of his people were involved in the Messiah craze and the ghost dance uprising. His white blood was probably no more than a fourth but his adaptation to white ways had been complete despite a boyhood in the remotest wilds. His lectures and books have done much to interpret his people.

A recent book on the Sioux people comes from one of the first group from Rosebud reservation to attend Carlisle Indian School in the year of its beginning. The author, Luther Standing Bear, prefers to spend the remainder of his life in Los Angeles rather than in his own Dakota land. His adaptation to the ways and beliefs of the white man seems thorough and sincere.

In Wichita, Kansas, is an American Indian Institute whose head is a Winnebago Indian, the Reverend Henry Roe Cloud, whose name in part testifies to the early training and encouragement received from a devoted missionary family. His degrees from Yale and other universities equal in number those demanded from the head of any white institution of learning; but more important than these is the fact that in any discussion of racial achievement his name is sure to be mentioned as an example of the best in Indian development and character. Yet little more than forty years ago he first

saw the light in a smoky tepee. Another Winnebago,
Peter Paquette, who was for years Indian Superintendent at Fort Defiance, Arizona, was a child of the tepee
and the baby-carrier.

A young member of so remote a tribe as the Navaho
admitted to the bar and in the practice of his profession;
Pueblo lads venturing as far from their ancestral home
as Chicago and filling acceptably clerical and mechanical positions; Chippewa and Cree girls becoming public
health nurses under the State Board of Minnesota —
such things as these, and they are not too rare, do not
savor of " going back to the blanket."

Civilization does not come to any race in a moment.
Many of our efforts in that direction have been futile,
many of them foolish. Indian education has proceeded
by the trial and error method. The wavering and
changes of policy which afflict all our endeavors have
been potent here as elsewhere. Even today there are
well-meaning people who deplore the fact that the Indian should learn anything. He should stay in a state
of picturesque savagery for the ethnologist to study, for
the artist to paint, for the literary genius to exploit.
These protesting folk should have impressed their views
upon Columbus, for with his first footstep upon the
shores of San Salvador life began to change for the Indian. Even the ghost dancers who prayed for the return
of the old life did not contemplate giving up the horse
and gun, the wool and cotton, the sugar and flour the
white man had brought to them. These changes they
had long since accepted; their benefits had long been
enjoyed.

Today the old Indian clings to his old ways as older
people do in any race. The young people are seeking
and experimenting as young people do in all times. Con-

ditions vary sharply from tribe to tribe, but even in the
dirty grass hut of the sullen and recalcitrant Mexican
Kickapoo one sees pinned to the wall the certificate of a
child who has passed his school grade, or a map or drawing some teacher has praised.

This is an era of changing educational theory. Each
new idea has its proponents who think they have found
the solution of all human ills. None of them have as yet
evolved a completely satisfactory statement of the purposes of education, much less of methods by which the
purpose may be attained. The white race is even now
dimly approaching a concept of education. It is not
surprising that the red man still lags a trifle behind.

CHAPTER XIX
The Red Man and the Land

I

IT WAS inevitable that a land-loving people of the type that spread the United States flag from sea to sea should misunderstand the Indian's attitude toward the soil. Every treaty proclaimed the misunderstanding; yet it persisted as strongly as ever. The contention of the Dreamers who counselled Chief Joseph was an exaggerated statement, it is true, of the red man's feeling about the land. Yet in spite of the exaggeration it gave a far truer picture than that drawn by the white man from his own feelings.

So fixed, however, was that erroneous interpretation that as the wave of sympathy for the Indian and his wrongs grew higher and higher, more and more powerful became the popular conviction that sure relief lay in individual ownership of the land. The argument ran thus: The Indian has been deprived of his ancestral acres. On the reservation he has only an undivided share in the land that is left to his tribe. If he is given a part of it for his own personal use and holding, he will be proud to claim it and so will become an independent and self-supporting member of society.

It was putting the cart before the horse as so many apparently good arguments do. The English love of the soil was probably the result and not the cause of an agricultural stage of development. Men had not left the hunting stage of life because they loved to sow and

365

reap.   But turning through necessity to sowing and reaping, they had learned to think of the land as the source of all their comforts and the supplier of all their needs.

A few, but not the greater number, of the Indian tribes of the North had started toward that stage.   Their progress in that direction might have been more rapid if America had remained undiscovered.   Many of the plains tribes have legends which point to a prehistoric period in which agriculture was a feature of their livelihood; but when the horse and firearms made hunting so much more profitable than before, the cornfields were deserted.

Now the white man, attempting to read into the Indian his own psychological peculiarities, was sure that dividing up an Indian reservation into farms would make each Indian a farmer.   Each year the pressure of popular demand for such action grew stronger.   In one or two cases it had been tried by special law or treaty for a single tribe.

One of the earliest instances had been the Isabella reserve in Michigan, parcelled out among a group of Chippewa.   Much of the land had slipped from their hands, and in practically every case titles had been all but hopelessly clouded with liens of one sort or another. This experience suggested the need for a period during which the alienation of the land would be forbidden by law.   In this trust period the Indian would, it was thought, grow up to the full stature of a landowner.

In 1878 the Commissioner of Indian Affairs outlined the plan which finally won acceptance; but it was nearly ten years more before it became law, in the Dawes Act of February 8, 1887. By this enactment each head of a family was to receive a piece of farm land not to exceed

160 acres; each adult single person one-half the portion. The land was to be held in trust for a period of twenty-five years, inalienable and exempt from taxation during that time.

The Indian receiving this allotment of land, however, was to become a citizen from the date of issuance of the trust patent. From that time he was to be amenable to the laws of the United States and of the state in which he lived.

The plan testified to the white man's faith in law as well as in land. These two powerful forces combined were in a quarter of a century to work the transformation of the roving hunter into a settled farmer.

During the decade which saw the most active consideration of this legislation there was an overwhelming torrent of public discussion on Indian matters. Public sympathy for the Indian mounted to such heights that the raids of Geronimo and the Meeker murders served only to raise it further. Mrs. Jackson (Helen Hunt) saw, indeed, in the outbreak of the White River Ute only an occasion to appeal to public sympathy because the government threatened to withhold rations from the band until they surrendered the murderers of Agent Meeker and his employees. Mrs. Jackson was reminded by another citizen of Colorado that the culprits had taken all the contents of the warehouse and therefore could not be starving.

Her answer was a *tu quoque* — a recital of the story of Chivington's raid at Sand Creek in 1864. Even a devoted lover of all Indians could scarcely have maintained that the Ute band was avenging an old injury of their inveterate enemy the Cheyenne. But this point of logic was slighted.

In " A Century of Dishonor " Mrs. Jackson, who as

"H. H." had won literary laurels in less controversial fields, wrote an impassioned brief in favor of the Indians from Columbus's day to her own. This found a receptive audience. But a brief, however impassioned, could not awaken the widespread interest that was generated by her novel "Ramona," in which she wove a thread of romance and human suffering into the story of the dispossession of the Mission Indians of southern California. This "Uncle Tom's Cabin of the Indian" carried its burning message to a multitude of readers.

It was a day of lectures, and Sarah Winnemucca made her appeal to audiences throughout the East, carrying back to Nevada with her the funds with which she established and maintained for a few years a school for Indian pupils. Susette La Flesche brought east with her Standing Bear, the Ponca chief, to protest against the removal of his people from Nebraska to the Indian territory. Miss La Flesche was an educated woman of mixed Winnebago and French blood, and her perfectly good name was an honest inheritance of generations; but for platform purposes she was "Bright Eyes."

In the early eighties began the conferences at the hospitable Mohonk Lake Mountain House of Albert K. Smiley. Each October for a generation friends of the Indian were invited there to discuss Indian problems with the Board of Indian Commissioners, of which Mr. Smiley was a member. Many a plan for legislation, many an impulse to private benefaction grew out of these conferences.

Great was the rejoicing at the Mohonk meeting in 1887, the year that marked the passage of that "Magna Carta of the Indian," the Dawes allotment act. The conference interpreted this to mean that the Indian was now to be a man instead of a ward of the government;

that he was to have the protection of law and the rights of citizenship; that ultimately the tribe would be abrogated, the reservation abolished, and the Indian "on an equal footing with other citizens of the country."

Senator Henry L. Dawes, author of the bill, did, it is true, sound a note less triumphant.

"What is this change? It is not any transformation of the Indian. The law has only enacted an opportunity and nothing more."

II

THERE had been allotment here and there before the passage of the Dawes Act. Miss Alice K. Fletcher, an ethnologist, had studied the Omaha Indians in Nebraska, and in the course of the study had become convinced of their readiness to receive their lands in severalty. Under a special law this had been done, with Miss Fletcher herself as the allotting agent. Her purpose was to assign tracts of land to the heads of families in such a manner as to bring about contact with the surrounding whites as far as possible.

Miss Fletcher's experience led her to feel that a general law for allotting Indian tribes was undesirable. Each tribe was to her a separate problem, to be studied independently. Location, surroundings, tribal characteristics were all factors to be weighed in making a decision.

But this painstaking attitude was not the kind to appeal to those who were filled with the enthusiasm of the day. When the general act was passed there was a great rush for the parcelling out of Indian reservations everywhere. The tribe thus receiving lands in severalty might be one which had been settled for a generation among the white man and habituated to his ways, or it might be fresh from the warpath, as were the Cheyenne, the Apache, the Comanche, the White River Ute.

The Jicarilla Apache, receiving their allotments and thereby becoming citizens, went their own roving way none the less. In a few years it was discovered that they had obeyed their tribal taboo against revealing their names to an outsider. Consequently it was impossible to identify the nominal owners of allotments by the names they had given to the allotment agent. The result was that a second distribution of the land was necessary, from the standpoint of the official records if not from that of the Indian. The Jicarilla Apache today are still semi-nomadic dwellers in tepees, harmless though scarcely useful members of society.

To some of the tribes the new law could not of course apply. The New York Indians, for example, were outside its purview. The line between their tribal rights, those of the state, and those of the United States had never been drawn. It is a question of which courts and lawmakers have fought shy. The matter is as undecided today as ever.

The Indians of the Southwest had come under the United States by virtue of the Treaty of Guadalupe Hidalgo at the end of the war with Mexico. In the case of the roving tribes the treaty merely handed over a series of wars. But the settled Indians of the pueblos had land rights by grant from the Spanish crown many centuries before. By virtue of the treaty, too, they had from the outset American citizenship. The Supreme Court of the United States, in a case brought against one Antonio Joseph who purchased land from the Indians of Taos, that " they have a complete title to their land, and are not an Indian tribe within the meaning of the Acts of Congress."

MISS ALICE FLETCHER URGING CHIEF JOSEPH TO
ACCEPT AN ALLOTMENT — FORT LAPWAI, IDAHO

Photo by Miss McBeth

JACK WILSON — PIUTE INDIAN
*who started the Ghost Dance Religion. Taken near his home
in Mason Valley, Nevada in 1924 by T. J. McCoy*

Courtesy of Malcolm McDowell

Greatest of the exceptions to the allotment act, however, was the country of the Five Civilized Tribes, that wide stretch of land across the eastern part of the Indian territory. In its confidence in the permanency of all things, the United States had given the Five Tribes patents to their lands as a whole. That the arrangement was full of difficulty and danger had long since become evident. But if the tribal acres were to be broken up into individual holdings, some further agreement was necessary. The tribes must give their consent to the change. This was not to be obtained quickly nor easily.

So the Dawes Commission — headed by the author of the allotment act — was sent down to the Indian territory. Its mission was to bring Creek and Cherokee, Choctaw, Chickasaw, and Seminole to agree to the abrogation of tribal governments and the distribution of their land.

Kiowa, Comanche, Arapaho, Cheyenne, Pawnee, Ponca, Shawnee, Sauk and Fox, Kickapoo, Apache, Oto, Missouria, Tonkawa — within the nineties they found themselves citizens of the United States and owners of ample farms. As the law directed, the surplus lands of each reservation were sold for the benefit of the Indians; and thus thrown open to white settlement.

Oklahoma Territory thus emerged in the twinkling of an eye, filled with white people who had swarmed from all parts of the country to acquire a share in this cotton-growing section. Good land was becoming scarcer in the United States by 1889. The frontier days were practically over. The magic of free land, the magic that had made America, was working its last spell.

III

STILL the Five Tribes delayed and the Commission labored in vain. At this awkward moment, Congress conveniently discovered that it had been acting unconstitutionally all along. It had never possessed the right to create these Indian "nations" and set them up in quasi-independence. Itself a body of delegated powers, it could not lawfully delegate these powers to others. Who said " Indian giver " ?

First Congress by formal resolution declared that it was a national duty to provide a stable form of government for the Indian territory. The next step was to extend to the section the jurisdiction of the federal courts. Finally in 1898 came the Curtis Act, authorizing the Commission to draw up rolls of the members of the tribes and to proceed to allot land to each individual.

There was little question of the necessity for some intervention of the Federal Government. These Indian nations might have been able to handle their own internal affairs, with no more disturbance, say, than are offered by the gang regions of New York or Chicago. But their country had been unfortunately seized upon as a refuge for outlaws of all sections, who saw here a rich chance of escape from the inconvenience of the white man's laws. The intercourse acts of 1834 forbade the entrance of unpermitted whites into Indian country. But the tribal governments gave many permissions, for one reason or another, and adopted many whites formally into their ranks.

If the United States endeavored to expel one of these hundreds and thousands of so-called "intruders," there was nothing easier than to set up a claim of tribal permission and right. There was at hand no impartial authority to gainsay the contention.

Matters had gone from bad to worse for many years. The " intruders " were a vast body of people, living in a country where for the white man there were no laws, no courts, no schools, no means of control.

The Dawes Commission now faced the unenviable task of deciding how many of these claimants should rightfully be enrolled as members of the Five Civilized Tribes, entitled as such to receive allotments of land. It was a stupendous work. Two hundred thousand people presented themselves before the Commission. The rolls as finally approved carried about a hundred thousand names. About half the claims had been adjudged valid.

On the rolls were Indians of all degree from the full-blood to those claiming a one hundred and twenty-eighth portion of Indian blood; the non-Indian portion being sometimes white, sometimes negro, sometimes both. There were also the " freedmen " who by the treaties made at the close of the Civil War had been admitted to equal rights with their former masters. And there were those of entirely white blood who had been adopted into the nations or had married members of the tribes — intermarried whites, these were called. And now, the names having been duly written down, the lands were to be appraised and apportioned.

Many refused allotment to the last. Crazy Snake and his band withdrew belligerently to the hills. Organizations of " Nighthawks " protested against the breaking up of tribal power and ownership. But in the end it was all divided. Those who desired allotment of course came forward in due course and made their selections. The

374 THE STORY OF THE RED MAN

unreconciled ones received their farms, willy-nilly, from
what was left.

So it came about that a few years later the more
progressive members of the tribe found themselves the
owners of the good farming land they had chosen, while
the adherents of Crazy Snake and his sort, given their
allotments in " the sticks," were frequently the proprietors of the rich oil wells whose discovery changed the
face of Oklahoma.

The Osage, north of the Five Tribes country, received
their allotments a little later. With them the agreement
was made that the mineral rights should be reserved for
the tribe as a whole, only the surface of the land going
into individual ownership. This is the reason why,
although in the Five Tribes there are the very rich and
the very poor, among the Osage there is an equal distribution of the great oil royalties. Every Osage on the roll
as it was completed in 1906 receives a share of the huge
annual income of the tribe.

And when allotment was completed, all the members
of the Five Civilized Tribes and of the Osage nation
became citizens of the United States as the tribes to the
west of them had already done on the receipt of their
trust patents.

Citizenship alone was not enough for the budding
State of Oklahoma. If the bulk of the land of the state
was to be exempt from taxation, it was difficult to see
how the machinery of government could be kept in
motion. There would be whole counties without the
means of getting funds for county officials, for courts,
for roads, for schools. The only remedy was the " removal of restrictions," and by the Act of 1908 this was
done.

Freedmen, intermarried whites, and those of the Five

Tribes having less than one-half Indian blood were permitted to have patents in fee to all their lands and to dispose of them at will. Those having half to three-quarters Indian blood were to retain under trust patent a part of their land as a homestead. Those having three-quarters or more Indian blood must have their lands held in trust for the entire period, unless sooner released by a certificate of competency issued by the Secretary of the Interior.

Thereafter there was vast trading in lands, and many were promptly landless. Especially in the question of inheritance by minors and incompetent Indians, there grew up abuses which aroused a great storm of protest. The close co-operation between Oklahoma county courts and the guardians whom they appointed to oversee Indian estates became a widespread scandal.

Every now and then a public demand is made that the United States take back to itself the powers it granted in 1908, even as it withdrew earlier grants of power to the tribes. But so far the remedy has been left to time, which yearly diminishes the number of acres and people upon whom exploitation can be successful.

IV

FROM the start the allotment plan as set forth in the Dawes Act suffered modification. There were some amendments almost before its application began. A vital change was made when the decision was reached to allot land to each individual member of the tribe instead of on a family basis. In the light of the results, this came perilously near to a reversal of the entire scheme.

Heads of families, and single persons of adult years,

might within reason be supposed to become farmers, or at least to benefit by the responsibility of property management. No one could allege that infants could rise to the rights and responsibilities of ownership, nor that any family could profitably use a farm for each individual member. So far as the Indian owners were concerned, the greater portion of the land was thus inevitably doomed to disuse.

But the white men who came in when the surplus lands were sold looked upon the unused Indian portion and found it good. In general it was the better location, the first choice; and it irked any farmer or cattle man to see it unused while his plough must turn over an inferior section. Demand arose for the leasing of the idle farms. So the Indians who could not or would not till them might receive money for their use.

At first the law provided for the leasing of land only in case the Indian owner were incapacitated in some way from farming for himself. After a decade of amendment and variation the leasing was thrown wide open. Any Indian land might be leased. So it remains today. An Indian proprietor may lease his land at will; the government employees oversee the contract, assure him payment, collect it for him if necessary. The result has been that in untold cases the Indian has become, not a farmer, but a landed proprietor who has his estate under capable management and concerns himself only with the disbursement of the proceeds. The land which was to teach the red man self-support has instead become a strong factor in delaying that condition of independence.

Another of the rights and privileges that did not work out according to schedule had to do with the matter of liquor. From earliest days the Indian had both loved and feared the white man's fire-water. Treaties had outlawed it; legislation had forbidden its introduction into Indian country everywhere. Theoretically it could not be brought across the borders of the Indian territory, or into any Indian reservation throughout the land. The sale of liquor was forbidden by statutes of the nation and of many states as well.

But now the allotted Indian was a citizen, as soon as he received his trust patent. And these were the days when the white citizen was at liberty to buy a drink whenever he had the money and the inclination. The new status of the Indian must certainly grant him the same boon.

Citizenship did not then, and does not now, necessarily carry with it the right to vote. But no one doubted that it carried with it the right to buy a drink. So the Supreme Court decided when the matter finally reached that tribunal.

This was in 1905. Eighteen years under the Dawes Act had indicated difficulties as well as benefits. The following year saw the passage of the Burke Act, under which allotments have ever since been made. This new legislation provided for the delay of citizenship until the end of the trust period. But in the case of an allottee deemed fit to handle his own affairs a " certificate of competency " might be issued, conferring citizenship and a patent in fee to his land.

Before the passage of this Act, in many sections, the greater part of the allotment work had already been done and citizenship already granted to Indians from the shores of Puget Sound to the lower Arkansas. Most of them found the new status not greatly unlike the old. The Supreme Court duly approved the double condition of citizenship and wardship as no more incompatible in an Indian than in a minor. Discharge of the Indian's technical minority would come with the issuance of a patent in fee to his land.

A decade after the Burke Act, a new declaration of policy was made. Certificates of competency were to be issued more liberally than before. By this time many of the trust patents had run their course and the time for the issuance of patents in fee was at hand. The Indian was to be thrown on his own responsibility whenever his capacity seemed to justify such a course.

A versatile Secretary of the Interior under whose jurisdiction this came even prepared a picturesque little ceremony of shooting the last arrow and taking up the handle of the plough, to impress upon the red man's mind the significance of the change. For some years the number of Indians receiving full title to their lands grew apace.

At the same time, the number of acres under Indian ownership tended to decrease. From the time when the Isabella Reserve in Michigan was allotted, in the middle of the last century, it had been very plain that most Indians would dispose of their lands as soon as they were at liberty to do so. A bird in the hand was always more desirable than the two in the bush. Attaining some knowledge of the white man's formal procedure, the red man was still without any inner appreciation of the real value of land ownership.

The policy swung back again. Today the practice is to extend the trust period. Lands already held in trust for a quarter of a century are to be so held for ten, fifteen, even twenty-five years longer. At the close of the extended period the original allottee will often have passed out of federal guardianship to the happy hunting grounds where land titles give very little concern.

V

THE PAST few years have seen another wave of public interest in the Indian — not such a vast sweep as overspread the country half a century ago, but enough to make a considerable impression on the shifting sands of our Indian policy. The storm first broke over a bill concerning the land titles of the Pueblo Indians along the Rio Grande.

The Supreme Court had long since decided that the Pueblo Indians held a title to their lands higher, as it was earlier, than that of the nation itself. They were not " Indian country." The Pueblo folk could sell their lands and they could buy intoxicants.

It was the latter feature of the situation which led to a clause in the state constitution, when New Mexico at last gained statehood, to the effect that these lands were henceforth Indian country. Just what that might mean, no one considered very deeply for some years.

These were the times of active enforcement of the laws against selling liquor to Indians. " Pussyfoot " Johnson was gaining his name and reputation as a Chief Special Officer of the Indian Bureau. These Indians of the Rio Grande had not been devotees of the white man's fire-water. Their habit of making a native wine of their own was as a rule the worst of their offending.

In time a case was brought up to the United States Supreme Court and a decision handed down. This declared that the government, by giving the Pueblo Indians schools and farm implements, by exercising a certain quasi-guardianship over them, as shown by the appointment of agents and teachers, had created a condition of wardship. They were therefore under the dominion of the liquor laws.

By this time the decision was perfectly academic, since prohibition for both red and white had become the order of the day. But while this had little to do with land, it seemed to add another complication to the already confused and confusing status of the Indian villages.

For centuries the towns of their Mexican cousins had been beside the Indian pueblos, for better protection of both against the common enemy — the roving Navaho and Apache. During these years, since it was a land of little water, there had been competition for the small portion of irrigable soil. There had been sales and transfers. There had been disputes and encroachments. But most of it had gone on under the easy-going Spanish law and left little written record for the legalistic American mind to brood upon.

They are brooding upon it now in the form of a Pueblo Lands Board which was created as the final outcome of much discussion. This court has already been at work for years and will for years more be busy with hearings, surveys, and investigations of Spanish law and Spanish history. Few more intricate questions than this are ever presented for solution.

The public impression of the matter was a vague one, but it centred upon the denunciation of the Indian Bureau as an organization deliberately designed to despoil the Indian of his property. The following year Oklahoma guardianship matters came in for some well-deserved criticism and the discovery was made that the Indian had fared more perilously at the hands of the state than of the nation. Obviously the greatest need of all was a better understanding of affairs by people generally.

The Secretary of the Interior appointed a Council of

One Hundred, chosen from among people who were interested in Indian matters but without official connection with the administration of affairs. In December 1923 they held a two-day session at Washington discussing many phases of Indian life and development. A series of resolutions brought the usual close to American endeavors. We seem to be so constituted that laws and resolutions satisfy our aspirations.

More recently a research bureau conducted a survey of Indian administration. The bulky volume published as a result of the visits of ten investigators to various Indian reservations and schools contains a great deal that is of interest to the student of Indian matters. To the reader who understands the background of Indian history it emphasizes the striking picture of a governmental agency called upon to perform the health and educational and social services considered requisite in this generation, with the technical and legal equipment provided for the administration of a property trust of a half century ago. The feeling today is undoubtedly for the human side of the problem; but the approach is still legalistic.

So the law of June 1924, which declared all Indians to be American citizens, satisfied many people that the "Indian problem" was at length finally solved. Two thirds of the Indians, it is true, were already citizens. Citizenship did not necessarily give them the ballot; did not remove the restrictions from their lands; did not break their bondage to tribal ways. In many cases it was difficult to see any effect whatever. But a law had been passed and things must therefore be greatly improved. So ran the general reasoning on the subject.

But the red citizens, newly made or otherwise, went on their several ways about as before.

CHAPTER XX
The Red Man at Home

I

SOME three hundred thousand people all told seems a small number beside the teeming population of our larger cities. More than one immigrant group in New York or Chicago might outnumber them, and present quite as many problems for the student of mankind. It is not surprising that the public in general is quite unmindful of the red man and his story. Those who think of it at all are prone to think of it as a story whose last chapter has been written. The "vanishing American," they believe, will soon have vanished completely.

In a sense this will some day be so; but the Indian will vanish not by extinction but by dilution. Each generation finds the Indian blood spread out farther, mixed more completely with the other races about it. One member of a small group is pointed out as the last living full-blood Miami. In some tribes the dilution has gone so far, as in eastern Oklahoma and in the French-mixed peoples of Wisconsin and Minnesota, that in a large proportion the Indian blood is a tradition rather than an actuality. In others, particularly in the Southwest, the mixture is less apparent. But even here it exists, less obvious because the newer racial strain is also dark, and so there is little change in physical appearance.

As there are all degrees of blood mixture, so there may be found all degrees of adaptation to the ways of the white man. In the two dozen states where Indians exist in numbers justifying government activities on their behalf, one may see hut or mansion, ignorant idleness or ambitious intelligence. A glance at the red man in his home, with the dust of warfare a generation behind us, will not come amiss.

II

Up in the northeastern corner of Utah, a hundred miles from a railroad, is a country that was once bare and waterless. Friends of the White Mountain Ute complained bitterly of their exile to this wilderness when the indignation of Colorado people over the death of the Meeker party brought about their removal. The Uintah and Uncompaghre Ute, it is true, were already here; but as they were friendly and brought no notice upon themselves by battle, murder, and sudden death, their plight was less heeded.

Irrigation has made this once barren region a beauty spot. In autumn the trees are laden with delicious apples; the corn sags with the weight of the ripening ears; the fourth cutting of alfalfa is ready for the mowing; the flocks of young turkeys strut about unmindful of the approach of Thanksgiving Day. And while many of the fertile fields are in the hands of white lessees who reap from them a living for their own families and for the Ute owners too, a not inconsiderable portion is occupied and tilled by the Ute themselves.

And here, to one's surprise, is found Tony, a young man from the Pueblo country. It is a long trail that has hailed him up to the land of the Ute.

Tony was a lad of promise when he attended the little day school at the village of his birth. When he had passed through its studies there were boarding-schools available for the higher grades. Santa Fé and Albuquerque were nearby; Pueblo pupils made up the greater number of their attendants. At a farther distance were the bigger schools of Phœnix, in southern Arizona, and Sherman Institute at Riverside, California. At these a high school course might be completed and much learned about farming and fruit growing in a sunny subtropical land. Tony chose to go to the California school, a long journey from the terraced villages on the Rio Grande.

Pearl had come a long journey too, from her broad acres in the Uintah Valley, to reap the advantages Sherman Institute had to offer when she had completed the earlier grades at the boarding-school on the Ute reservation. Perhaps among the greatest of the school benefits Tony and Pearl counted the fact that it brought them to the decision to cast their lot in together when school days were ended. Commencement and wedding days are happy days, and happily combined.

It was the custom of Tony's tribe for the husband to go to the home of the bride and become one of her people. Even if it had not been, Tony's share in the small tribal field of his people apportioned to him by the cacique of the village could not compare with the wide stretch of fertile soil, the ditches flowing with an unfailing stream, to which Pearl had claim by reason of her Ute lineage. The young couple went to Utah to set up their new home.

An attractive little home it is; simple enough, but showing that Pearl's school training has not gone amiss. Curtains hang at the windows; a geranium flaunts its bright color between. The floor is freshly scrubbed; kettle and stove are shining with cleanliness.

A mile or two away, in a house as well built as this,

but bestrewn with a disorderly litter of rubbish, a stalwart Ute sits crosslegged on the floor. His glazed eyes stare before him, unseeing. His right arm beats upon the skin drum as a monotonous droning chant issues from his throat. Soon he will pass entirely into the peyote dream he is wooing with his incantations and will see beatific visions of ineffable delight.

A few miles farther on, in a part of the reservation not yet under ditch, a withered old squaw is bending over an open fire whose flames and smoke are mingling in the preparation of a meal of buffalo berries, stewed with sugar in a battered old lard pail that has evidently seen long and hard service. This meal is to be a feast, for another decrepit can sends forth an aroma that suggests coffee — of a sort. The dirty toddler who creeps behind the grandmother's dragging calico dress at the sight of a stranger, will enjoy this fare. Tony and Pearl might feel otherwise about it.

Indeed, they are centuries as well as miles away from such a scene as this. Their neat home, their well-kept garden, the fields of corn growing brown with ripeness, all tell a story of industry and purpose that are admirable in any race. Tony has been too busy with his harvest to attend the county fair; but the government farmer has taken some of Tony's produce, and has brought back blue and red ribbons that make the young man's brown cheeks flush with pride. The couple are full of plans; fall preparations for another year's crops; the disposition of the flock of young turkeys busily pecking about the fields; a bridge over the irrigation ditch, so that access to the road may be easier and more stable.

Life seems to stretch out rather pleasantly before these two young citizens.

III

THE LAND of Tony's nativity is the delight of poet, artist, and ethnologist. Small wonder that they hate to see its age-old beauty develop new features. It has the magic of the primitive and the romance of old Spain; and a loveliness all the country's own to which words can never do justice.

All along the Rio Grande we find these close-packed villages of white terraced houses. Each village has its own story and its own organization. We visit the governor and are greeted with soft Spanish syllables and a courtesy such as a grandee of Spain might offer. We see the two canes that are symbol of his authority — the older one from the Spanish government of centuries ago, the newer one given by Abraham Lincoln in 1862. Both are modern as Pueblo tradition goes. For this is held to be the land of conservatism, of ancient ceremonial and the ways of the fathers.

Noteworthy among them all is Acoma, the city in the sky. Valiantly indeed did the Spaniards fight to conquer it, and again to reconquer this massive mesa of rock after the rebellion of 1680. It is a natural fortress with approaches few and very difficult. And on that sheer, bare rock, three rows of the tiered houses were set, century upon century ago.

Earlier still, tradition says, Acoma folk dwelt upon the top of La Mesa Encantada, before a landslip destroyed the approach.

The old Spanish mission church on the edge of the cliff at Acoma was rebuilt, so they say, after the re-conquest. How many miles the little brown men sweated and toiled to bring the great logs from far-off forests and tug them up the steep rocky pathways, how many thou-

XII. DISTRIBUTION OF INDIAN TRIBES TODAY

sands of loads of dirt bowed their backs before the rectangular churchyard was filled to suit the plans of their spiritual fathers, history will never tell. But imagination pictures an endless line of these toilers of Acoma, unbelievably docile, superhumanly patient. The old church is evidence of an all but incredible accomplishment.

In this fabricated churchyard they bury their dead as the old padres told them; but according to rites that are far older than the coming of the " wet-heads," as they named the introducers of baptism. Always must the body be wrapped in the finest ceremonial blanket, perhaps a priceless old bayeta of flaming scarlet; always must the head be set toward the east and the rising sun; always, when the earth has spread its cover above the new guest, must the ceremonial jar of water be broken above the spot. With this and with much other ceremonial Acoma says farewell to her own.

She must greet them, too, for your true Acoma woman, wherever she may be, returns to the high rock that her baby may be born in the home of its ancestors. And throughout their days of life certain times of feasting and ritual bring the Acoma people back to their city in the sky. Surely here conservatism has its fullest power.

But there is another side to the picture. Except for ceremonial seasons, the traveller is apt to find Acoma all but deserted. A few of the village folk greet the guest who reaches the top of the rock breathless and dishevelled from the long climb. They present a paper which indicates that an admission fee is to be paid. Acomans are not insensible to the commercial value of their picturesque city.

On this summer day, however, it is almost a silent city. You may stand in front of the old church and ponder upon the lesson of that strange burying ground; or you may look out from the roofs toward Katzimo, the Enchanted Mesa. You may walk in the narrow streets that separate the three rows of dwellings; but they are quiet streets indeed. Only the little group that has met you follow you about the empty village, not unfriendly, but quietly watchful of all you do and say.

Far off across the sands is the greener village of Acomita where lie the farms that feed these little folk; and here the families of Acoma spend their summers and often winters as well.

Still more distant is a village with the prosaic name of McCarthy's. It is nearer the railroad, and many children of the rock work there for a wage which buys them the comforts and enjoyments they desire. Not so picturesque, perhaps, is the man of Acoma in blue overalls wielding a pick or a shovel. But it may be that he does not realize that his purpose in life is to be picturesque. For that you may go up on the rock and pay your admission fee. He has not yet come to the point of staging a dance for the tourist, as the Blackfoot do, but prefers to earn his own living by commonplace labor.

You have to be careful, perhaps, as you go about the streets of Acoma, to use your camera only for the church, the houses, the enchanting views. Remembering the courtesy due to any stranger, you do not essay to point your lens toward the party of Indians.

But the woman of the group, attractive in the black wool and white buckskin and gleaming torquoise of the native attire, is always close at hand when the button is pressed. Now she offers a tray of small bits of pottery and you choose and purchase; now she balances upon her head a huge jar of bewildering design. Still you resist the temptation. At last she says a word to the interpreter; he repeats it to you.

" She would like," he says, " to have you take a picture of her."

It is done. And who is she, we wonder; thinking we shall hear some romantic Indian phrase or some soft Castilian words. The name gives us something of a shock. She is Mrs. Frank Johnson.

After all, even here on the ancient Rock of Acoma, old and new are mingled inextricably.

IV

FAR TO the west of Acoma lies Hopiland, whose high mesa villages never again readmitted the Spaniard after that bloody year of rebellion, 1680. But between the two there rolls and billows the vast ocean-like sweep of that expanse of sand and rock that is the Navaho country.

A ride of a hundred miles across the desert may show you only a distant glimpse of a half-hidden hogan, or a gleam from the bright blanket about the shoulders of a young girl trailing across the landscape with her herd of sheep. Groups you will not see, of either people or dwellings. " No Navaho is happy if another lives within a mile of him," is the saying here on the desert. We have gone back to Biblical days, when Father Abraham roamed with his sheep across the Asian sands.

Only so far as that ? Some contend that this is one of the oldest countries known to mankind.

Go up the Cañon de Chelly and see the remains of the little homes where once the cliff-dwellers lived; from which hundreds, thousands of years ago, they flung their rocks and rude weapons down upon the heads of the

ancestors of these hardy Navaho, before the fierce nomads drove them from their strongholds and took possession for themselves. Or up Monument Valley, where
a people still older than the cliff-dwellers lived and discovered basket-making and packed their dead and
fragments of their utensils into the crannies of rocks for
the dry climate to keep inviolate for us. All about you
in this weird country are evidences of days and peoples
long since passed away.

Here, in a green corner of Cañon de Chelly, between
high walls of stone, sits a Navaho woman at her loom,
skillfully weaving bright colors into a pattern made
once and never to be repeated; a pattern woven from a
picture within her own mind, complete though unseen.
Yet the rug must not be quite perfection; the powers
beyond man's ken will not have it so. Somewhere you
will find the slight imperfection which propitiates the
jealous watchers from the spirit world.

This, too, seems of another age, as does the weaver
herself, in her long voluminous skirt of calico and her
velveteen jacket bedecked with silver buttons. But
silver and loom and wool date no farther back than the
Spaniard, who brought them to America; and to the
Navaho rovers they came by way of Pueblo captives
from whom they learned the arts of the weaver and
the silversmith. This pastoral age of the Navaho, therefore, is easily of historic date.

And as the whole people adapted themselves to the
new opportunities and necessities when they were discouraged from the following of the warpath, so individuals are proving themselves adaptable in many ways.
They send their children to school unwillingly indeed, for
that means the loss of a youthful shepherd and a reduc-
tion of the flock which is the livelihood of the family.

And when those who do fare forth to school come back to their own, there are ceremonial "sings" of many nights' duration, to exorcise the evil spirits that have been engendered by the sojourn among the white people.

Despite all this, one encounters the alert face of many a young Navaho man or woman away from the great pasturing ground that is their home, and finds a seeking intelligence and ready industry.

The man who is guiding you is a Navaho, borrowed for the day from his employment at the government school near the mouth of the cañon.

"I was twelve years old," he tells you, "before I ever saw a white man. I had heard of the white man's school and wanted to see what it was like, but my mother was afraid; she told me they would kill and eat Indian boys.

"But a cousin of mine went away, and in a year or two he came back. He had not been eaten, so I persuaded my mother to let me go to Grand Junction, in Colorado, where there was then a school for Indian boys. My wife went to school too. Since we finished school we have been always working, most of the time in the Indian Service.

"In the winter our little girl goes away to school, to public school with the white children. She is in the sixth grade and stands high in her classes."

He does not boast, but gives this as a simple matter of information. Reflection shows this a rather remarkable advance for a single generation.

Among the many taboos of the Navaho in his unschooled state is a prohibition against the eating of fish. Some unspecified but dire calamity descends upon the head of the unwary person who partakes of the forbidden food.

Luncheon time comes, and among the viands which

have been prepared by our guide's wife is a tin of sardines. Her spouse attacks them without a sign of hesitation. A quizzical grin spreads over his brown face.

" If my mother could see me now ! " he exclaims, as one and then another sardine slides down to its predestined fate.

v

LEAVE the trail of the *conquistadores* and follow the northern *coureurs de bois*. Come from the land of cloudless blue sky into the deep shadows of the forests; from the desert where a drop of water is worth a king's ransom to the country of a thousand lakes. By their dwelling places alone you can know how different are the Navaho and the Chippewa.

Minnesota, some years ago, offered a striking illustration of the complications to which Indian laws may give rise. The White Earth region was a rich timber country and lumber companies looked upon it longingly. By the " Clapp amendment " to an appropriation act it was provided that Indians of mixed blood should be permitted to sell their timber.

An orgy of selling began. Presently it appeared that there were none other than mixed bloods in the entire White Earth country. Many who had proclaimed themselves all Indian now discovered a mixture for trading purposes. The speedy dissipation of the timber, and the equally speedy dissipation of the funds it brought in, gave White Earth a sudden notoriety.

Investigations were made; discrepancies between the degree of blood claimed at the times of allotment and of sale were obvious enough. It was thought for awhile that suits might bring about the successful recovery of

much Indian property, conveyed by Chippewa who had
been quite ignorant or unmindful of its value.

Little, however, came of the well meant endeavor, for
it proved impossible to establish the quantum of Indian
blood by evidence satisfactory to a court of law. In a
word, the Chippewa were indeed all mixed bloods —
and in common sense as well as law this is a reasonable
conclusion. Four centuries of French contact, to say
nothing of later strains, have left their impression on
practically every member of the great tribe.

A recent student of migrated Indians, in a survey
made by the Institute for Government Research, recorded the impression that " in Saint Paul and Minne-
apolis most of the people claiming to be Indians have
but a slight degree of Indian blood." She characterizes
them as " whites whose dash of Indian blood permits
their enrollment as Indians."

From such people, self-supporting in professional,
clerical, and mercantile pursuits, one may in the same
state and the same tribe pass down the scale to the
dwellers in wretched huts in the forest, who cling as far
as may be to the " old wild life " and eke out a living by
acting as guides for hunters or selling trinkets to tour-
ists.

Up on Wild Rice River, as September is drawing to a
close, a picture of the old life is still to be seen. The rice
harvest may be for some a real source of income or food
supply. For others it may be the annual vacation outing. Chippewa of many degrees of development gather
here when the brown grains of native rice are ripe for
stripping.

They bring back their gleanings to camp, and they
are parched above open fires in great iron pots that might
have been purchased from the Hudson's Bay Company

in its palmy days. When the old guardian of the kettle has done her work, the rice passes to the ministration of two or three men, who place it in a wooden tub or barrel sunken in the earth and prod it with long poles of peeled birch until hull and grain are separate. Then it is spread on flat birchbark trays for winnowing.

The picture is a primitive one; not so primitive, however, are the trucks of the dealers drawn up to purchase this crop at thirty to forty cents a pound. The Chippewa is fortunate in that he may combine holiday making with profit.

Less pleasing is the sight of two lads, staggering with drink, shouting obscenities as they reel down the pathway and cover themselves with muddy water in an attempt to cross the narrow stream. Less pleasing is the sight of the native missionary who deplores their condition but lacks the courage to take a stand against this and other untoward doings of the days and nights in camp.

But we can turn from this to things of better promise — to the neat homes of the Chippewa who work in the Cloquet paper mills, and to the attractive Chippewa boys and girls in the public schools there; to the fine young Chippewa women travelling about on nursing business for the State Board of Health; to the Chippewa forestry expert who is superintendent of the still unallotted Red Lake reservation and who has made its roads and its woods a model of beauty and care.

Here, as elsewhere, light and shade forever intermingle.

VI

WESTWARD again to the land of the Oregon Trail, whose marks still lie upon the unbroken prairie sod, along the

course of the Snake River. Here where old Fort Hall
once reared its adobe walls and spoke of civilization to
weary travellers who had left the dwellings of men a
thousand miles behind them, there remain but these
signs of old travel and fording of streams, and out in
the tall rank reeds a tiny granite stone set up not long
since by the Historical Society of the state as a belated
memorial of the old days.

Two summers ago there were few who could find
that stone; few indeed who knew of its existence. Yet
it was but ninety years since Fort Hall was in its heyday,
and its adobe walls resounded to the cheers of mountain
men when they saw the faces of those brave wives who
were the first white women to make the long journey
across the Rockies.

Today none visit the spot and around it on all sides
the country is covered by a vast sheet of water. Miles
down the river, at the American Falls, a huge dam, finished in the fall of 1926, is storing up water for irrigation and power. The Snake River valley that once knew
the tread of the pioneer is fast becoming a great inland
lake.

Much of this is on the land of the Indians of the Fort
Hall jurisdiction — those Shoshoni and Bannock folk
who were neighbors, though not by any means friends,
when Buffalo Horn returned from the march in pursuit
of Chief Joseph to start out on a little war of his own.
No one lived in this lowland along the river, but it was
frequently a place of winter feeding for their horses.
The Shoshoni and Bannock dwell on their irrigated
farms where autumn brings rich harvests.

For the overflowing of the Snake River valley, however, the Congress has voted the Indians a payment of
many, many dollars; and in this summer of 1926 they

have left their harvesting and come in to the agency, a dozen miles north of the city of Pocatello, to confer with various officials as to the disposition of these funds.

The superintendent is there, a man whom they scarcely know. They are still a turbulent people, these Bannock, and for one reason or another they have had three " agents," as they still call them, within the twelve-month. The district superintendent of this northwest country is there; a man of long experience with Indian work, trained in the days of General Pratt at Carlisle. The general superintendent of Indian affairs is there; a man who for a generation has advanced the education of Indian boys and girls at Haskell Institute in Kansas. All these hope to persuade the Indians to accept a building and implement purchase programme which will turn their new funds into better homes and more productive farms.

The Governor of Idaho is there; he has come for a look at these constituents of his. He sees them, hears them talk, observes the manner which more than once carries a hint of hostility and aggressive distrust. He shakes his head.

" We must march ! " he says, to the one who sits beside him. " We must march ! I realize it as never before."

One by one the Indians rise to speak. The nearer ones are seated on a bench; beyond, they are spread out on the green grass. There are a few women, with bright kerchief or shawl giving a hint of Indian color. The men are dressed as countrymen of any race might dress, but long black braids are seen, and moccasins are not infrequent. They have heard the propositions put forth by their white advisers and now it is their turn to answer.

The manner of speaking and the burden of the talk

are typical. There is the general complaint of encroach-
ment and loss of territory, of the hunting that is no more.
The buffalo has been gone for half a century but tears are
shed for him whenever a council gathers. Some of the
younger speakers, obviously of as much white as Indian
blood, become denunciatory and fiery. The older men
speak in the Indian style, grave, dignified, with the
simplicity of children in earnest talk among themselves.

Opinions seem to vary; the speakers generally recognize the value of the building programme presented; but
it does not appeal to them half so much as the immediate
receipt of a large sum of money and its disbursement in
accordance with the desires of the moment. Many more
generations will have to pass before the true Plains Indian learns much of prudence and foresight. The Hopi
on their rocky mesa learned such a bitter lesson through
a succession of cropless years that they were obliged
to sell their children to the Mexicans for corn enough to
carry the elders through the winter. Today every Hopi
house has its room piled with ears of six-colored corn.
The time of famine will not come again.

But these erstwhile buffalo hunters of the Idaho
plains have not had such a need to give them the forward look. The Great White Father has been too near
with his ration roll. The payments that come easily
go more easily still.

One by one the Indians rise and talk; for at their beloved councils all must have a chance to speak. One old
man, possibly the oldest of them all, rises to his feet. He
is wrinkled and unkempt. He voices most pitifully
the mood of complaint that is strong in the assemblage.

" I am old," he says, in that eloquent strain that never
fails of appeal. " I am old and poor. My clothes are

ragged. Sometimes I am cold. Sometimes I am hungry. I am very old — I am very poor —

"I want that money here — right in my hand — to buy myself an automobile!"

VII

IF MEMORIAL DAY finds you in the Puget Sound country, follow the highway northward and cross the slough to the little section, sometimes island, sometimes peninsula, which is known as the Swinomish reservation. Here between two and three hundred Indians maintain themselves by labor of various sorts — fishing, logging, agriculture.

Since their timber was not so valuable as that of their brethren at Tulalip, farther down on the sound, they have not been able to have the neat and well-appointed bungalows one finds to the South. But the wretched shacks along the water's edge which once housed them are now practically deserted and better homes are being built on their allotments up the hillside.

Their business contact with white men has given to these Indians not only a fair command of English, but also a comprehension of business method that is unusual in the race. Their children go across the slough to the white town of La Conner, where they attend the grammar and high schools. The dress of young and old is the common dress of the average white citizen.

This little community boasts a town hall, a "community center," which the Indians themselves have financed and erected. "The Society," as they call the organization through which this was effected, is practically the adult citizenry of the tiny reservation. Community activities such as this are to be recommended for villagers everywhere, white as well as red.

The hall is long, with movable benches of wood. To-day these have been lined up outside, under the trees, and long tables are laid inside the hall, for this is The Society's day of festivity.

But first comes the assembling at the gateway of the community church, and the procession of all, bearing flowers, along the dusty road and up the hill to the little cemetery. For days workers have been setting it in order for this annual ceremony.

The flowers are piled upon the graves and heads are bowed for a word of prayer. Then voices join reverently in a familiar hymn and the procession moves down again toward the community hall.

Here all gather on the benches arranged as for council, and talks are made, both in their own language and in the English tongue. Visitors are called on to speak, and are received with rapt attention. Their own leaders speak, gravely, simply, in friendly fashion.

The talking over, all assemble in the hall for the community dinner. It is a picnic feast of pies and cakes, rolls, pickles, fruit, lemonade. Crowning the board are the immense platters heaped with salmon that has been caught the night before and baked in the earth. It is good eating.

Some odd roots that once formed a larger part of the Indian diet are produced and sampled. The story of them is as new to the young people, it seems, as it is to the white visitors. Their adaptation to modern diet seems almost complete.

When feasting is done, there is an afternoon of plays and games, with the competitive sports so dear to boys and girls.

"We spend the morning," the chairman of the day had explained in his careful English, "in remembering the ones who have gone before. We go up to the cemetery to place flowers on their graves, as a memorial to them. Then we come down here and talk to the grown people, to remind ourselves of the old days and of the things we do today. Then we partake of our dinner. After that is over, we spend the rest of the day with the young people, the children, in games and playing. First the old ones, then the people of today, then the ones who are to come after us."

A beautiful memory for the past, a substantial provision for the generation of today, and for the young — happiness.

It seems a not unreasonable philosophy.

BIBLIOGRAPHICAL NOTES

I

THIS first chapter, as a brief summary of two and a half centuries of development, is necessarily general in character. Authorities for particular aspects of the period are many.

For the French aspect, the " Jesuit Relations " are invaluable. A selection of these and allied documents, edited by Edna Kenton (New York, 1925) is the form most generally available. Parkman's " Half Century of Conflict " should not be overlooked.

On the Spanish side possibilities range from the beautiful and all but unattainable translation of Benavides' " Memorial " by Mrs. E. E. Ayer, to No. 605 of The Little Blue Books — " The Indians of the Pueblos." Leo Crane's new book " Desert Drums " (Boston, 1928) reviews portions of the Spanish mission history of the Rio Grande pueblos. A government pamphlet of 1923, giving the Senate hearings on bills 3865 and 4223, is a good guide to a study of the Pueblo historical and legal background.

A study of colonial Indian relations, French, Spanish, and English, is found in Alice Fletcher's monograph (Ex. Doc. 95, 48th Cong. 2nd Sess.) published for the Bureau of Education in 1888. On the entire colonial period there is of course endless material in the accounts of early explorations and settlements.

Archæological and ethnological studies of the pre-Columbian Indian are innumerable, though as a rule they dwell much more thoroughly on the Indians of Central and South America than on those of our own region. Radin's " Story of the American Indian " (New York, 1927) is, despite its misleading title, an excellent account of the history before history began. Verrill's " The American Indian " (New York, 1927) is an ethnological study.

Dr. Hodge's " Handbook of the American Indian " (Bulletin 30 of the Bureau of American Ethnology) is invaluable as a reference on matters of many sorts throughout the entire historical period, though its main interest and importance are ethnological, as is also E. S. Curtis' monumental work, " The North American Indian."

Ahlee James' " Tewa Firelight Tales " gives an interesting light on Indian folk lore and the home life of the Pueblo Indians.

II

On the events covered by this second chapter Parkman's " Conspiracy of Pontiac " is so admirable that little else is needed to make one familiar with the scene and its actors. Cadwallader Colden's " History of the Five Indian Nations," Bouquet's " Expedition Against the Ohio Indians " (Cincinnati, 1907), and Wraxhall's " Abridgement of the New York Indian Records " (Harvard Historical Studies, XXI) are of value and interest to the student.

III

From this point on the way is charted by Kappler's " Indian Affairs: Laws and Treaties " (3 vols., Government Printing Office, 1904) and Royce's " Indian Land Cessions," an Ethnological Bureau report, with many maps. Murchison's " Digest of Decisions " (vol. I, published 1901, series not completed) adds much useful information. The codification of Indian laws is regularly urged, but Congress has so far failed to authorize it.

The five volumes of " American State Papers: Military Affairs " and the two of " Indian Affairs " add greatly to our knowledge of this period. Paxson's " History of the American Frontier " (Boston, 1924) summarizes admirably the western movements in a volume as important as it is of engrossing interest.

For the New York Revolutionary story there is nothing secondary of better value than Stone's " Life and Times of Sir William Johnson " and " Life of Brant." The two large volumes of each chronicle are filled with much first hand material — letters, documents, speeches, and councils. " Old Fort Johnson " by W. Max Reid (New York, 1906) and " The Old New York Frontier " (New York, 1901) are of interest. For a British story of New York in the Revolution " Gentleman Johnny Burgoyne," by F. J. Hudleston of the British War Office (Indianapolis, 1927) is American enough to have had its first printing in this country, and unconventional enough to make a very living tale of an old period.

It is good to observe that George Rogers Clark is now getting some of the attention justly due him. " George Rogers Clark:

BIBLIOGRAPHICAL NOTES 403

His Life and Public Services," by Temple Bodley (Boston, 1926) is a sympathetic biography with many valuable citations of original material. In recent months there has been published in Chicago a "Life of George Rogers Clark" by James Alton James, the fruit of years of research.

IV

"The Journal of Lewis and Clark" is of course the final authority on all of this journey. Oral tradition from some of the tribes visited adds a bit of interest here and there. In "The Nez Percés since Lewis and Clark" (Chicago, 1908) Miss Kate McBeth, a missionary to that unusual people, recorded some valuable tribal reminiscences.

In this connection it should be mentioned that recent researches on the part of the State Historical Sociey of North Dakota have brought out strong evidence that the name of the Indian girl who guided the explorers is properly Sakakawea rather than Sacajawea, as previous writers have transcribed it. The form Sakakawea appears on the monument in Bismarck, North Dakota, while that in Portland, Oregon, bears the older form. I have used the more familiar spelling in this narrative, although the weight of evidence is in favor of the form Sakakawea.

V

From this point on there is a good source of biography in McKenney and Hall's three volumes, "The Indian Tribes" (Philadelphia, 1844). Unfortunately, this is long out of print and all but inaccessible, and the volumes, with their carefully executed portraits, are so huge as to make their perusal a matter of muscle.

The official papers and documents tell the Tecumseh story in detail. Drake's "Life of Tecumseh" is founded on these. "Tecumseh, a Chronicle of the Last Great Leader of his People," by Ethel T. Raymond (Toronto, 1916) is a tribute Canada may well pay to the Indian who did more than any other leader to save the land for the British Empire.

VI

Mrs. Dunbar Rowland's " The Mississippi Territory in the War of 1812 " (New York, 1926) gives a lively picture of these times. George Cary Eggleston in " Red Eagle " relates the Billy Weatherford story for young readers. Halbert and Hall made a study of " The Creek War of 1813 and 1814 " (Chicago, 1895) which covers the ground faithfully. The many lives of Andrew Jackson, from Parton's on, give illuminating discussions of the period. A highly fictionized version is found in " Hearts of Hickory," by John Trotwood Moore (Nashville, 1926).

VII

Schoolcraft's " Indian Tribes in the United States " now begins to be of use to the student. Long's " Journal " of his trip is necessary. H. H. Chittenden's three volumes on " The American Fur Trade " are of first importance. " Astoria " and " Captain Bonneville," by Washington Irving afford a lively picture of Indian ways. John G. Neihardt has given poetical form to a splendid picture of these times in " The Song of Hugh Glass " and " The Song of Three Friends " (New York, 1919 and 1921).

The final recourse of the student is always to the official papers of the Executive and the Congress. Thomas Hart Benton, in his " Thirty Years' View," gives instructive summaries of these as of other governmental matters, from 1820 to 1850.

" Wau-Bun, or Early Days in the Northwest," by Mrs. John A. Kinzie (Chicago, 1901) is spirited and illuminating, though its facts occasionally limp a little.

VIII

" Old Fort Crawford and the Frontier," by Bruce Mahan, published by the State Historical Society of Iowa, deals largely with the period of this chapter and the preceding one. McKenney and Hall present many of the people of this period. Black Hawk's own " Autobiography " cannot be missed by anyone who wishes to know the story, though it can be comprehended only in the light of a wider historical summary such as is contained in the second volume of the " Centennial History of Illinois." Benjamin Drake's " Life and Adventures of Black Hawk " (Cincinnati, 1849) takes us closer to the times and the actors.

IX *and* X

For the events in these two chapters the best reliance is on the executive papers, the Congressional debates, and the judicial decisions. For their real understanding a wide general reading of the history and politics of the period is needed. Interesting light comes now and then from " The Diary of John Quincy Adams "; its fruitful twelve volumes, seldom available to the general reader, are the source from which a single volume has been recently culled by Allan Nevins (New York, 1928). George Catlin's two big volumes with their quaint pictures should be consulted from now on. They must be considered as propaganda rather than history, for Catlin idealized all he saw and studiously ignored all that was not beautiful and noble. " The Cherokee Indians," by Thomas Valentine Parker (New York, 1907), is a careful outline of the legal aspects of the Cherokee migration. " Red Patriots," by Charles H. Coe (Cincinnati, 1898) and " The Seminoles of Florida," by Minnie Moore-Wilson (Philadelphia, 1896) are two small volumes telling about the Seminole warfare.

XI

Good material on this period is plentiful. With the coming of the white man to the Far West the many great volumes compiled by Hubert Howe Bancroft become a source of reading matter, if not always of authentic fact. Bancroft's compilers seem unable to distinguish between fact and fancy, and many of the volumes are distorted by most unhistorical prejudices. In the case of the natives this takes the form of assuming at times that the Indian is the natural man, simple, noble, and unspoiled, of virtue all compact; and within the briefest of periods this child of nature is represented as so low and degraded a creature that the writer cannot find words scathing enough to condemn the policy pursued by the Hudson's Bay Company officials of marrying the daughters of the tribes. Neither attitude makes for historical accuracy. One must take careful account of these and similar obliquities of vision in weighing the contents of these books.

Rev. Samuel Parker's "Exploring Tour Beyond the Rocky Mountains" (Ithaca, 1844), Alexander Ross's "Adventures on the Oregon," and "Fur Hunters of the Far West" (London, 1844 and 1855) are among the earliest — Parker's earliest of all — of the first hand narratives of the Oregon Trail. Parkman's "The Oregon Trail" covers only the early part of the journey and at a later period, but is valuable as the record of a trained writer and observer. Frémont's "Reports" of his first and second expeditions, in 1842 and 1843, are almost as fascinating today as they were when they first stirred the American public to a realization of the land beyond the mountains. Ghent's "The Road to Oregon" gives some additional material on the emigrations to the Far West and the experiences of the early settlers with the Indians.

There is a great deal of material, much of it highly controversial, on the Cayuse outbreak and the murder of the Whitmans. "Marcus Whitman," by William Mowry (Chicago, 1901) is only one of many that might be cited. "Memoirs of the West," by Eliza Spalding Warren (Portland, 1916) was written in her old age by the daughter of the Nez Percé missionaries. At ten years of age she was among those taken captive by the Cayuse at the time of the massacre, and was interpreter between the savage and the whites who came to the rescue, through many trying scenes.

XII

THE story of Bent's Fort is comprehensively given in Volume XV of the "Kansas Historical Collections." George Bird Grinnell has done valuable service in gathering together the record of that outpost in the wilderness.

For the Mexican War there are many authorities. Luckily the Indian part of the story is less involved in controversy than that which concerns the whites. "Notes of a Military Reconnaissance," by W. H. Emory, printed in 1848 as Executive Document No. 41, Thirtieth Congress, First Session, and "Doniphan's Expedition and the Conquest of New Mexico," by John T. Hughes, published in Cincinnati in 1847 and reprinted as Senate Document No. 608 in 1914, give several diaries of the march across the plains to New

Mexico and to California. From Frémont's "Memoirs" (vol. I, Chicago, 1886) comes the dramatic story of Klamath and Delaware in the California mountains. Among the accounts of the Pueblo uprising, that in Ruxton's "Adventures in Mexico" should be consulted. A great deal of interesting material is found in Twitchell's "Leading Facts of New Mexican History" (Iowa, 1911). A recent publication of the "Diary of Susan Shelby Magoffon," edited by Stella Drumm of the Missouri Historical Society, is a valuable and thrilling picture of the westward journey and of Santa Fé.

XIII

Now the printed reports of the Commissioners of Indian Affairs become generally available, and for the next forty years the volumes grow in bulk, containing not only the reports of the Bureau head in Washington, but the more intimate revelations of the agents and farmers and teachers in daily contact with their Indian charges. The amount of drama in these reports would never be guessed from their commonplace black bindings.

In his later years Commissioner George W. Manypenny wrote of "Our Indian Wards" (Cincinnati, 1880). He told the story of some of this treaty-making. Hazard Stevens in his "Life of Isaac I. Stevens" (Boston, 1900) has given a boy's recollections, fortified by official records, of his father's extremely important and interesting trips among the Indians of the Northwest. Kit Carson's own narrative, edited by Blanche Grant and published at Taos, New Mexico, in 1926, gives much that is valuable. Edwin L. Sabin's "Kit Carson Days" (Chicago, 1913) should not be missed by anyone wishing to gain familiarity with the western scene. Its appendices contain as well reprints of much first hand material.

XIV and XV

BESIDES the official sources for this decade, including the 1867 "Report on the Condition of the Indian Tribes," there are memoirs of many generals of the day. Custer's "Life," (New York, 1870), "Our Wild Indians" by Colonel R. I. Dodge (Hartford, 1883), and "The Sioux of Dakota," by Captain R. C. Poole (New York, 1881) may be instanced. From a missionary standpoint we have

"Mary and I," by Stephen R. Riggs (Chicago, 1880), for many years a worker among the Sioux; and Bishop H. B. Whipple's "Lights and Shadows of a Long Episcopate" (New York, 1899), which tells of a life devoted to the Chippewa. George Bird Grinnell's "The Fighting Cheyennes" (New York, 1915) gives the tribal story as the Indians themselves know it; and a more recent volume, "Kit Carson," by Stanley Vestal (Boston, 1927) gives further traditions of the same tribe.

A poetical but none the less accurate narrative of the post-Civil War history of the Sioux and their Cheyenne allies is to be found in "The Song of the Indian Wars," by John G. Neihardt (New York, 1925).

XVI *and* XVII

MANY volumes deal with the Indian events of the seventies. The series edited by Cyrus Townsend Brady contains two volumes, "Indian Fights and Fighters," and "Northwestern Fights and Fighters," (New York, 1904), which give a many-angled view of a number of these encounters. In many of his books but especially in "My Life and Experience Among Our Hostile Indians" (Connecticut, 1907) General O. O. Howard brings the reader close both to the Southwest and to the Department of the Columbia during their most thrilling times. The "Personal Recollections" of General Nelson A. Miles (New York, 1897) tells the closing chapters of the Apache story. A recent book, "Some Memories of a Soldier," by General Hugh Lenox Scott (New York, 1928) is a valuable sequel to this story and to the adventures of others of the plains tribes. "My Friend the Indian," by James McLaughlin (Boston, 1910) comes from one who knew the Sioux intimately, and other tribes well, throughout a long lifetime. "Life Among the Piute," by Sarah Winnemucca (Boston, 1883) will always repay its reader with its revelation of character as well as its story of events. A recent volume, "Memoirs of a White Crow Indian" (New York, 1928) written by Thomas Marquis from recollections of Thomas La Forge, gives some interesting side-lights on these events.

In the magazines of about thirty years ago are to be found many articles dealing with these conflicts, written as a rule by those who had taken part in the warfare.

XVIII, XIX, *and* XX

THOROUGHLY characteristic of the period which saw the rapid advance of school opportunities for Indians and the inauguration of the allotment system is "A Century of Dishonor," by Mrs. Jackson (Helen Hunt). It is eloquent not alone in its recital of the wrongs perpetrated upon the Indians but in its masterly suppression of anything that might to the slightest degree extenuate the white man. It is amusing to compare its quotations from official reports with the originals and find sentences cut in half in order that the good accomplishments of the Indians may appear to be entirely unaided or the wrongs done them entirely unprovoked. The reports of the Mohonk Conference discussions are the best illustration of the popular sentiment of the decade.

A fictional picture of transition days in the Indian territory is found in two novels, "Wild Harvest," and "Black Jack Davy," whose author, John M. Oskison, is himself possessed of Cherokee blood. A recent Indian autobiography, "My People the Sioux," by Luther Standing Bear (Boston, 1928) tells the story of an early Carlisle pupil and his reaction to new conditions. Dr. Charles A. Eastman's many books give much interesting light on the Sioux people.

In preparing to write such a book as this, one necessarily reads and studies hundreds of books and consults many hundreds more. I have not tried to list more than a small portion of the volumes which have been my study for years past. I have merely tried to indicate some which will be of value to the reader who wishes to carry his knowledge of Indian history further than the scope of this volume would make possible, and who wishes to refer to the original sources from which this narrative is mainly drawn.

INDEX

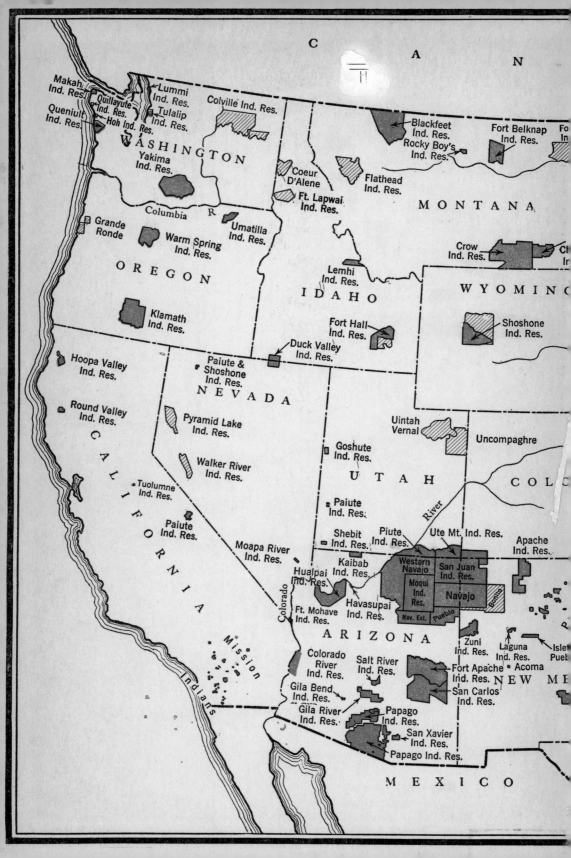